A Most Hostile Mountain

The 1897 passage beneath dangerous hanging glaciers.

A Most Hostile Mountain

Re-creating
the Duke of Abruzzi's Historic
Expedition on Alaska's Mount St. Elias

Jonathan Waterman

HENRY HOLT AND COMPANY   NEW YORK

Henry Holt and Company, Inc.
Publishers since 1866
115 West 18th Street
New York, New York 10011

Henry Holt® is a registered
trademark of Henry Holt and Company, Inc.

Published in Canada by Fitzhenry & Whiteside Ltd.,
195 Allstate Parkway, Markham, Ontario L3R 4T8.

Library of Congress Cataloging-in-Publication Data
Waterman, Jonathan.
A Most Hostile Mountain : re-creating the duke of Abruzzi's historic
expedition on Alaska's Mount St. Elias / Jonathan Waterman. — 1st ed.
p.   cm.
ISBN 0-8050-4453-1 (alk. paper)
1. Saint Elias, Mount (Alaska and Yukon)—Description and travel.
2. Mountaineering—Saint Elias, Mount (Alaska and Yukon)
3. Waterman, Jonathan—Journeys—Saint Elias, Mount (Alaska and
Yukon)   I. Title.
F912.S15W38   1997   97-8314
917.19'1—dc21

Henry Holt books are available for special
promotions and premiums. For details contact:
Director, Special Markets.

First Edition 1997

Designed by Paula R. Szafranski

Printed in the United States of America
All first editions are printed on acid-free paper. ∞

1   3   5   7   9   10   8   6   4   2

To Mom and Dad, who worried.

ACKNOWLEDGMENTS

I am indebted to Gary (the Captain) and Jeff Hollenbaugh for accommodating me on the sailboat and the mountain. Jeff was kind to share his reflective journal entries for the book. The Captain's magnanimity in teaching me how to sail and then letting me single-hand our *Heaven Sent* the last six hundred miles is appreciated, particularly since I have now gone public about cuffing the reef and getting caught in a whirlpool.

To those who weathered rough drafts and shared their impressions—Susan Golomb (my literary agent), David Hale, Michael Larkin, Lodovico Sella, David Stevenson, David Sobel (my editor), and John Thackray—thank you.

Julia Amari, Michael Larkin, Clotilde Sella, and Eliza Moran illuminated the Italian culture by translating otherwise inaccessible biographies, essays, diaries, and letters. Bernadette McDonald of the Banff Film Festival helpfully introduced me to her broad network of friends. The staffs at the University of Alaska-Fairbanks archives, the Bancroft Library in Berkeley, the Western State College Library in Gunnison, Colorado, the Italian Alpine Club Library in Turin, the Appalachian Mountain Club Library in Boston, the Historical Office of the United States Senate, the Sierra Club Library in San Francisco, and the American Alpine Club Library in Golden (to name only a few) were particularly helpful. Michael Larkin of Dorset and Dee Longenbaugh of the Juneau Observatory Bookstore also performed valuable library research for me in England. Paul Kallmes introduced me to the Sellas.

Walt Gove and Dee Molenaar shared photographs of the mountain and considerable knowledge. Michelle Ridgway and Justin Smith taught me the finer nuances of sailing and took my blues away; many others in Juneau were exceptionally hospitable. Dr. Ralph Bovard provided sensible medical counsel, the best of which warned me not to go. Another doctor (name withheld) wrote drug prescriptions, the best of which dulled our pain while in the throes of hunger during the descent. Ranger Rick Mossman of Wrangell-St. Elias National Park and Preserve provided crucial information after we got off the mountain, knowing that we insisted on being left entirely to our own devices while on the mountain.

Our sponsors (some gave us gear in exchange for photographs and testimonials; others sold us gear at wholesale) made an uncertain outing more comfortable and affordable. They include Backpackers Pantry freeze-dried food, Blue Water ropes, Bucci sunglasses, Garuda tents, Glacier Gloves, Patagonia, Summit Canyon, and Polartec (their generous grant did not help to defray the costs of our expensive sailboat, but the money kept hope alive by floating us in beer).

Katherine Elkins Kelly graciously shared her memories and a relative's letters about her great-aunt, Katherine Elkins, the duke's lover. Since Michael Shandrick's and Mirella Tenderini's *The Duke of the Abruzzi* biography had not yet been published while I researched and wrote my book, I could not study their work. However, they were kind to me. Michael's knowledge of his subject and the generous sharing of a source inspired me to research the duke's later life. Numerous Italian writings—particularly Gigi Speroni's *Il Duca Degli Abruzzi* and Filippo De Filippi's *The Ascent of Mount St. Elias*—

helped illuminate my subjects. Aldo Audisio and Roberto Mantovani of the National Museum of Mountains in Turin, Italy, reimbursed the entrance fee and steered me. The Provincial Administration Corporation in Turin supplied a translator and gave me a tour of the Cisterna Palace, which the duke grew up in.

Lodovico Sella and Clotilde Sella, of Fondazione Sella, generously translated and dusted off their long-dead uncle's (Vittorio Sella's) diary, photographs, and old letters to and from the duke. Since the duke's personal papers were burned after the War, and the duke's surviving relatives did not know him, the Sellas became the crucial link. Although I was little more than a stranger, this family opened up their doors, refilled my cup with the fruits of their Biella vineyard, and brought me closer to Vittorio Sella's lifelong *compagni,* the duke of Abruzzi.

AUTHOR'S NOTE

I refer to the 18,008-foot mountain of my own journey narrative as Yasetaca (as the Tlingit people named it). Within quotes or historical narrative, it becomes the commonly used Mount St. Elias. I have reduced proper Italian names—such as Luigi Amedeo Giuseppe Maria Ferdinando Francesco Di Sovia-Aosta, Duca Degli Abruzzi—to the duke of Abruzzi, the duke, or Luigi.

After completing my research and writing, it became apparent that the Italian biographies have omissions. These works (like mine) were undoubtedly diminished by the scarcity of surviving papers from the duke. Unfortunately, other information had been omitted, such as the duke's original tombstone epitaph, his lying in print about where he was born, details of the palace he grew up in, remarks in his correspondence to Vittorio Sella (and Sella's own correspondence and diary entries about the duke), his alleged fistfight, being pulled over for speeding, the correspondence of his lover's father, his so-called alpinist queen being hauled up mountains in a divan, and his jingoistic treatment by numerous Americans (particularly the press). In the interests of painting a genuine portrait of this elusive prince and his times, I have not withheld information that might be perceived as unkind to him or his country.

Although I dug deep and sourced all of the material used, this book is not intended to be a comprehensive biography of the duke. Given his aloof and princely manner, along with the dearth of anecdotes about his personality, the best way to find him was to launch onto his sort of cold seas and high mountain—then chase him down. While risking my own bacon on *A Most Hostile Mountain* and during the sail home, I had a glimmer of who Luigi really was.

Innumerable batteries allowed me to constantly shoot video during our escapades. Sometimes I filmed clandestinely. Other times my subjects got annoyed at the camera in their faces. Eventually my partners gave up and just started talking candidly. Although the shaking and blurred video images would be barred from any respectable film festival, the sound track enabled me to accurately record the lengthy and often anxious dialogue that follows.

Proverbially it is not easy to blow and swallow at the same time. So also it is not easy to combine mountaineering and sailing.

—H. W. TILMAN

A Most Hostile Mountain

Cape St. Elias (*on Kayak Island*)
Kayak Island

*Gulf of
Alaska*

Icy Bay
Mount St. Elias/
Yasetaca
Malaspina Glacier

Yakutat

Mount Fairweather

Lituya Bay
Cape Spencer
Cross Sound
Hoonah

Pacific

JUNEAU

Sitka

Admiralty Island

Petersburg

*Alaska
Canada*

Ketchikan

Dixon Entrance

Queen
Charlotte
Islands

Prince Rupert

Grenville Channel

Hartley Bay

Queen
Charlotte
Sound

1995 *Heaven Sent* route

Ocean

Dent Rapids

Vancouver Island

Strait of Juan de Fuca

Vancouver

Friday Harbor

San Juan Islands

Port Townsend

SEATTLE

AK
CAN

AK
CAN

CAN
USA

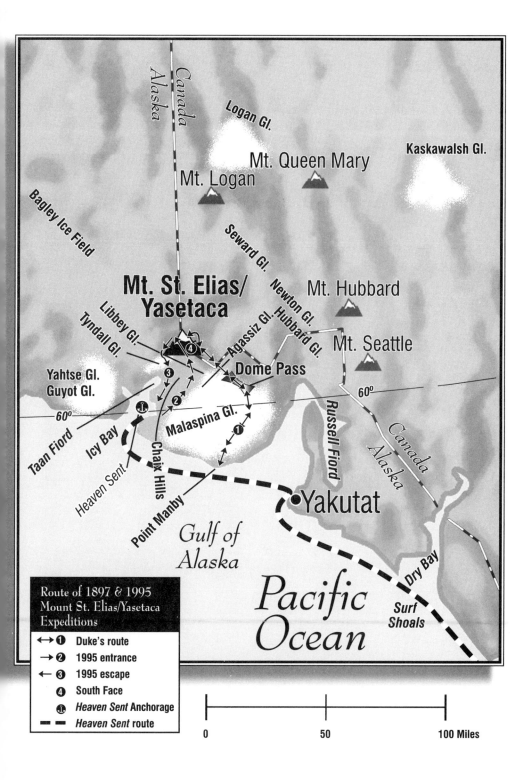

Canada
Alaska

Logan Gl.

Mt. Queen Mary

Kaskawalsh Gl.

Mt. Logan

Bagley Ice Field

Seward Gl.

Newton Gl.

Mt. Hubbard

**Mt. St. Elias/
Yasetaca**

Libbey Gl.

Tyndall Gl.

Agassiz Gl.

Hubbard Gl.

Mt. Seattle

❹

Dome Pass

Yahtse Gl.
Guyot Gl.

❸

60°

60°

Taan Fiord

❶

❷

Russell Fiord

Canada
Alaska

Icy Bay

Chaix Hills

Malaspina Gl.

❶

Heaven Sent

Point Manby

•Yakutat

Gulf of
Alaska

Dry Bay

**Pacific
Ocean**

Surf
Shoals

Route of 1897 & 1995
Mount St. Elias/Yasetaca
Expeditions

↔ ❶	Duke's route
→ ❷	1995 entrance
← ❸	1995 escape
❹	South Face
❶	*Heaven Sent* Anchorage
– – –	*Heaven Sent* route

0   50   100 Miles

PROLOGUE

Yasetaca rises from the Gulf of Alaska as an ivory-steeped pyramid. Its broad eastern and western escarpments form abrupt shoulders, while the summit cone rises the last several thousand feet in languorous symmetry. Unlike any mountain in the world, it culminates 18,008 feet—or 3.4 miles—above the ocean, all within 8 miles of Icy Bay.

In its beginnings, the land was forced skyward by a sublucting cataclysm of continental plates, sculpting the mountain into a Himalayan-sized peak. As it cooled, the region was blanketed by the largest ice fields outside of today's polar regions. The 1,500-square-mile Malaspina Glacier sprawls to the east, 140 miles of ice field form moats to the north, and North America's most tempestuous stretch of Pacific Ocean batters the south.

Tlingit people who lived on the coast told of the mountain's ice running like a river down to the sea. The people often used Yasetaca (pronounced *Ya-see-tah-sa*)—surrounded by swamp (Yasé), head of a bay (ta), beneath a mountain (ca)—to guide them on their journeys, like a ghostly triangle in the sky. They sang about the mountain because it put happiness in their lives. European navigators mistakenly substituted "St. Elias" from a nearby island named by Vitus Bering, then supposed its "smoke" (from frequent rockfalls) to be volcanic steaming.

Until the end of the nineteenth century, it was thought to be the highest mountain on the continent, enticing alpinists everywhere. In 1891, six climbers drowned in thunderous surf beneath Yasetaca before they could step upon land. Today, 5 percent of its suitors have died (mostly in avalanches)—making it one of the most dangerous mountains in the world; only 3 percent of climbers have died on Everest.

Depending upon the viewing angle, Yasetaca is reminiscent of other, more celebrated peaks, such as the broad-shouldered Ama Dablam, the rounded Mont Blanc, or the pyramidal K2. Imagine enlarging New Hampshire's Mount Washington times three, swaddling it with glaciers, and moving it to the northern tip of Labrador. The difference is that Yasetaca will remain unpopular and difficult, offering climbers a 70 percent failure rate and abundant hanging glacier avalanches. Famous alpinists avoid Yasetaca.

Its international summit lies 240 miles north of Juneau and 280 miles east of Anchorage, submerged in the heart of America's greatest unpaved and uninhabited subarctic playground. The mountain's southern toe falls into the sixtieth latitude, while the northern half shadows Canada's Yukon.

Twenty million square acres belong to the largest parks in North America (Wrangell–St. Elias National Park and Preserve and Kluane National Park)—the grandest legislated wilderness in the United States (the size of Missouri), managed by the greatest entanglement of red tape anywhere (the Department of the Interior). Most people have never heard of the place.

This *place* is regulated, however, by the collision of ocean and glaciers. As warm and wet air masses build and are pushed northward by the Japanese Current, they stall up against the refrigerated mountain, then inundate it with snow. The meteorological station from the surrounding Yakutat area averages 134 inches per year of precipitation. So if the viewer is lucky enough to study the mountain on a moderately clear day, it is like exiting from a cave into a solarium: one cannot stare without dark glasses.

Yasetaca foretells storms with a lenticular cloud banner, produced by high-atmosphere winds capping the summit cone and placing the peak into a vacuum. Tlingits see giant brown bears running from it. Icebergs are pushed twenty miles across Icy Bay. Schooners are demasted. Eventually this porcelain-smooth lens cloud envelops the mountain and the wind reverberates as if it is alive: outrunning avalanches, flinging shale off ridges, and bridging crevasses. The upper half of the mountain is scoured to bare ice, until this wind cyclones out into the surrounding seas of brine and ice, then expends itself.

In 1897, after five attempts, the mountain remained unclimbed. That summer, ten Italians cursed at the fog from their steamboat, listing with sixty crates of equipment and towing a yacht with eleven American porters. Everyone was anxious about the competition: Henry Bryant's American climbing team had departed two weeks earlier. The Italian leader, Luigi Amedeo of Savoy, duke of Abruzzi, wanted to plant his country's flag atop St. Elias more than he had wanted anything in his life.

Most of the team was seasick. One of the porters was vomiting blood. And the Italian climbers—a handful of guides, a photographer, a doctor, a lawyer, and two naval officers (including the duke)—were equally listless. For thirty-seven days they had paced back and forth on steamships and express trains, ducked pestilent reporters, and smoked countless cigarettes while awaiting their calling with America's penultimate Alp.

If the duke had been merely an inexperienced climber willing to suffer, he would still have had a chance to climb the unclimbed St. Elias. His guides were the finest in the world and could have dragged him up the mountain, if they could have first foreseen the complex logistics involved in crossing the fifty-mile-wide Malaspina

The duke of Abruzzi, and members of his St. Elias team. From left to right: Filippo De Filippi, Francesco Gonella, the duke, Umberto Cagni, Vittorio Sella.

Glacier. As an adolescent naval cadet Luigi had assimilated the art of navigation. For his dream peak, he had personally marshaled the team's equipment to a meticulous strategy, more akin to naval battle than early alpinism, unintentionally perfecting the "expedition-style" (fixed camp, load shuttling, supply depot) mountaineering that is still in use a century later.

As the fog lifted up one finger after another, the duke, sporting a boy's downy mustache, calmly studied landings through the surf. The twenty-four-year-old's politeness masked a relentless ambition. He had confided to one American that "we will not fail on St. Elias." His generosity—as well as his sad eyes—drew companions to his side as if he were the heir apparent (he was sixth in line to the throne).

Vittorio Sella, an accomplished alpinist and the world's foremost mountain photographer, wrote frequently to his philoroyal wife about the duke. Sella was initially kind in his appraisals of the duke (at least until the terrible labor of hauling sledges began), to the extent that Sella fretted about being "humiliated because I am not worthy of capturing this exalted Princely life with my photographs." Or: "The Prince gives us every day an example of his exceptional moral and physical strength."

Sella was not a sailor, and like the guides, he had spent a lot of time gagging over the rail and seeking his balance. But when the fog finally parted to reveal their mountain filling the northwestern horizon, everything changed. "The Prince is in a good mood today," he wrote, and the men rose from their torpor ready, if necessary, to follow their tall, long-faced leader anywhere.

That day the mountain filled them with inexplicable momentum. "To me," Sella wrote his wife, "this is a painful journey except for the vision of St. Elias. . . . The first time I saw St. Elias I forgot all the suffering past and found the moral strength to be enthusiastic in the landing." Sighting this behemoth from the sea was enough to abandon the rest of the world. They pulled into big surf—dwarfed by the mountain—and fell in behind their young prince.

Part One

The Sea

His portrait provoked me almost as much as Yasetaca. He looked too dandyish, too impossibly regal and poker-faced proud to grovel up such a peak. Alaskan mountains reduce climbers by scorching solar reflection, subzero winds, and prodigious snowfall—no place for a twenty-four-year-old millionaire in a jaunty fedora and a finely knit sailor's sweater. He seemed as different from me—emotionally, intellectually, and culturally—as any man who had ever swung an alpenstock. The only goal we bore in common was the mountain.

To bigger-is-better peak baggers, the 18,008-foot Yasetaca is eclipsed by North America's highest, the 20,320-foot Denali (Mount McKinley). I know this because Denali occupied me—as a ranger, guide, and climbing bum—for nearly two decades. That whole time I avoided Yasetaca.

Yasetaca is unique because it has not become a trophy peak for guided clients—although the duke was accompanied by guides during his first ascent of the mountain. Royalty did not climb *Le Alpi* without guides, so he employed them as load bearers, step choppers, and trailbreakers. They became lifelong friends.

The loyalty of the duke's companions, the great breadth of his explorations, his interest in science, and his World War I admiralcy—all spoke to his sense of destiny. He did not confine his adventuring to the polo matches and sailing regattas that fill the appointment calendars of other princes.

In a day when alpinism was in its infancy, and after the Italians wrote their *Ascent of Mount St. Elias* book, the duke's party attempted to reach the North Pole, beating the previous "farthest north" record of Dr. Fridtjof Nansen. The duke and his partners finished the work of Livingstone, Burton, and Speke by traveling to the Nile's source and climbing sixteen virgin peaks in the Ruwenzori Mountains of Africa. He then attempted the second-highest mountain in the world, K2, and set the high-altitude record (which stood unmatched for a dozen years) by reaching 24,600 feet on Bride Peak in the Himalayas.

I believed that there was something to be learned from this distant yet somehow heroic figure. By attempting to repeat his style of climbing Yasetaca from the sea, I hoped to give life to forgotten history. By abstaining from the cheat sticks of modern mountaineering—airplanes and radios—I could attempt the mountain by "fair means," and perhaps better understand what made this duke tick.

Yasetaca was not climbed again until 1946, by eight alpinists and one military C-147 transport plane, which bombed the mountain with three thousand pounds of supplies—an accepted ethic among 1940s American climbers. For the sake of convenient access, the modern climbing history of Alaska, including six more routes on Yasetaca, became dependent on aircraft. Consequently, modern alpinists rush in, climb, then flee, learning next to nothing about Alaskan mountains or their first ascensionists.

While retracing the duke of Abruzzi's path, I was also chasing familiar personal demons, and hoping to escape the rut I had fallen into. *Midlife crisis* is our society's collective explanation, but I have been climbing in and out of similar ruts and going on expeditions since

I was a teenager. If it takes until midlife for people to begin question-
ing their mission in life, the term might be more accurately described
as *complete-life crisis*. Besides, midlife is that time when we all convince ourselves that we'll be feeling better in another week or two.
And my salvation had always been based on modeling my actions and
taking inspiration from the accomplishments of others. So if I could
understand Luigi, and the methodology of his own *dream-catching*
life, it could shed some daylight into my own dimly lit fantasies.

L uigi Amedeo, initially called "the Spanish Baby," was
born in Madrid. In the two years that his father had
been king of Spain, there had been two assassination attempts on
their family.

Thirteen days after Luigi's birth, on February 11, 1873, his father,
Amedeo di Savoy, abdicated the throne of Spain. Spanish loyalists
celebrated the departure of the Italian they called "Don Macarrón."

Luigi's mother, Princess Maria Vittoria dal Pozzo della Cisterna,
was wheeled to the waiting train in a wheelchair, exhausted from
birthing and raising their three sons, including two-year-old Vittorio
Emanuele and four-year-old Emanuele Filiberto.

The duke of Aosta had reluctantly accepted his assignment as
king of Spain from his father, the king of Italy, in November of 1870.
A Spanish military junta had deposed Queen Isabella in the interest
of establishing a liberal government under a monarchy. The king of
Italy, Vittorio Emanuele II, was pleased that his son was crowned—
the rest of Europe figured any charismatic figurehead could lead the
Spanish people—but for his part the king of Italy was happy to see
his House of Savoy (from Turin, in the northwestern Piedmont
region, considered by many to be more French than Italian) gaining
further prominence. After deposing the Catholic Church as a papal
state in 1870, then taking Rome, Vittorio Emanuele II figured that
the duke of Aosta's promotion to king of Spain would only increase
the House of Savoy's stock—until Amedeo abdicated.

The former king of Spain, now the duke of Aosta, slunk back to Italy and told a journalist, "I want to live in the dark shadows." So Luigi's family retreated to Turin's Palace of Cisterna, bequeathed to his mother, the final heiress of an old Biella family (his mother and father's wedding had been customarily "arranged" by the two families). According to Gigi Speroni's *Il Duca Degli Abruzzi,* the king and queen gave the duke of Aosta a triumphal reception, named him inspector of the army, and bequeathed him a four-hundred-thousand-lire-a-year annuity.

This modest and blocky fifteenth-century palace, two blocks from the magnificent and turreted House of Savoy palace, was then renovated to keep up with baroque Turin (known for its palaces and still a center of Italian wealth today). Luigi's parents commissioned artists to paint frescoes, while workers added stairways, knocked out

The Palace of Cisterna in Turin, the duke's boyhood home.

windows to bring in more light, and planted a large garden in the rear patio—the princess wanted to inspire her young sons.

Luigi's later interest in mountain climbing developed partly because he was an exacting boy with an affinity for the visual—a characteristic shared by most alpinists. He would develop a fascination for photography, his eyesight was nearly perfect, and much of his future could be foretold by his mother's deliberate efforts to inspire him. Luigi, just old enough to walk, watched the ceiling frescoes being painted. One showed the four elements—fire, water, wind, and earth; the other, a Pompeian-style mural, showed figures at war, at sports, and at love. Both frescoes would preordain the essentials of Luigi's (but not his older brothers') outdoor-warrior life.

His mother also hung a recently completed oil, *Glacier of Mont Blanc* by the well-known Piedmont artist Giuseppe Camino, on the living-room wall. It was a huge and visually arresting canvas, the sort

Giuseppi Camino's "Glacier of Mont Blanc,"
the painting that inspired the young duke.

of work that no young boy (or alpinist) could look at without feeling awe or inspiration. The brightness of the glacial landscape was true to life, and in the left-hand corner, a dozen alpinists groveled amid crevasses like mere Lilliputians beneath the dazzling Giant. Luigi, as it turned out, couldn't resist it.

M y first climbing experience was as a sixteen-year-old Outward Bound student in North Carolina. Tying in, then groveling up a seven-hundred-foot cliff was exhilarating and kaleidoscopic for the way it allowed you to see the world below through a different lens. This perspective is common to many first-time climbers, but up on the rock, engaged in my own style of stumbly ballet, I also decided that conventional sports and college and a nine-to-five career were pedestrian compared to this world of wind raking the mountains, sun warming the premature bald spot on my head, granite rasping my fingertips, and a wild planet curving out of sight and beckoning me on beyond the smog of the Appalachian Mountains.

This exquisite movement made my body feel as if it had existed in only robotic form until I started moving on the rock. Several hundred feet off the ground, to dispel fear and to prevent falling, I had to concentrate on fluid body movements—no easy task for a gangly teenager. Of course, I had danced to bands, but the cliff, and the pines below and the scudding clouds above, contained a music unlike anything I had ever perceived. It was as if I had become a musician: the rock held the score, my passage gave it voice, and the wilderness around me became an audience rapt. I wanted to climb as well as to experience wild places that could filter out the noise of the city. I wanted to lose myself in this symphonic dance.

My climbing heroes all came from books, and I never climbed with any inspirational mentors. But I was looking for one. My early rock-climbing instructors were merely sharing experience and fleeing to the mountains with the 1970s back-to-nature counterculture.

They smoked pot and spoke ad nauseum about safety and issued the vegetarian, back-to-nature party lines.

I climbed up the brick walls at high school, got kicked off stone churches by police, climbed atop the field house and—while crouched out of sight—shouted condemnations to the mystified coaches (who had implored me to rejoin the football team).

In the winter, I learned how to build igloos, ice-climb frozen waterfalls, and stay warm in thirty-below temperatures. My parents grounded me for leaving climbing-shoe skid marks and greasy fingerprints alongside the drainpipes, moldings, window ledges, and doorsills and atop the doorknobs of what had become my practice climbing walls.

On walls greater than those of our two-story house, my fear of heights at first threatened to overwhelm me. I tried to shut it out of my mind, like one does when driving over high bridges. Instead of peering down I just looked up at the sky and hummed. However, I was so scared on my first ice lead—taking the rope up a five-hundred-foot, narrow blue gully, shaking too hard to twist in the ice screws and clip them to the rope to prevent me from falling all the way to the ground—that I fouled my pants. Subzero weather has a way of freezing your mistakes, and my partner George didn't comment when he joined me at the first belay other than mentioning how quickly I had led the pitch.

I didn't conquer my fear (which is climberspeak for an ephemeral state of adrenaline production more hallucinatory than real), but the dance and the sensual textures drew me on: walking fast enough so that my twelve-pointed crampon spikes would squeak rhythmically in frozen snow; the binding-up feeling of icicles on my beard; staring up at the whirling grainy texture of my bamboo-shafted ax (which I frequently restored with linseed oil); and the acrid-wet smell of my Dachstein wool mittens (almost counteracting the soiled knickers) thawing above the Ashley woodstove. In these sensory attractions, the goal-oriented, mathematically minded, and very Catholic duke of Abruzzi and I (once sent to summer school for flunking math) were not at all brothers.

Despite my mother's attempts to introduce me to the Protestant church, I found spirituality in the mountains instead. It came while climbing Maine's Katahdin: rainbow auras circled our shadows, projected up on the clouds from a knife-edged ridge in midwinter. I felt afire with beauty—the loveliness of rime-ice feathers clinging to rocks and alabaster clouds billowing above and below—and I began dedicating myself to mountains because I felt closer to sublimity and my companions and the saneness of the world up on that knife-edge than anywhere else. Including church.

Winter became my domain. Bad weather in particular appealed to me because clouds often hid the void below. While on rock, I greased the holds with sweat and was too anxious about the void to become a real technician, so I concentrated on mountaineering—combining climbing, aerobic fitness, navigation, campcraft, and winter survival into my own brand of off-kilter art.

L uigi's mother was tiny, delicate of features, and fluent in several languages, including ancient Greek. She raised her sons as strict Catholics, inflicting upon them numerous masses and prayers, as if to retaliate for their uncle's (the king's) sin of taking Rome and being excommunicated by Pope Pius IX.

At twenty-nine, Princess Maria Vittoria contracted tuberculosis and died in her seaside villa as a worn-out, elderly-looking woman. Luigi, now three years old and bearing a striking resemblance to his mother, appeared at the funeral dressed in the blue-ribboned petticoat sailor garb of the day.

One of the many Italian biographers of the duke, Gigi Speroni, wrote about a "gloomy" upbringing, marking Luigi as a "taciturn man, that will be reflected in eyes veiled with perpetual melancholy." Speroni did not mention that they were also bedroom eyes. Luigi was precocious, and physically—by his straight-backed stature and his disarming, sad, yet sensuous eyes—he commanded attention.

According to the *New York Times,* a wandering Gypsy approached Luigi in Turin and told him: "Your Royal Highness will have a brilliant future. You will one day sit on the throne, and your papa will get you the most beautiful Queen in the world."

"Rot!" replied the duke. "A lot you know! I shall be a sailor and I shall sail all over the world and marry whom I please."

Luigi's widowed father was at a loss in raising his three young sons. Within months of his wife's death, he lost his father, Vittorio Emanuele II, to pneumonia. The beaten and grieving duke of Aosta could not have provided much love, let alone have been a good father figure for his young sons, in particular the impressionable four-year-old Luigi.

After Umberto I inherited the throne, the duke of Aosta, now brother of the king, had increasing court and travel duties, which further distanced father and sons. The three young sons were privately tutored, while their forty-three-year-old father married Letizia Napoleone, his twenty-one-year-old niece—scandalizing the House of Savoy.

Eventually, Luigi's older brothers went into the army. Six-year-old Luigi was enrolled as a navy cabin boy and asked to clean toilets, swab decks, and kowtow to the officers. His father had told the vice admiral overseeing Luigi that the boy should be given no preferential treatment.

Luigi thrived. Cast out to sea, aboard the rollicking decks, he felt a freedom unlike any he had known in the darkened Turin palace. A quick learner who shared his mother's intellect, he became a student of language and history. He read the classics in their original Greek (like many privileged Italians), and also learned French, English, German, and Spanish, and some Arabic. During his early days at sea, he kept Jules Verne's *Twenty Thousand Leagues under the Sea* beneath a pillow, but his inclination was more to the science than the fiction of that story.

By age eleven, first in his class, and showing athletic prowess while climbing the yardarms (and from competitive games while growing up with older brothers), he received his first instruction on a warship. He was being catapulted out of boyhood and straight into the tasks of manhood. As a postpubescent, he sailed all over the Mediterranean and into the Atlantic with the Italian navy.

Photographs from this era show him almost sneering—it was difficult and unprincely to maintain a smile in front of the first, slow-shutter-speed cameras. This regal hauteur may also have been partly attributable to impatience (judging from his drive to succeed), as well as to an oversize and loose upper lip. Even at fifteen years old, his premature widow's peak and stern face—pinched and narrow—project taciturnity.

Luigi discovered a happiness and an abiding love of adventure while aboard naval ships. Out on the world's great oceans, he rode through gales and found a precision in the crashing waves and thunderstorms. He learned the science of navigation while observing the teeming sea life of the Mediterranean. His travels to new and strange places awakened him to the regimens of quantifying, exploring, and identifying, but not with any poetic sensibility. The arts bored him.

His middle brother, enrolled in the army, later told a reporter, "My brother the Duke of Aosta is the dandy, my brother the Duke of the Abruzzi the learned man, and I am the *bon vivant*—the gay boy." Luigi's candid intellect became apparent during his final exams. His history teacher, Camillo Manfroni, inadvertently assigned an essay to the young prince: a critical examination of Carlo Alberto's disastrous military campaign of 1848–49. The embarrassed Manfroni caught his mistake—Alberto was Luigi's great-grandfather—and suggested that Luigi take on another essay; he refused, and scripted an illuminating and critical analysis of the poor battle strategy devised by his own flesh and blood.

While it was a point of pride to honor one's forebears, the only greater point of honor for a noble Italian, and a member of the House of Savoy, was that of country. Luigi would later throw himself upon peaks, toward the North Pole, and into war—sacrificing fingertips, romance, and even family—for this zealous sense of duty to country.

The task of modernizing the Italian navy's fleet had fallen to Benedetto Brin, the minister of the Naval Academy. In 1889, the sixteen-year-old Luigi earned his degree in mathematics and was promoted to midshipman. The Italian fleet had expanded from fewer than 100 scows to 273 warships in a decade, which allowed the king to tout Italy as one of the naval powers of the world—an ideal that unduly affected the young midshipman and filled him with patriotic pride.

In 1889 Luigi embarked upon one of the newest warships, the *Vespucci*, across the Atlantic, to South America. At Rio de Janeiro, according to his biographer, Speroni, Luigi remembered:

> I was getting ready to go ashore when I heard a discreet knock on the cabin door. I went to open it and found myself facing the commandant: he had come alone instead of sending for me—an unbelievable occurrence. He had in hand a dispatch that he handed me in silence.
>
> Immediately I had the presentiment that something very serious must have happened. [He read the dispatch.]
>
> The King has communicated that my father was dead.
>
> [Commandant Falicon said:]
>
> Immediately His Highness asked my permission to withdraw and I left him alone with his immense grief. A few minutes later he came to me with a dispatch to Turin.

Luigi had addressed the telegram to his oldest brother, Emanuele Filiberto, now the duke of Aosta.

> I cannot find the words to express my state of mind. Cruel fate does not enable me to place a final kiss on [his] cold brow. Besides the family wreaths, please place on the memorial grave a special wreath, with just my name and that of the port where now I find myself. This separate wreath will show my immense sorrow about not being present at his last moments.

Please tell the King that this calamity brings no change in the campaign of the *Vespucci:* duty must come before sorrow. A kiss to you, to Vittorio Emanuele, console Letizia as much as possible. Please write details of the last moments.

Luigi

On his deathbed with pneumonia, his forty-five-year-old father had looked a septuagenarian, and whispered in his oldest son's ear: "Kiss for me little Luigi."

He was now officially named the duke of Abruzzi (a region in central Italy, far from the northern Piedmont, but the House of Savoy was broadening its influence amid the newly expanded and unified country). Luigi bore his duties with alarming nonchalance. His portrait photographs show the same sort of impatient yet unruffled composure that would have made him a superb poker player. He had become handsome, tall, and bronzed by the sun. He was said to be kind. He spoke little. And he listened assiduously. For a scion of royalty, this seventeen-year-old (going on forty) carried few privileges, only a fierce patriotic pride, and the crushing knowledge of an impermanent and love-shorn world.

Luigi would develop a heretofore undescribed and understated sense of humor, blackened by his abbreviated childhood. His nephew would write: "He had a very good sense of humor (without it members of Royal families could not survive!!)."

The arresting feature of this manchild's portraits, outside of his Eurasian eyes, was an outsized head and his ungainly ears, sticking out like wings before the headlong flight of his life.

I first saw Yasetaca from neighboring Mount Logan. I was twenty-one and singularly focused on climbing Logan's unclimbed West Ridge. I had recruited three older partners, all on the strength of a photograph of this sinuous ridge.

Mountains were my life. The love of a mountain is strange and exhilarating, a kind of contact high from spending too much time becoming acquainted with wilderness and estranging yourself from people. It might not have happened if I hadn't been so full of youth and dreams, and, as they say about most juvenile climbers, *hormonally imbalanced.*

In the sometimes deluded geography of mountain climbers' minds—where you perceive physical challenge and beauty and happiness as one—the contours of the twenty-five-mile-distant Yasetaca enthralled me. Unlike sprawling Logan, Yasetaca had graceful form. Its western side would go magenta during midnight sunsets. And the ominous lenticular clouds sitting over its summit warned us of approaching storms. Though my interest stopped short of crossing over into obsession, the mountain did become something of a talisman for me. Lacking the ability to actually touch it, I worried it in my mind.

In the dawns, as I leaned out of the tent into subzero air to fill the cooking pot with snow, I began studying Yasetaca. I studied it over my shoulder while resting my screaming calves from frontpointing (kicking crampons toe-straight) up steep blue ice. During the bright evenings, I studied Yasetaca burnished by starlight.

Its northern shape called to mind a lion crouching upon a pedestal. During the day, the mountain was wind-blurred and bluish, as if I were looking at it under water. Just before the sunsets I tried to imagine what transcendence I would feel up on an unclimbed route in that long evening light, braced against the wind. Surely it would change me.

I was never entirely content. My partners and others described me as pensive, although mountains seemed to be my source of joy. It never occurred to me that this was abnormal. On the contrary, it

Yasetaca (Mount St. Elias) in twilight, as seen from Mount Logan.

seemed fortunate that I knew what made me happy. I believed a greater transformation would occur if I plunged into that surreal light. I wanted to touch the summit, but I also wanted to be high on the mountain, pushed to my limits because Yasetaca would somehow make me more whole; my partners thought marriage or career might be a more sensible way to accomplish the same objective. My partners, by the way, put up with a lot.

After several weeks of crabbing across that four-mile-long, unclimbed West Ridge of Logan, I collapsed a huge cornice—wrenching me inside like a cardiac defibrillator. Only blind luck made me jump back onto solid ridge. I closed my eyes, then was hit by the swirling backblast of two tons of ridgeline avalanching thousands of feet to the glacier. When I opened up, I was thinking about how good it was to be alive, and studying Yasetaca.

It was beautiful.

For seventeen years I wanted to go. I carried my talisman-peak everywhere. I aborted trips there twice. I was scared about giving myself to the mountain and also knew it had to be done respectfully. You can't think about your dream peak for that long, then just fly in and mow it down and tack it up on your wall and boast about it.

By climbing all of the mountain's 18,008 feet from the sea, I could pay homage to it. I would also prove that there is in fact a thin line between fantasy and reality if you choose to make it that way—I believe this is the essential condition of the mountain climber's mind. (It would have saved alpinists a lot of explaining if George Leigh Mallory had just said, "Because *my fantasy* is there.")

Given the potential consequences, it is crucial to understand your motivations if you are drawn to big, foul-weathered peaks. Being out of touch with your feelings is like asking for that big blade to whistle down from the sky, sharp as a descending lens cloud; climbers call it "getting the chop." If you don't understand your emotional motivation—be it fame, ego gratification, adrenaline addiction, witnessing beauty, or the thrill of conquest—it's a good policy to make out your will before you leave. That's why I had to dig deep before I could finally make myself go. It took me seventeen years to come up with a good reason, a foundation for the many peculiar reasons that head cases like me climb mountains.

This is what I figured out:

I wanted to attempt Yasetaca, and by fair means, so that I could let the memory of the mountain and my former strength sustain me as an old man. I had not squandered my youthfulness, but if I could put this climb inside me—put it in my past—I would be able to gracefully *stop* climbing big mountains.

It is rare nowadays for climbers to attempt difficult Alaskan peaks without communication devices, airplane support, and other benefits of modern technology. The sanctity of wilderness and the opportunity to rediscover our remnant instincts are short-circuited by technology.

Far too many climbers are resorting to satellite global positioning systems (GPSs) instead of good map-reading and mountain-route-finding skills. Others are demanding helicopter rescues over their cellular telephones instead of practicing self-sufficiency. Most climbers carry radios to arrange aircraft pickups or weather forecasts, rather than walking out the glaciers or learning to read the sky (or a simple barometer). Many contemporary mountain expeditions have become crass exercises in commercialism and overindulgent sponsorship. Nowadays, expeditions to Mount Everest—the largest and most over-hyped mountain in the world—cart televisions, VCRs, and Walkmans; download their daily progress onto the Internet; and insulate themselves so thickly with modern technology and cashy clients that they never have a chance to experience the mountain itself.

I didn't want to impose any contrived agendas upon this trip. My game plan of sailing up to and then trying to climb the mountain ("Yasee-*what?*" or "Mount Saint *A-what?*" my friends asked) without a GPS, cellular telephone, computer Web site, handheld radio, or aircraft support probably seemed frivolous to the uninitiated. Furthermore, the mountain is considered obscure because it's only the second highest in the United States, and fourth highest in North America.

Among most altitude-status-conscious climbers, let alone the nonclimbing public who have borne the hyperbole about Mount Everest, Alaskan peaks are considered a mere training ground for the Himalayas. Alaskan veterans argue that you needn't travel halfway around the world only to risk high-altitude illness, amebic dysentery, and porter strikes when you can find all these challenges here in North America. By using a sailboat as a base camp, and vying for the 18,008-foot summit of Yasetaca, you effectively gain more elevation than anywhere Himalayan. Everest is only 12,000 feet above its base camp.

Out of hundreds of major Alaskan ascents each year, one can count the number of pioneer-style (ski-in-and-out, dogsled, or sailing) ascents on one hand. It is not altogether different from shaving: most people use electric razors because a straight edge takes more time and might nick you. Climbing Yasetaca correctly, I figured, was all about following the duke, stepping back in time to discover how to make progress. In accordance with Santayana's "Those who can't remember the past are condemned to repeat it," I was going to study my predecessor—then artfully climb around his footsteps.

After eighteen months of cruising around the world in the *Vespucci*, the duke had graduated from his menial cabin-boy and ensign apprenticeships. He had visited Italian colonies in the Americas and Africa, seen the lights of Paris, and experienced the ballyhooed underground trains of England.

In February 1891, while the *Vespucci* was docked in Venice, his old professor visited him and found Luigi looking older than his eighteen years. He "is friendly with all," recalled Camillo Manfroni for Speroni's biography, "officers and men, most natural, but little inclined to salaciousness, having a bent for reflection."

Although Luigi had been exposed to the arts and to poetry as a boy, his life at sea predisposed him to science and natural history. While his uncle, King Umberto, was busy trying to quell unhappy demonstrators in Milan, the duke of Abruzzi had his eyes on horizons other than the political chicanery and social inanities of his House of Savoy. Ashore briefly enough to keep his sea legs, he was promoted to second lieutenant of an eighty-ton torpedo boat, and spent the next year cruising the Italian coasts.

After three years at sea, Luigi was granted a ten-month leave. He avoided the fashionable balls and nightclubs and was characteristically reserved with the women who approached him. By contrast, his brothers, Vittorio Emanuele and Emanuele Filiberto, were rakes; King Umberto was regularly betraying his queen.

The king's aide-de-camp, Paolo Paolucci, noted in his diary that "Emanuele Filberto appears to be a ladies' man and every day received a lady at home." But Paolucci was struck by Luigi, who was of course younger, more widely traveled than his older brothers, and less inclined to gossip, and who spoke with a solemn precision about his experiences at sea.

According to Speroni, Luigi spent time with his aunt, Queen Margherita, who was considered a mountain climber, and encouraged her nephew's interest. Margherita, Paolucci wrote, frequently partook in "bold excursions with skirts custom-sewn with seven meters of cloth and allowing ample room to permit more comfortable movements." Her Highness was frequently hauled up these mountains in a divan—an act officially denied by the royal family.

Although guides would teach Luigi his craft, Franceso Denza (a meteorologist belonging to the Barnabite order of Milan) had been instrumental in developing Luigi's passion for mountains. Father Denza had often taken the young prince for long hikes, sharing lessons of mountain topography, and speaking of alpine bliss. Denza had told the impressionable boy how he could become closer to God from the summits. But despite the father's (and his mother's) best efforts, Luigi did not worship God on mountains so much as he developed his own spirituality. He was of mathematical logic, and although he was said to be more religious than his brothers, what he could not see, he could not prove.

His photographer companion on St. Elias, Vittorio Sella, first saw the prince in 1884, as an eleven-year-old, hiking with Father Denza in the Alps. It wasn't for another decade that the photographer talked to him. "I am very inclined to think that, at 22," Sella wrote, "it was already in him to explore the great mountains of the world. That day made me desire to become a devoted friend and companion with him in his explorations."

The duke of Abruzzi had dedicated a plaque to his father, but Luigi confided to the queen that while his father had intended Luigi's destiny to be on the sea, to which he owed his thanks, he had now uncovered a second great love: mountains.

After the fashion of the day, many of the European gentry hired guides. These nimble mountaineers had herded sheep and plowed fields until mountain climbing transformed the mountains above their villages into a sporting playground and a new employment opportunity. Traditionally, the House of Savoy had supported mountain climbing: Luigi's grandfather, Vittorio Emanuele II, and great-grandfather, Carlo Alberto, had financed Italian guides. (Sella's uncle, Quintino Sella, had started the Italian Alpine Club thirty years earlier.)

In July of 1892, the Italian Alpine Club registered Luigi's climb up Levanna's eastern summit—a casual half-day scramble in which the duke was shepherded by the well-known lawyer and director of the Turin section of the Italian Alpine Club, Francesco Gonella, and a famous Courmayeur guide, Emilio Rey. A week later, they climbed Levanna Central by its north face (which the Alpine Club's 1898 guidebook described as "difficult and laborious, as many steps have to be cut"). The duke also stayed with Margherita at the queen's hut at Pointe Gnifetti.

The duke convinced Gonella—who was already impressed by the prince's quickness, endurance, and judgment—to take him up more challenging routes. By summer's end, they had traversed both Mont Blanc and the Matterhorn, and climbed the Dent du Ge'ant, Grand Paradiso, and the Breithorn. These climbs were important because they involved the full gambit of alpine experiences: rock gymnastics, snow climbing, and logistically complex traverses. All played an important role in his development as an alpinist.

Gonella reported to the president of the Italian Alpine Club about the hardest of these climbs:

> Advancing we found the crest in bad condition. The rock, growing steeper and steeper, was covered with a coating of light fresh snow. [The guide] proceeded surely and with the greatest calmness, cutting steps continuously in the solid ice and prying the thin layer from the rocks. The Prince, appreciating the gravity of the situation, showed himself calm and undisturbed throughout the ascent, never once slipping, and already giving promise of becoming a bold and skillful mountaineer, in no wise betraying the ancestral courage of his race.

R elative to the prince, I was a pauper. Somehow I had to find a sailboat, borrow the money to buy it, and learn how to sail if I wanted to climb Yasetaca stylistically. First on the agenda, however, was finding a partner.

Since I didn't know how to sail, my partner had to be a sailor. Next, he had to be able to withstand the rigors of cramped tent or boat quarters, bad jokes, and personality differences. Thanks to my own absence from climbing for several years, I needed a partner who could lead steep ice or rock, break trail, carry more than his fair share, and be (or at least act like) an eternal optimist.

Age was also a consideration. A partner halfway through life like myself wouldn't be "hungry," hormonally driven, or as likely to commit all to reaching the summit. Most forty-something partners would have nothing to do with a month before the mast in Alaskan waters, let alone slogging in a week from the sea—which could be so neatly remedied by an hour's ski-plane flight. Add to this that many modern climbers aren't interested in risk taking, a long-dead duke, or the debauched lifestyle of mountaineering. The new vision involves absolute safety, easily accessed roadside crags, and rendering climbing into an official Olympic sport. Candidates weren't exactly knocking down my door. Most Alaska-bound climbers were more interested in the famous Denali anyway, a place that I had spent too much time with already.

The last time I climbed North America's highest mountain, I got to know Jeff Hollenbaugh: a six-foot-tall, lanky, kind, and deferential fellow who made up for his youthful naïveté with directed energy, a knack for organization, and an assumption of goodwill toward everyone he met. At first glance, his round, wire-rimmed glasses and self-composure gave him an intellectual air—which was hardly true, but spending more time with him did make me wonder how I had misspent my own youth. He was barely of legal drinking age on that trip, yet severely motivated and technically adept. Cheerfully, without complaining, he voluntarily escorted a sick climber back down the mountain while I went to the summit on the first good day for a week. Then Jeff sauntered back up to the summit at midnight, returned for breakfast, and began his descent with a crippling pack—all before I could take down my tent. Jeff had also climbed Denali previously (with his father), as well as other subarctic mountains, so he was no intern.

Inviting Jeff to Yasetaca, it turned out, was a package deal that included his father. Gary was a semiretired optometrist, one of Jeff's closest friends, and vital in selecting, let alone sailing, a small boat 1,200 miles north from Seattle. Gary was forty-eight years old and accompanied Jeff most places. Little was taboo between them. They could easily be mistaken for regular accomplices until you overheard Jeff being addressed as "son."

During high school, when Jeff was partying and doing whatever he pleased without listening to his parents, Gary gave him a father-to-son talk about being an officer in Vietnam and how troops Jeff's age always took his suggestions. That impressed Jeff and brought him closer to his father, or so he said; such a statement of authority would have crumbled my own adolescent relations with my father.

While many Vietnam veterans might carry the war as a badge or a cross, Gary would not flaunt his combat experiences. Politically, he was left of center, more dove than hawk, yet he held no grudge against McNamara, Nixon, Westmoreland, or LBJ. Once he arrived back from Southeast Asia he had to wait a while before he could shoot a rifle again, and since his two sons weren't too interested in hunting, he quit rifle hunting because he "didn't like to see the light going out of the animals' eyes." He still regularly volunteers for the National Guard.

He was a slight, five-foot-eleven, unlikely looking, graying adventurer wearing large glasses. Underneath an aw-shucks country-boy affectation, he read books voraciously, would not admit to chronic seasickness, and rarely hired a mechanic.

Jeff had reluctantly shared his own war story with me. It happened to him and a climbing buddy in rural Peru, on the back of a *colectiva* open-backed truck. Jeff and Mike had hitched a ride along with a score of villagers. No one knew that the Shining Path guerril-

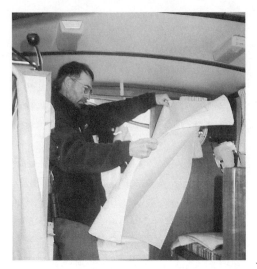

Gary Hollenbaugh,
finding our position.

las had declared that particular day off-limits to all traffic. Suddenly Jeff heard what sounded like firecrackers, and then the people next to him were inexplicably moaning and a baby started screaming, until their voices abruptly ended. Everyone dove under blankets and hid. Then the gunfire stopped. Voices approached the truck. The truck driver got out and began arguing with the voices, who began poking gun muzzles at the truck's human cargo. Jeff was certain that he would be executed, but fortunately he and Mike—the only gringos—were hidden. The guerrillas let the truck pass and none of the passengers spoke for what seemed like hours, until the truck arrived at the next village. It all felt like a nightmare to Jeff; the bodies didn't look real, so he avoided looking at them.

Afterward, when Gary picked him up at the Denver airport, Jeff immediately held forth. There wasn't much his dad could say or do, other than suggest that telling his mom would cause undue worrying. (When I picked up Jeff to leave, Marilyn pulled me aside, apologized for the tears running down her face, and said, "Please take care of them, Jonathan.")

Gary referred to his own retirement as a time to adapt Jeff's sort of lifestyle: living simply in order to pursue his primary passion (climbing). And Jeff so constantly referred to "Mom and Dad" that one might think he was still living in the nest.

On the eve of departure, not wanting to worry my own mother and father, I told them I was going to sail up to an Alaskan mountain. This time, with the boat, versus climbing, I could at least claim some genetic impulses: my grandfather had been a Hudson River pilot and my uncle Will had roamed the world until his fifties as a merchant marine. On my mother's side, I was related to Sir Francis Drake. Dad determined that his ancestors had sailed over to Plymouth Rock three years after the *Mayflower,* but liked to keep us from feeling high and mighty by reminding us that we were also direct descendents of the Revolutionary War traitor Benedict Arnold.

The cognoscenti of alpinism commonly debate whether training or your gene pool alone—known as "climbing off the couch"—prepares you for a hard climb. But I wasn't taking any chances, so I had scared myself witless bashing knuckles against the ice (fear makes you overdrive your ice axes) while following my friends up frozen waterfalls. Climbing short, vertical ice pitches is always good psychological and technical preparation for the long, moderate ice faces found on mountains like Yasetaca.

During a ten-day sortie to Ecuador, I earned a splitting altitude headache trying to guide some friends up Chimborazo within a day of climbing Cotopaxi—peaks slightly higher than Yasetaca. Back in Colorado, I spent several sleepless nights on fourteen-thousand-foot peaks, in hopes of gaining some high-altitude acclimatization. Jeff and I staged one twenty-four-hour ski-walking marathon, twenty-nine thousand feet up and down our local ski mountains.

We often met to peruse the tattered 1-to-250,000 scale five-hundred-foot-contour-interval map (left over from the Mount Logan climb I had done in the St. Elias Range when Jeff was in kindergarten). The map itself was undetailed and small-scale for our purposes, but our imaginations easily made up for the mysterious landforms presented by inadequate mapping. By now, we were generally oblivious of most of life's normal routines because we were so busily running fingers over maps and ogling photographs of Yasetaca.

The mountain soon emerged from our one-dimensional references as if I were confronting and worrying my three-dimensional talisman all over again. The Hollenbaughs and I each customized a mountain for our own private yens, something to fill the vacuum of tapping keyboard or nails or eyeglasses, something that can make you quit your job and leave your girlfriend or wife, then commit yourself to inexplicable desire. We had created our own Moby Dicks.

In the bustle of preparation, building any further upon the foundation of "why" I climbed mountains, even though I had a specific "retirement" goal for Yasetaca, would have distracted me. Besides, it's a question universally disdained by active climbers. Although my marriage had just ended traumatically, the event was not entirely connected to my motivation for attempting Yasetaca: I had originally asked my wife to come with me. Climbing the mountain, I figured, would simply put some balance back into life. I had stopped seeing a therapist, because I was long overdue (as she had suggested) "to start taking care of " myself, even though she recoiled at the potential "death wish" of my Yasetaca plans.

The therapist counseled me that travelers deliberately select the length and difficulty of their journey relative to the amount of pain they are suffering. I denounced her observation about the same time I left both therapy and marriage.

But the thought occurred to me, as Jeff's dad loaned me enough money to become his sailboat partner, that I had designed the longest, costliest, and most challenging and convoluted expedition of my life. The therapist had been right, except for one thing: Everyone must choose his own method of healing.

Sailing 1,200 miles north from Seattle to the mountain would take us at least three weeks. The duke's team covered the same distance in ten days with a steamer, racing to catch up to an American team. But the Italians first had to cross the Atlantic and the North American continent, so getting to the shore below St. Elias took a total of thirty-eight days. Attempting the mountain would take Jeff and me another three weeks (the duke spent five weeks), while getting the boat home might take another month (or two, if Gary would let me single-hand the boat back to Seattle). I could expect to be gone for four months—just like the duke.

The first 1,000 miles up the Inside Passage is an archipelago ripped by tides, thick fogs, and contrary winds. "Inside" is a bit of a misnomer because there are several crossings exposed to open ocean, and many of the passages act as natural conduits for the wind. Some of the straits are so large that they create their own localized storms and huge waves; locals call them "gulfs." And the last 200 miles out in the open ocean to Alaska's Icy Bay beneath the mountain promised some foul seas. It wasn't Cape Horn, but we weren't Joshua Slocums either. (See map on page 2.)

My two partners and I also could have been justifiably set back by the last open stretch of Pacific—uncharted reefs, williwaw winds sweeping from the mountains along the Inside Passage, infamous tidal whitewaters and whirlpools, and collisions with stray timber and ice chunks—or by my knowing nothing about sailboats. But at the moment of departure, in the last week of March, our primary preoccupation involved leaving the confines of our Seattle marina without ramming one of many yachts, squeezed into their slips like purebreds in a lavish dog kennel. We had already spent the first few hours of our journey unable to start the engine; one of us finally figured out that we'd left the choke handle up.

Certainly, Gary was more concerned than I. He wanted me to be fully involved in the piloting of the boat, to let me feel useful. Without words it was understood that it would be better to have me (rather than the experienced skipper) "T-boning" a neighbor's yacht.

Gary awarded me the wheel, trying to accommodate my philosophy that we were embarked upon an adventure with all of its uncertainties. I had insisted that spontaneity had certain advantages over planning and whatever happened was simply *whatever happened.* After all, the boat was insured, and I had already verified that we were all good swimmers. He undoubtedly was pondering the fact that most of the hulls around us were constructed from lightweight, and in some cases *translucent,* fiberglass.

He and Jeff watched with concern as I shoved it in reverse and goosed the gas lever of our four-cylinder, forty-horsepower Perkins 108 engine. Fortunately, the Hollenbaughs were deft with boat hooks, and they frantically began poling us off the other boats, generally in the opposite direction that I was mistakenly steering the boat, hoping to gain the canal, only forty yards off. In reverse, our heavy-keeled sailboat responded as well as a 1958 Grand Coupe with busted tie-rods, flattened tires, and no steering pin.

Passersby on the Ballard Bridge above watched us bounce like a pinball between the other boats. Once we finally popped out into the canal, sweaty palmed all, pretending not to notice the growing assemblage of boat owners in the marina behind us—brandishing boat hooks and contemplating a call to the harbor police—it dawned upon us that it was some kind of a miracle that all boats, particularly our own, were still afloat. No one suggested changing our boat's name, *Heaven Sent*, again.

Judging from our first hundred-yard gain, we were going to need all the help we could in the next 1,200 miles just *approaching*, let alone *tackling* Yasetaca. The possibility of sinking the boat was foremost in my mind. Now that we were under way, dreading the coming night's moorage, I realized there might be some glory in turtling over in a storm or upon a distant reef—but we had now learned it was more likely to happen at a cramped marina or a fuel dock, under the unforgiving gaze of yachtsmen polishing their teak, fishermen coiling their nets, or the eagle-eyed Coast Guard itself.

It is always in those first moments of calamity that everyone's role and rank in the greater team, as well as the subtle channels of communication, become known. In our case, there were few words spoken, but it was clear that Gary had become the *Captain,* Jeff remained *son,* while I became *cabin boy.* Becoming the odd person out is always something to guard against on expeditions, particularly if you're traveling with a father and son. I had already been dressed down by the Captain for forgetting a set of wrenches.

Truly, this expedition was my idea, and I had invited Gary and Jeff. But on this first seaborne leg, the Captain's military background, his superior mechanical abilities, and his sailing experience would demand acquiescence from anyone of lesser experience aboard decks. I shrugged. After all, I knew nothing about sailing, and assuming the role of subaltern might be the best way to learn.

Our friends and family figured that we might be able to climb Yasetaca, but our supporters were skeptical about three mountain men sailing up to Alaska. Yet the Captain was determined.

We would enter British Columbia two days north of Seattle, then southern Alaska after another ten days. It was tingling cool, spring-with-a-winter-hangover weather. Late March is too cold for most recreational boaters, which would reduce obstacles as we practiced tacking and jibing.

As we cleared all potential collisions in the several-mile-wide Puget Sound, the Captain asked Jeff to haul the sails. Jeff showed me how to unbutton the covers, clip on the halyards, and haul white sails into blue skies. We felt the boat "lifting" as the wind rushed down the lee side of the sail like an airplane wing—rushing to catch the higher pressure to the windward side of the sail, heeling the boat over to a disconcerting twenty-degree angle, and pushing us along as fast as our former motoring speed. The Captain killed the idling engine. I lurched for a handhold. Nobody spoke. Doors on the fore-berth and out of the cabin were framed under five feet eight inches. Since I'm six foot two, I had three eggs on my head as we snuck into Port Townsend at dusk. As I shut *The Handbook of Sailing*, the Hollenbaughs wrote in their journals.

I asked Jeff, "What you writing about?"

"Today's mishaps in marinas."

"Are we getting any better?"

The Captain spoke up: "Well, we haven't hit anything. Yet."

For me, keeping a journal was a way of venting emotions. Sometimes I wrote letters unintended for postmarks. I wrote down dreams, dabbled in poetry, and pondered how dissimilar I was from the duke of Abruzzi. If there was a common denominator for my journal and letters (a loosely bound collection of notebooks, computer diskettes, spare napkins, toilet paper, the back of maps, the back of a divorce contract, and end pages from bad novels), it was expunging fear, seeking truth, and getting closer to my dreams.

I wrote in my journal:

Dear Luigi,

You're long buried, taken by a cancer more insidious, more dangerous, and undoubtedly, more heartrending than all of your expeditions put together. Your 60 years were fuller than most men would even dream of living.

Enough patronization. I am going to find you up on Yasetaca. You were 24 years old then and although I know nothing about being a prince, I do know about the hormones and demons and desires that drove me up unclimbed mountains at that age—I once understood obsession and calculated risk, and although I am scared silly to revisit the halcyon days of my own youth, that's the only place I am going to get close to you.

You led 24 men into the unclimbed Yasetaca—none were younger than you. If you had led men by virtue of your position in life, or even with money, you would have failed as the more mature, influential, and monied leaders Kerr, Swatka, Russell, and Bryant all failed before you on Yasetaca. You reached the summit because, as you confided to one man, "You could not fail"; and because men saw that fire in your eyes and wanted to share it with you. I am going to find you up there.

[signed] Jonathan Waterman, No Count

In 1893, Lieutenant Luigi of Savoy, duke of Abruzzi, was second-in-command of the gunship *Volturno,* moored in Taranto. Following an incident involving the stabbing of an Italian officer in Somalia, the Royal Navy began bombarding the port of Merca and several surrounding villages. The *Volturno* sailed across the Mediterranean, down the Suez Canal, and into the Indian Ocean to support these punitive actions.

The commanding officer, Lieutenant Ruelle, was considered "inflexible," as well as quite anxious. Like most men who felt responsible for the young scion's safety and were afraid of answering to the king, Ruelle didn't want to expose His Royal Highness to danger. To Ruelle's relief (and the duke's disappointment) the uprising had been quelled by the time their ship arrived off Somalia.

The duke made several exploratory trips into the interior, but passively, unlike his more militant countrymen, who would lord it over their Somalian colonies. Here he learned of the safari style of traveling that is the nucleus of expedition-style mountaineering, as well as developing a lifelong fascination for Africa.

He was also developing an innate ability not only to lead men, but more importantly, to follow, while commanding the respect of his peers in a fashion that had little to do with his royal lineage. While offshore, the *Volturno* lost a man overboard. The duke rescued him, a complex maneuver under heavy seas because the ship had to quickly turn around, locate, then pluck the man from the big waves. Luigi was obviously quite bright, but he was also "one of the boys," never condescending, and a sailor who put the lives of his companions above all.

In a French book the Italian Aldo Bonacossa wrote about this period in the duke's life:

> This was a prince not like the others. He would have been a great man even had he not been a blue blood. As young as he was, he was already a leader. He knew how to form a team of companions who would be devoted to him throughout their

lives. He was sometimes a little exacting in his demands, and he never ceased to be a prince [maintaining aloofness], but he held a special place in men's souls, and above all, he set an example by hard work and struggling against danger.

Back in Venice, Ruelle filed a report about the duke living as modestly as his shipmates, not pulling rank, and disdaining princely invitations that didn't include his fellow officers. His charm and his composed cool under fire drew men both young and old to his side. Many of these men—Cagni, Petigax, Gonella, Rey, Sella, and De Filippi—became the sort of companions called aides-de-camp or guides, well educated and leaders in their own right, but they stuck beside their prince because they were also his friends.

Being at sea gave the duke plenty of time to observe the men under his command and under the often stressful call of duty. His later successes could be attributed to his powers of observation, his judgment of character, a leadership style more democratic American than monarchical Italian, and a good ear (during decisive briefings of his World War I admiralcy, an English naval officer frequently observed the duke of Abruzzi *listening* while other officers argued). His time at sea, while doing nothing for his aerobic fitness, was also superb psychological preparation for the spartan lifestyle and objective hazards of mountaineering.

During an 1894 shore leave, he had a fantastic season in the Alps. He took Gonella and an educated but not very accomplished Courmayeur guide, Giuseppe Petigax, known as "la Bionda" (because of his blond beard). He climbed Mont Blanc—a moderate albeit arduous outing. Then, above Chamonix, he traversed difficult rock routes on the Gre'pon and the Aiguilles des Charmoz. He climbed the Petit Dru and the Aiguilles du Moine. Above Zermatt, he climbed a dangerous route exposed to rockfall on the Dent Blanche, then the Zinal Rothhorn.

After this tour de force, he met two acclaimed English climbers, Albert F. Mummery and Norman Collie, at Pointe Gnifetti. Mummery, a self-made man from the queen's England, disdained royalty, but told the duke: "I have heard people speak highly of you."

The duke characteristically smiled and thanked him.

Mummery then extended an invitation to climb a difficult route up the Matterhorn, baiting the duke to come without his usual retinue of guides, testing to see if he played only by royal conventions. Luigi eagerly accepted.

A few days later, Mummery telegraphed him that the weather was good. The duke sped to Zermatt, alone. His aunt, the orthodox Queen Margherita, was concerned (her baron admirer had died during a mountain outing from a heart attack, so she had given up "alpinism"). But she was always looking for ways to spotlight the House of Savoy, and a young prince boldly accompanying such luminaries of alpinism as A. F. Mummery up such a European icon as *Il Cervino* (the Matterhorn) would only burnish the crown.

Mummery had initially been blackballed from the prim and proper Alpine Club of England. His willingness to confront absurd difficulties, rockfalls, and avalanches grated against the old guard's traditions. Besides, he made his money from a tannery. But no one could debate that he had become the alpinist of record, so eventually they had to nominate him as a member. He also disdained the tradition of hiring guides, and was the first "amateur" climber who practiced on short cliffs in order to apply "rock gymnastics" to the mountains. The famed climber and explorer Sir Martin Conway called Mummery "the finest climber of his or any preceding generation."

Mummery, Collie (who discovered neon, and took the first medical X-ray photographs), an apprentice guide named Pollinger (taken along as a porter), and the duke stole a few hours of sleep behind a stone wall bivouac, then left before dawn on August 27. In all of Collie's many climbs with Mummery, they only slept in huts twice. Mummery had a bad back, which made him invent lightweight gear that was decades ahead of its time, as well as carry next to nothing, which impressed the duke.

In a letter to Gonella, Mummery—who rarely climbed a peak without a bottle of cheap red wine—wrote:

> Heavy clouds that engulfed the Dent d'Herens threatened to defeat us. It was clear to us that the only probability of success lay in completing the climb before the weather broke. The load was distributed among the party, of which his Highness took the safety rope, we climbed very rapidly towards the principal ridge. . . . A short ice slope separated us from the crest, but we decided to abandon one of our bags, and the wine and major part of the supplies. Lightened by such drastic measures, we spiritedly attacked the rock teeth. . . .
>
> The rib we found very cold and exposed to strong wind. . . . After a tiring climb up through a chimney by an ice wall, we reached the Zmutt Ridge, secure that we have overcome the most serious difficulty.

They reached the summit at 9:50 A.M.—completing the third ascent of the Zmutt Ridge (Mummery had cut his teeth on the bold first ascent fifteen years earlier). He closed his letter to Gonella with the story of the duke getting happily soaked in a rainstorm as they sauntered down to Zermatt that evening, and attributing their speed to both the threatening weather and "the ability and the dash of the Prince."

It was Mummery's last alpine climb. In the book *My Climbs in the Alps and Caucasus* that he wrote that winter (securing his fame), Mummery concluded that "it is not likely the ascent will often be made as rapidly." Enthralled by companions known as the elite alpinists of the day, the duke had learned about pushing his limits, an important lesson in any serious climber's career. At the same time he found a role model in Mummery.

Mummery nominated the duke of Abruzzi to the Alpine Club and broadened his networks and sense of purpose as a mountaineer. Early alpinism was a highbrow, clubby affair practiced by the gentry, but mountains also gave the twenty-one-year-old the opportunity to follow his passions. Climbing also provided welcome respite from his sometimes oppressive princely duties, which required him to project an image of nobility, restrain actions or comments that could be misconstrued by the press, and be courteous at all times as a representative of the House of Savoy. As a ranking officer in the Royal Italian Navy, he was also trained to set a proper example for the men he was to lead—many of whom were older and more battle-seasoned than he. The duke of Abruzzi was acutely aware of his position, of the need to maintain a regal posture, but while mountain climbing he could cut loose from the royal vestments, trundle boulders down mountainsides, and earn the respect of his companions by pulling toward a common goal—the summit—without pulling rank or royalty. Membership in the prestigious Alpine Club of England also gave his mountain outings an air of international orthodoxy, as well as providing a political tie to England for the House of Savoy.

Gonella reserved his criticism of the audacious climb and sugarcoated the Matterhorn outing in a letter to the king and queen: "This climb demonstrates how His Royal Highness interprets alpinism in its noblest form and his accomplishment is one which few brave men dedicate themselves to."

But it was his partner on that climb who changed Luigi's life. Mummery—charismatic, ape-armed and ham-fisted, forever bumbling with his owlish glasses—encouraged Luigi to cast off the pose of royalty and to take risks in the mountains. Most importantly, Alfred Mummery became a friend who cared little for royal status, but appreciated Luigi for his daring. Through Mummery's example, the duke found the inspiration to seek out difficulty for its own sake in the mountains and to initiate his expedition to St. Elias.

At the Captain's "O-five-thirty," he awakened me by brewing a liter of midnight-black coffee several feet from my head. On this, our first morning out, we motored into the thirty-mile-wide strait named after Juan de Fuca, who first plied these waters in 1592. Forty miles to port lay the bouncing Pacific; Seattle lay out of sight, thirty miles to stern.

Our pilothouse had a tendency to catch the wind, but comfortable headroom seemed more important for sailing to wintry Alaska. The *Heaven Sent* is five times as long as I, and one and a half times as beamy. The boat's 12,500 pounds and 195 feet of underwater volume implied that it should be more stable. To dilettante sailors in choppy seas, it felt like trying to stand atop a cantering horse. The keel was almost half the weight of the whole boat, so in any current, chop, or swell, the boat performed like an upside-down scale, swinging back and forth to balance itself out. Theoretically this lead-ballasted keel, which weighed as much as an unloaded pickup truck, would prevent that part of the boat above water—the equivalent of a loaded pickup truck—from broaching onto its side. The rocking and constant rolling activity was not the sort of movement that most steady-footed mountaineers would describe as comfortable.

The *Heaven Sent* drew five feet (which, the Captain explained, meant that we should not try to transit reefs with three feet of water on top unless we wanted to leave behind two feet of our keel). The Perkins diesel engine had a fifty-six-gallon fuel tank, and a small propeller that made six knots of engine speed sound like a race car stuck in a snowbank. Our humble sloop also carried an outdated loran radio positioning device, a marine VHF radio, two fire extinguishers, one taped-together fishing rod, the usual complement of running lights, compasses, buckets, scrub brushes, assorted cans of varnish, oil, cleaning solutions, flotation vests, a five-foot Achilles rubber dinghy, $1,200 of nautical charts, two months of supermarket bulk food, a month of freeze-dried food, an incomprehensible autopilot, and a broken depth sounder. Add four berths, a head (which the Captain forbade the use of in favor of a bucket), two anchors, winches, two foresails to complement the mainsail, a snug galley, a gimbaled propane stove, a nongimbaled diesel oven, a barometer, and, tied onto the backstay, a ten-foot-long, yellow-pennanted, floating spear for marking crew who went overboard.

Apparently Alaskan boaters had certain prerequisites for transiting icy waters, which we did not meet. We did not have survival suits, a global positioning system (our loran radio positioning device was unreliable), a wind meter, or an emergency inflatable raft (our rubber dinghy was considered subpar).

Marilyn had discreetly mentioned that her husband would drive for days to avoid flying, and since the liquid antacid she had asked me to stow on board was for "Gary's upset tummy," I suspected that all of us were going to be holding tight to the reins. Jeff assured me that his dad was a veteran sailor (upon Colorado lakes).

The water was friendly that day. As Jeff hauled the mainsail into a fresh breeze, white-sided dolphins arose to welcome us into Canadian waters. The Gulf Islands resembled the hills rising out of New Hampshire's lakes. Mount Baker arose to the stern as a huge saffron cloud, marking the northern United States. That world behind me— of saccharine therapists and painful breakups—that whole clanking web press of binding office work and call-waiting telephone conversations, faded into a seemingly distant past. Sailing consumed us all.

When the wind died and we reluctantly ran under power, there were hours to kill between watches. I consulted De Filippi's *The Ascent of Mount St. Elias,* the duke's own two-volume book about attempting the North Pole, a series of turn-of-the-century newspaper clippings, various *Alpine Journal* articles authored by (and about) the duke, and numerous other writings about the journey that we were attempting.

After his stellar season in the Alps, the duke of Abruzzi, now twenty-one, went back to sea on the *Cristoforo Colombo,* circumnavigating the globe and acting as public liaison for the Italian monarchy and the Royal Navy. In January 1895, he stopped in Calcutta and rode to Darjeeling—spying Kanchenjunga and several other eight-thousand-meter peaks beckoning along the skyline. Several months later, he learned that his friend Mummery had been killed in the Himalayas, on Nanga Parbat, while taking a shortcut over an avalanche-prone pass. The duke had been so strongly influenced by Mummery, he announced that he would attempt Nanga Parbat in the spring, after another season at sea.

One of his six Italian biographers, the geographer Giotto Dainelli, wrote:

> It is said, and truly, that those who love and understand and know how to conquer the mountain often remain indifferent spectators to the beauties of the sea, and that those who feel the fascination of the sea often remain without the slightest understanding of the divine majesty of the mountains. But he who has the full and complete understanding, both of the mountains and of the sea, must possess a remarkably keen and wide soul.

In 1895, the duke sailed to the United States and was feted in Philadelphia, New York, Niagara Falls, and Boston—where Italian Americans held parades and dinners in fond recognition of the Italian monarchy.

The duke had corresponded with Israel Russell and read his account about his St. Elias attempt in the *National Geographic.* Russell, an American, had nearly reached the summit during his second attempt in 1891, losing six companions in a surf landing. The duke had also carefully studied the two other attempts on the mountain written up in the *Alpine Journal.* Like most climbers, his competitiveness made him fantasize about being the first to climb St. Elias, thought to be America's highest peak—it wasn't until 1897 that the *New York Sun* published a letter declaring that Denali was higher.

In the summer of 1896, while the *Colombo* was moored in Victoria Harbor, Vancouver Island's towering forests and the vast tracts of northern wilderness put him close to Mount St. Elias. Settling the score for Mummery, however, was the first order of business. In late December, the duke returned to Italy and began organizing for the Nanga Parbat climb, until the governor of India telegrammed the duke about the bubonic plague, which made overland travel to the Himalayas unthinkable.

A month later, with his trademark spontaneity and energy, he announced that he would attempt Mount St. Elias instead. The king and queen responded enthusiastically and agreed to support the fifteen-thousand-dollar trip. Their nephew had already gained notoriety for his climbs in the Alps, and if he climbed one of the highest peaks in North America, the resulting media attention could help put the rising Italian monarchy on the world map.

In March, for training, he and Gonella made the second winter ascent of Monte Viso—significant in that the duke was still stretching himself, seeking to find his limits, as well as testing the equipment they would need for subarctic Alaska.

To research his climb, the duke had been corresponding with American alpinists Professor Charles Fay and Professor Israel Russell; the latter provided information grudgingly because he supported a fellow countryman who also had his eye on St. Elias—Henry Bryant. The duke did not learn about this competition until after he had announced his own climb.

"I do not claim to be a skilled mountaineer," Bryant wrote to one of his colleagues, "but have had some experience in climbing in Switzerland." Like many geologists of the day, they were accustomed to adventuring out in the field, getting away from the stuffy norms of Victorian society under the pretense of bringing back scientific knowledge of the world. Russell went so far as to tell a reporter that Bryant "will probably reach the top of the mountain." Russell did not like the duke (who in turn graciously disregarded

Russell's antipathy), and he wrote to another geologist, Professor George Davidson:

> I fancy they [the Italians] intend to land at Icy Bay and try the south side of Mt. St. Elias. If they reach the summit of that route they will have done some fine climbing. I wish Prince Luigi all success, but think that Bryant has the best chance, as his party is much more compact and he himself is not afraid of hard work.

Bryant was "a man of wealth" who would typify the gentlemanly beginnings of the American Alpine Club—modeled after the Alpine Club of England, and somewhat more exacting in its membership requirements than the more plebeian Appalachian Mountain Club. He was vice president of the Geographical Society of Philadelphia, had supported two of Peary's North Pole reconnoiters, and had explored the Great Falls of Labrador—so his interest in climbing St. Elias was one part sport and one part scientific exploration. Then, with the entrance of the duke, a race of nationalistic promptings began. Most newspaper reporters did not understand the abstractions of alpinism, but *could* relate to a big race, so the newspapers presented it as the Americans versus the Italians.

Bryant's feelings about this were mixed, as he expressed in a May 5, 1897, letter to Davidson:

> The probable presence of the Italian party in the same territory this summer I cannot but regard as a most serious complication. On learning of their plans, I felt that I had already gone too far in my preparations to withdraw simply because others had selected the same field of operations. I regret exceedingly the possibility of international rivalry, and a possible duplication of the work.

Bryant sanguinely expressed his interest in "scalping" Mount Logan if his attack on St. Elias was successful; then, in a naive flourish of optimism about traversing the sea of ice, he wrote to Davidson about traversing out of the range and floating down the Chitina River to the Pacific. While Bryant gestured toward the moon and stars, the duke focused on a singular incisive mission: climbing St. Elias.

On May 17, Luigi left Turin with Umberto Cagni, Gonella, four Italian guides, the photographer and explorer Vittorio Sella and his assistant, Erminio Botta, and Dr. Filippo De Filippi. In London, they spent four days shopping at Edginton's Store, Edwards and Company, Eastman & Company, and Wratten & Wainwright. They purchased five Whymper tents, 99 pounds; two lightweight Mummery tents, 28 pounds; five oilcloths for the tent floors, 35 pounds; five tent rugs, 20 pounds; five folding iron bedsteads, 70 pounds; two cooking stoves, 30 pounds; an iron case with kitchen utensils, 30 pounds; a dozen bags of clothing, 575 pounds!; ten alpine ropes, 50 pounds; photographic supplies, 90 pounds; meteorological gear, 40 pounds; and sanitary supplies, 40 pounds.

Sella purchased sixty twelve-by-sixteen-inch glass plates for his large-format camera (he would only expose one plate), one ten-by-eight camera with assorted lenses and six hundred films, and one seven-by-five-inch Kodak with twenty rolls of thirty-two-exposure film.

On May 19, 1897, Sella wrote home to his wife, Linda: "Don't think of me as a man without a heart and occupied only in the ambition to succeed in this journey." Already the duke had shown his singular focus, and the men were stepping in line behind him. Sella complained to his wife about his seasickness while crossing the English Channel, and told how the duke reassured him that the Atlantic would be a calmer crossing in a big steamship.

De Filippi wrote in *The Ascent of Mount St. Elias* about steaming across the Atlantic:

> Our guides showed an indifference to their surroundings only to be compared with that of Arabs. Hurried away from their quiet valleys into the tumult of London, and thence on board, none of the strange new sights they saw roused them

from their apathy. Of course they were sick during the first hours at sea, but speedily recovering, spent whole days in the second-class smoking-room playing endless games of cards.

They arrived in the New York quarantine station on May 28 and "were instantly attacked by the first American reporters, who swarmed on board with the Health and Customs officers." The Italian ambassador had already pulled strings in Washington, D.C., effectively preventing customs from opening up over fifty crates of provisions—which would have delayed the Italians for days.

Professor Fay arrived and told the duke that his American competition, Bryant, had a two-week head start. As a sporting man, the Duke was determined to close Bryant's lead. The *New York World* headline read "Race for Big Mountain Top." One reporter misunderstood the duke and wrote that he had never climbed mountains before. To another New York reporter, the duke tried to downplay the race and spoke directly about his motives:

> We do not care to have our expedition considered in the light of a braggadocio. The members of our party look upon mountain climbing as good sport, and it is in that spirit that we propose to try to ascend St. Elias. . . . It must not be understood that we are undertaking a scientific expedition. It is purely what we are pleased to term a pleasure trip.

But most papers were not nearly so objective. A May 25 *Seattle Daily Times* headline, "Race of Governments for Exploration Honors," picked up a story from the wire that ran in several other American newspapers:

> There is another incentive, and that is that great honor must not be left to be carried away by the young man whose one important distinction entitling him to world-wide notice is connection with the nobility of a European country. To beat

the "Dago Prince" is undoubtedly the greatest incentive to the present activity in the Bryant expedition.

Similar stories ran in other newspapers. How the prince would be "disappointed . . . to find the matchless banner of the stars and stripes" already atop St. Elias. Or that Bryant, in the interests of international fairness, should wait for Luigi "below grim old St. Elias" in order that they could race for the top at a given signal. And that Americans should celebrate once Luigi reached the summit, for unlike "marrying rich American girls or negotiating heavy loans of American money," he could not carry the mountain back home with him.

The duke's right-hand man, Umberto Cagni, thirty-one, was introverted and quiet, indisposed to madding crowds, but able to make the duke laugh with his trenchant humor and quick intelligence. They had long been friends, so when Cagni saw how the press had entered a feeding frenzy, and after the duke was misquoted in the *New York World,* Cagni shielded the duke and became his spokesman. The duke was fluent in English, and after reading the erroneous stories, he maintained a lifetime disgust and aversion for journalists.

It took them three days in an express train to reach California. Cagni jousted with a *San Francisco Examiner* reporter. The duke was described as cheerful and referred to the climb as "no more serious than a *stipple shase.*" Cagni choreographed the interview for the reporter:

> Lieutenant Cogni [*sic*], known for short as Chevalier Tenente di Vascllo Umberto Cogni [*sic*], laughed with eyebrows and shoulders and elbows at the idea of a serious purpose or a possible contribution to scientific literature. . . . "What is it you would have of me?" he began, speaking English well, but with an effort. If a word failed him he dived into a little red dictionary and ran his finger frantically up and down its pages leaving the sentence suspended in midair and

the audience tense with nervous excitement, till a rapturous smile broke the suspense, and the sentence went on from the very syllable at which it had stopped.

"What can I give you?"

"Two thousand words if you will."

"Two thousand! But I could not say so many in a week."

"As many as you wish, then, and we will make up the rest."

"Yes, and how should I come out? Half Italian sportsman? Half American young lady! Do you understand French?"

"If it is baby talk."

"But we do not scale Mount St. Elias in baby talk. No, we will keep to English."

Cagni turned to the maps and showed their route north. Then he began explaining the pile of gear surrounding the reporter.

> The supplies of the party weigh some 2,000 pounds, and are of a luxuriousness that would suggest the amateur explorer to the American mind, which considers indifference to comfort the first sign of the professional. . . . But the nephew of King Humbert [sic] prefers to risk his life in well-fed comfort, and the outfit of Prince Luigi contains all the comforts of a first-class hotel.

They carefully packed their food into fifty tins, welded them shut, and placed them in canvas bags with more food. Each day's ration (canvas bag and tin) weighed fifty-three pounds and would feed ten Italians: cigars, chocolates, tea, coffee, three pounds of sugar, two pounds of cheese, three pounds of soup paste (mock turtle, oxtail, or chicken gumbo), forty biscuits (five hundred reserve pounds of biscuits would be left on the yacht), a small pot of English mustard, nine pounds of different meats (varied with tongue, ham, and salmon), assorted other foods, and a three-quarter pint of rum.

De Filippi packed a thirty-six-pound medical chest containing "a small box of ophthalmic tabloids, one of drugs for subcutaneous

injections, some tubes of lanoline, powders for curing snow dermati-
tis, a few tubes of ethyl chloride for a local during slight operations,
and other medicaments of secondary importance." Several para-
graphs later, he suggested that climbers carry darker sunglasses, but
in case of snow blindness "the sufferers were all quickly cured by
applications of cocaine."

A few days north of Seattle, we swirled into British
Columbia's Seymour Narrows. This riverine section of
Inside Passage waters is squeezed through a bottleneck between
Vancouver and Quadra Islands. Over one hundred vessels have been
destroyed in whirlpools or tidal currents here—two dozen of them
large seagoing ships. I pulled out *Sailing Directions,* a book that we
consulted whenever dazed and confused, or whenever the helmsman appeared to be getting drowsy. I read aloud to the Captain:

> "Small vessels have been capsized with loss of life while
> navigating Seymour Narrows even near slack water and in rea-
> sonable weather conditions. . . . Precautions should be taken
> to maintain adequate stability and trim even when planning to
> transit at slack water. All crew members should be alert and
> ready to cope with any emergency."

Jeff ran up to the bowsprit and hung over the rail watching eddies
toss our bow ten degrees to starboard and port. The Captain flung
three life vests out of the lazaret. I closed *Sailing Directions* and
started another round of coffee.

A week north of Seattle, we anchored next to a logging operation at
the north end of Vancouver Island. Smoke and flames wafted
upward as Jeff and I took our first exercise in a week: a ten-minute
walk on our new sea legs. Our aerobic fitness and our balance were

severely diminished. I kept tripping. The trees seemed to be swaying. Twice I landed in a push-up position amid devil's club and nettles. Jeff was having the same problem, as if seismic activity were shifting the ground beneath us.

We quickly fell back into our bathtub-sized dinghy and began rowing out to the *Heaven Sent*—narrowly avoiding a capsize as I stood up to relieve a cramp in my leg. Jeff and I didn't talk about walking into Yasetaca with hundred-pound-plus packs, or about our dissipating fitness. We had enough to worry about just getting to Alaska.

Once we were aboard the bobbing boat, the trees stopped swaying and a clean ray of light isolated our schooner in a soft glow against the gathering darkness. It seemed as if all those things dark and unknown awaited us abeam. This way, the unfamiliar path, was smoking madness, with apocalyptic-looking clear-cuts and glacier tongues refrigerating the sea. Abaft, to the south, I saw only the welcoming light of the sun and gentle familiarity.

The Captain raised his porter and we toasted our nightly thanks to Neptune for sparing us yet again. Tomorrow was always in question. I wondered what I was getting myself into.

We first hit the big swells of the Pacific outside of Queen Charlotte Sound. Dall porpoises jumped ahead of us, but no sooner did I get out on deck than they fled. We were running on our small storm foresail and a shortened or reefed mainsail. A faint smile lit the Captain's face as I pointed out the black cloud wall racing toward us. I opened *Sailing Directions* and read aloud from a description of a sheltered cove, several miles to stern.

The Captain wouldn't alter the course. I held my tongue.

"Well," he said, "guess you guys better secure the cabin and throw me some storm bibs." No sooner had he pulled them on than it was upon us: the wind kicked up ten-foot seas as the boat heeled over and I checked the knot meter: six knots. Leaning to port, I noticed our starboard teak was running in the water; pots and books and plates crashed all around us. Jeff shouted, "Mom will never let him do this!" He looked as white as I felt, knowing that we were fifteen miles from the next sheltered anchorage.

The Captain shouted in: "You wanna take it, Jonathan?" I was out in a flash. Once at the helm, I marveled at big sets rolling in from the ocean, long and gentle furrows plowing in from the west instead of the short-wavelength chop of the Inside Passage. With the ocean in our teeth, Yasetaca seemed somehow closer as I threw down the dodger and father began throwing commands to son and they braced themselves under the mainsail and threw in a second reef for mom. A feel for the boat came to me then, that sweet point where the rudder held true while swinging the wheel against a weathered hull (when steering into the wind, the sails pull the boat out of a steady course), and as I closed my eyes, the Captain shouted from the foredeck: "Don't hit that reef!"

I swung it another ten degrees into the wind and felt the sail lift as we picked up another knot of speed and the boat heeled over a few degrees, banking neat as a jet, carving water like air, and billowing out milky contrails from the bow. With the engine off, the valleys between waves felt electric. My fingers had turned white numb but the metal wheel felt hot to the touch. I licked brine off my lips as the rhythm of the big swells and a contrary wind pushed us north.

During Jeff's watch I went to the foreberth and listened to the bow cleaving the Pacific with the same unmistakable swishing smoothness that big rocks give to a river—entirely the opposite of the slapping noise while being pushed by our engine. I opened my eyes and wrote in my journal:

> April 7 / We all come alive when the sails go up. I love the clicking drive of the winches ratcheting up the main, ratcheting in the jib. I love this sailing water noise against the hull, and if I had more time I would catalog the difference between water caressing the hull on a beam reach, a broad reach, close-hauled, or fighting the current. . . .
>
> But I feel somehow dumb on this boat, almost drunken in clumsiness and newness to sailboat machinations. Broke a

shelf today by yarding too hard. Simple tasks such as positioning the pot grabbers on the gimbaled stove evade me. I have
been hitting my head an average of 2 X per day on light fix-
tures, doorways, and the like; if I brought a climbing helmet,
I'd be wearing it. Many bumps rising.

Have not fallen overboard.

Five days before the duke and his men arrived in Seattle, his chartered yacht, the *Aggie*, sailed north for
Sitka with eleven porters. Ten of these men were hired in Seattle by
Major E. S. Ingraham and would be freighting the Italian parapher-
nalia across the Malaspina Glacier to the base of Mount St. Elias.

De Filippi referred to them as a "queer group, such as could
scarcely have been got together in any other country." Seven Americans, a Swede, an Italian, and a German; five of them were sailors,
four students, and one thirty-five-year-old county auditor, C. L.
Andrews, who had left his wife and children in Seattle, hoping to
find new fortunes in Alaska. (Like me) Andrews wanted to learn how
to sail. Over the next two months—considering rollicking seas, rain,
mosquitoes, and snow—Andrews kept a remarkably tidy journal:

During night sailed 80 miles west and wind died out leaving us in morning just off the rocks . . . at morning of the 9th
June.

Lay all day in the [Queen Charlotte] sound in a calm. Sea
smooth and glassy except ground swell. Nearly everyone seasick. . . .

Mate let the boat jibe and the mainsail boom piece ripped
out of the rail. Had to double reef main and fore sail. Mate
Grant a crusty old fellow sometimes—tells me to do things by
sea names and kicks because I don't understand.

"Lend a hand here and make yourself generally useful[!"
he would yell.]

"Look out there that aint the right way pull on the throat halyards I tell you[!]"

"Helper you'd better go aft and lay down dont ye know anything about ships[!]"

Andrews closed that day's entry: "Hell going out to sea."

By day ten of our sail to Yasetaca, the only seafood I had pulled on board was a gray, mealy-looking, five-inch-wide starfish that had been clinging to our anchor. As the appointed fisherman, I was determined to set things right. We were anchored on the rim of a deepwater cove; fish dimpled the water left and right, while a family of bald eagles shrieked, beat the air with their wings, and dropped repeatedly into food-filled waters.

Under cover of darkness, I pulled out a week old slug of sausage, gone the same color as the starfish, and secured it to the hook by wrapping it tightly with brown thread. I swung it through the air off the stern, released the bale, heard a solid plop, and let the bait plummet fifty feet to the mud bottom. Fastening my rod to the wheel with a shock cord, I turned on my headlamp and peered into clear blue water surrounding an ever widening slick of summer sausage oil. As I adjourned to the foreberth, Jeff slung the contents of our toilet bucket just off the stern.

When the Captain's snores began softly ripping in rhythm to the waves, we heard line whizzing out of the reel. My head clunked both the foreberth and pilothouse doorframes. I tightened down the drag, yanked up the fishing rod, and quickly checked the fish's flight.

"So, Jonathan," said the Captain, "looks like you got us some breakfast." Jeff asked his dad where the fish identification guidebook was. They were both dressed in long underwear; I was shivering in a T-shirt.

By the time I flipped the dark object over the transom and into the cockpit, a low, inhuman grunt accompanied the squishy-sounding landing on the fiberglass deck. The Captain was holding the spotlight, and Jeff the fish guide. No one spoke, and it occurred to me that two men's fish was another man's *poisson*. The Hollenbaughs were undoubtedly thinking it was the ugliest creature they had ever seen: a crown of thorns wiggled like worms on its forehead, huge goggled fly eyes looked up at us accusingly, barbed fins were covered in slime, and five sharp appendages protruded from its groin.

I didn't care. My efforts would undoubtedly grace the breakfast frying pan, so I bent to remove the hook, but then Jeff shouted while pointing at the guidebook, "Don't touch! It's the spotted ratfish. Says here: 'Fins and five penises are venomous . . . and inedible.' "

Jeff wrote in his journal:

> 4/10/95
>
> Last night was the coldest yet and this rain is one step removed from snow. Midday we ignite the diesel oven for the first time. What a change in atmosphere. I shed two pile jackets and am comfortable in a tee-shirt. I get sourdough going and bake some muffins. The rain persists and the shifts at the wheel are cold and miserable. Taking the long afternoon shift, Dad brings us into Hartley Bay, a native settlement w/a dock pointed out to us by Paul [a Canadian sailor]. Paul's wife is very worried about us. She kept rolling her eyes, impressed and dismayed by our ignorance. They couldn't understand why we wanted to go climb St. Elias.
>
> I read the obituary for the Duke of Abruzzi. Motivated guy, ready for adventure. He was 24 when he climbed St. Elias, born 100 years before my time.

On June 13, after a furious day and a half in Seattle gathering their final supplies while trying to close Henry Bryant's lead, the duke and company boarded the *Topeka* steamship. They took bets on whether or not they would beat their porters' schooner *Aggie* to Sitka.

By their own admission to reporters, they were out for "pleasure," but the notion of a turn-of-the-century "sporting trip" was to beat out your competition. And one look at these "lean, gaunt-faced men accustomed to hardship," primed from first ascents in the Alps, belied the contradictions of their luxuriant rations, and of the prince's "boyish looking appearance." The duke and Cagni may have deluded various reporters with their lighthearted banter, but as navy men, they discreetly conducted their expedition as a military campaign for the glory of Italy. As the duke had confided to Professor Fay in New York: "We will not fail on St. Elias." De Filippi, however, was not a military man. As the prima donna of the Italian team, he complained about the cramped quarters of the steamship *Topeka*. Once leaving "the wretched hovels and vacant building plots leav[ing] ugly blanks in the spacious streets" of early Seattle, De Filippi wrote in *The Ascent of Mount St. Elias* that the enfolding scenery of the Inside Passage made up for their privations:

> Here the shores, vandyked in countless bays, are mossed with green pines to the water's edge, while towering in the background, the distant snow-peaks of the Cascade Range cluster round their monarch, Mount Rainier. . . . The entire coast, with all its islands, rocks, gentle slopes, sheer cliffs, and dark gorges, is so overgrown by dense forests of firs, that, from a distance, the whole seems one mass of velvety green.

Two weeks in rubber boots had given me the beginnings of what soldiers (after standing in trenches filled with cold water) had diagnosed as "trench foot." Under "Immersion Foot" in the third edition of *Medicine for Mountaineering*, I read:

> The cold induces intense vasoconstriction, which deprives the feet of an adequate blood supply. After a period of days or weeks permanent damage results, particularly to the nerves, and can be so painful that amputation is required. Sensitivity to cold is usually life-long.

In addition to the uniquely acidic odor that Jeff couldn't help but notice at night in the foreberth, my toes were as red and bulbous as ten Italian sausages. Walking hurt the least by hobbling on my heels. As a cure, I began wearing sneakers, regularly toweling my feet, and changing into dry socks twice a day. For the next few days, walking was not essential; swimming for shore from a sinking sailboat, however, seemed a fair possibility.

Jeff poked his head out of the cockpit and into the cabin: "What's cooking?"

"Lentil stew."

"Again? Great!" Jeff's enthusiasm was both stunning and magnified while living within constant arm's reach of one another. Up on the mountain such optimism could help us through all kinds of epics.

Jeff was twenty-four years old, pragmatic (like his father), and seldom outwardly disappointed. As far as I knew, he had never been brokenhearted in a relationship. He spoke with deference toward his parents. He withheld judgment in discussing mutual friends. And he wanted climbing to be his life. Like his father, Jeff never publicly complained, rarely second-guessed anyone's decision making, seldom vented his feelings, and was painstakingly polite.

We were different. After I asked Jeff, with the video camera rolling, "How do you *feel?*" he became frustrated and nervous. Both he and his dad needed to be asked how things *worked,* rather than their personal perception of events. Their strengths were prepared-ness, anticipation, general repair, and steady-handedness (mine were spontaneity, intuition, dreaminess, and recondite willfulness). Articulating emotion was no more a part of their family than engine repair was part of mine. Part of it had to do with the fact that father and son were well attuned to each other's thoughts and emotional rhythms, so discussion between them was limited and efficient. I settled into being the odd man out, an emotive chatterbox between two Victorian cowboys.

Their camaraderie was something I sought with my own father, who was content to stay home. The problem may have been my aberrant Uncle Will–Sir Francis Drake genes: I could not remain in one place, I was the black sheep of the family (although my parents never said so), and when my dad talked physics I swelled with pride even though the exact nature of his work eluded me. I watched the Hollenbaughs closely—and knowing that I would have to settle for getting whomped in tennis or walks on the asphalt, I tried to imag-ine Dad helping me reef the mainsail.

Other times, I wanted to scream because I had been nursing a dermatologic concern since leaving Seattle. It would have been unmanly to discuss this kind of thing with the Hollenbaughs. My crotch was afire down to my thighs—a reddened, mildewy rash that I scratched discreetly during the day. At night, I scratched the raw-ness in my sleep, beyond view of my companions, lest they think I had contracted crabs and would introduce yet another horrible form of sea life on decks.

I also had my "sea legs," which was supposed to be helpful, but felt disorienting. This adaptation to seasickness straightens out the conflict between your inner ear sensing motion and your eyes not seeing motion. So my balance center compensated for the swaying of the five-thousand-pound keel while I tried to stir a swinging din-ner pot on the gimbaled stove, or walked up to the foredeck in rau-cous weather, or pissed off the stern while hanging from the backstay cable running from the mast to the stern. If the Captain manned the helm, we used a pee bottle *inside* the cabin, because I had once underestimated a following wind while hanging behind him.

We had spent so much time aboard the jumpy *Heaven Sent* that we swaggered like drunks while walking on solid land. *Mal de debarquement,* or land sickness, caused a strange vasodilation, an ear-ringing rush of blood to my head. I would undergo a sensation of overheating and start sweating profusely, forcing me to strip to a T-shirt.

Shore leaves demanded concentration for other reasons too. As climbers upon a wilderness embarkation, we could not help waxing scatological and loosening our etiquette. To the scandal of prim and proper yachters, mountain climbers regularly descend into a state of food-sweatered teeth, stained clothing, and disarming body odors. It is not unusual for mountain climbers to hold flatulence contests, measure stools, and go on about the length of their ice axes as if they were another appendage. I made a mental note not to offend anyone abeam of the *Heaven Sent.*

In the huge port of Prince Rupert, I walked up the hill to a bait and tackle shop. By the time I had climbed the two-hundred-foot hill above our mooring, I was out of breath and the land was wobbling from left to right, then back again. I opened the door, walked past a clerk, and quickly grabbed some shelving so I wouldn't hit the floor. My face was flushed and beaded with sweat, I had a compelling urge to scratch my crotch, and it seemed likely that the entire store knew about my deficiencies in the bathing department. The clerk was staring at me as I stripped down to a T-shirt. A customer moved away. And to keep the aisles of sinkers and lures and plastic fish from jigging up and down, I stabilized it all by spreading my sea legs wide, then rocking back and forth.

The clerk—a nattily dressed and clean-shaven man who probably washed his hands after patting dogs—approached. "Can I help you?" he asked, as I thoughtfully took a step back and silently passed gas. No sense excusing myself—there was a small chance he would think it was another customer.

I said, "I need to try and catch dinner from our sailboat." Then I couldn't resist the rash any longer, so I gave my crotch a quick and casual-looking scratch, careful to suppress my sigh of relief.

"Have you caught crabs?" the clerk asked.

"Pardon me?"

"Dungeness crabs," he said, picking up a wire-mesh pot on an adjacent shelf, "are easy to catch."

"No"—I was blushing from the heat—"we're mostly interested in fish, like salmon."

"Have you tried flashing them?" he asked.

Jeff made his entrance, fielded a sonorous belch, and mentioned that he would be over at the liquor store. I suggested we go with three cases. The clerk continued filling my basket with an assortment of fluorescent lures, huge weights, and sharp hooks.

When we returned to the *Heaven Sent,* the Captain emerged from under the engine hatch. He wiped the grease from his hands, took one look at the grocery bag of tackle, and said, "Looks like they caught a real rube at the bait and tackle store." He summarily closed the lid on our Perkins engine and fired it up.

Leaving port, I felt myself relax, and started trolling with the new lures. As we bounced across Pacific rollers in the wide waters of Dixon Strait, the horizons expanded. Mountains grew bigger. The air got colder; we crossed the border into Alaska. Near sunset, no fish had yet hit the flasher.

Jeff turned to the loran and punched in the longitude and latitude for our position, then that of Yasetaca. For once the loran worked. It read: "600 miles." Halfway there.

Six hundred miles and years ahead of us, Henry Bryant and his seven companions slipped through the dangerous surf by coasting over a sandbar in lightweight Tlingit Indian canoes. For the long pull across the Malaspina Glacier, he had custom-built the same sort of heavy wooden sledges he had used in Labrador.

While the Italian team would swell to twenty-five men, Bryant's seven men began yanking and heaving 2,500 pounds up the convoluted surface of the Malaspina. Bryant had wisely enlisted Neil McCarthy, who had climbed high with Russell six years earlier, but unlike the Italians, the Americans were not trained alpinists.

Byrant had told a reporter from the *Seattle Daily Times:*

> In regard to the Italian expedition that is to follow . . . the promoters deserve no end of credit. They come from the other side of the world, almost, and take their lives in their hands to accomplish something that has a purely scientific value. I am not in the least prejudiced against the expedition. Alaska and the mountain are both big enough for several expeditions. I have furnished all of the details of my own equipment to the agent of my competitor [Major Ingraham], which does not seem as though I were jealous of my chances for success.

While the porters sailed up the Inside Passage on the *Aggie,* sighting on the North Star, the *Seattle Daily Times* printed a story of one of the porter-sailors, an Italian American working for Ingraham. Under the subhead "Will the Two Expeditions Scale Its Snowy Peaks This Year," Benno Alexander had written:

> Will Luigi of Savoy ever scale St. Elias' icy walls? That remains to be seen. One hopes for the best. And you American boys [referring to himself and the *Aggie*'s crew], who will have the distinction to be members of this Italian party, do your very best. . . .

Climb, heroes—sail!
Put your manhood to the test,
Sail and climb with mists abreast;
Some day you'll win your goal!
Some day the sunlit peak sublime!
The victory's yours in God's good time.
Climb, heroes, sail!
Mount St. Elias waits afar—
Mountains and seas shall naught avail
To eyes fixed on a star.

During our first attempt to leave the fishing village of Petersburg (after spending the previous night clandestinely moored at a fuel dock), we motored into Wrangell Narrows oblivious of the incoming tide. We were eighteen days out from Seattle, and two days south of Juneau. The Hollenbaughs and I were in fine spirits after celebrating Easter with greasy hamburgers and a disarming pancake breakfast. I was engrossed in *Sailing Directions*. The Captain manned the wheel.

Jeff called back from the foredeck: "Hey, isn't that the same cannery we passed a few minutes ago?" We looked up, checked our watches, then the tide book. The opposing current ran seven knots—faster than we could motor. We rechecked the cannery and it still seemed to be moving with us. The *Heaven Sent*'s bow bobbed back and forth, bucking a wind and gurgling at throaty full throttle against the current, but not making an iota of progress. The Captain silently executed a snappy 180-degree turn toward the fuel dock.

That night, after transiting the roiling Frederick Sound, rimmed by glaciated Alaskan peaks, we surfed one last wave into Farragut Bay's protected waters. As the Captain briefed Jeff on how and where to drop the anchor, I prepared chicken curried rice, shaky handed about the size of that day's waves. Remembering how the

Jeff hauling the foresail.

duke skillfully elevated the morale of his men, I poured a generous cup of Glenlivet Scotch and drank it neat.

The Hollenbaughs set the anchor after half an hour of gear shifting, backing, boat spinning, engine revving, shouting, chain rattling, and thumping on the decks above my head. The brown rice fizzed in the pressure cooker. My onion-raisin-curry sauce bubbled in the frying pan.

Jeff lowered the dinghy and began rowing ashore through the wind in order to find a horizon that wasn't performing jumping jacks. I discreetly pushed the bottle of Scotch behind a box of raisins as the Captain strode into the galley. "Smells like diesel fuel in here," he said, standing bowlegged, braced against a counter, seemingly alert to my expected indulgences.

"Could be an engine leak," I suggested, holding my breath and checking to see that I had hidden the bottle of Scotch.

He pulled back the rug and lifted the hatch for another snoop at the oil level (which had not changed a millimeter in weeks), and then began sniffing for leaking diesel fuel. "Nah," he said, "can't smell anything down here."

I passed him a beer and pointed to his son, a distant dot out the window. Jeff had reached shore a mile off—we had initially thought it to be merely a hundred-yard row—and the formerly tiny-looking stacks of crab pots towered over his head, while the "dwarf" spruce forest now appeared to be two hundred feet high.

"The Alaska factor," I said. "Everything's bigger than it first looks."

The Captain took a long slug of his Blue Ribbon. "Like making love near a lake." He held up his beer can, waving it back and forth to compensate for a loss of balance.

"Pardon me, Gary?"

"Fucking near water," he said, waiting for my laughter.

Ninety-eight years ago, De Filippi observed that the prevailing trees were Sitka fir. "Less numerous are the white larch, the pine (*Pinus contorta*), and certain varieties of fir. The yellow cedar (*Cupressus nutcanensis*), a much-prized wood, was nearly exterminated under the Russian rule."

For the duke and his companions, the voyage up the Inside Passage, while entertaining for its scenery, was an otherwise routine voyage for seasoned sailors. The duke spent his spare time charming the young women returning to Alaska from college, while the Italian guides and American miners swapped lies down in the second-class smoking section.

The *Aggie* arrived in Sitka five days ahead of the Italians. C. L. Andrews complained in his journal about performing pack drills for Major Ingraham with seventy-three-and-a-half-pound loads in a misting rain. De Filippi said the major possessed "great force of character." The major wrote about the porters being "husky fellows" (a poet, a teacher of the classics, and writers); they were all bored from waiting.

The major was considered an expert climber because of his ascents of Mount Rainier. He wrote a story for *The Mountaineer* newsletter in Seattle:

> Anticipating his arrival, we had hoisted the Stars and Stripes to the main truck and the Royal Standard of Italy to the fore truck. That gave the Prince his first opportunity to show his thoughtfulness and courtesy. Upon meeting him, about the first thing he said to me was, "Oh! I see you have my country's flag at your ship's masthead."

Meanwhile Bryant and his five companions had already reached the Malaspina Glacier, which took six days, thanks to the help of several Tlingits. Bryant wrote: "The difficulties of advancing equipments weighing 2,500 pounds a distance of thirty-six miles across a desert of snow proved formidable." Reporters referred to the duke's case of wine and sundry "dainties," but no one reported that Bryant was traveling considerably heavier, despite the use of lightweight silk tents and his condensed food.

Bryant's summit ambitions may have been doomed by his menu, which he called a "concentration of albuminoide [*sic*, i.e., water-soluble gelatin] and vegetable foods, compressed into strips eight inches by two and a half wide and one inch thick. One of these strips weighs eight ounces, and is sufficient food for two men a day." Because of its dubious nutritional value and potential for provoking gastrointestinal distress, the duke had not purchased any albuminoid—available only in England—during his own Liverpool shopping spree. As a military strategist, the duke deliberately chose a wide variety of food, as well as a flask of rum for each day's ration (an old British sailing tradition). He described his expedition drinking philosophy: "Only a small quantity of wine and spirits was taken, for if it is harmful to drink too much alcohol in the Arctic regions, a moderate amount is not only wholesome, but has also a decidedly moral effect by making the crew more cheerful."

As the Italians left Sitka for Yakutat, towing the *Aggie* behind the *Topeka*, buffeted by Pacific swells, Bryant's team wrestled their sleds up the Malaspina. Bryant wrote about the illness of a camp hand, "who succumbed to the hardships of the journey" (in all probability, the albuminoid rations; Dr. De Filippi later referred to the victim's problem as an "intestinal malady"). "Our invalid being unable to go farther," Bryant wrote, "it became necessary to leave Mr. Lathom, the officer of the United States Coast Survey who accompanied the party, to nurse him."

F rederick Sound was mirror still as we motored toward Juneau. The Captain had the mainsail hauled, like most mornings, even though there was no wind. I peered down to my reflection: bags beneath my eyes, creases on my forehead, and curry glued around my beard.

Two curious clouds sprang up over the water to starboard; pulling alongside, we found two humpback whales rising serpentinely every few minutes to expel a fetid wet cloud, inhale, then sink back under for another nap. Their ebony flanks were studded with barnacles, like cliffs showing their fossils.

I took a deep breath. We were breathing the same air! Under water the whales were undoubtedly talking or singing to one another, as the poet Mary Oliver wrote—"not for any reason you can't imagine."

Swarms of what appeared to be insects bore closer, until we realized it was a flock of snow buntings, northbound just like the whales, the seiners, the porpoises, and us. Even gentle movements of air had a glacial edge, cutting through our clothing and riffling the sail. The farther north we sailed, the more Yasetaca preyed on me. It was in the water, in the air, and on my mind. The mountain from the sea was going to be the ultimate realization of "the Alaska Factor"; the mountain would dwarf stacked crab pots, humpback whales, and climax spruce forests.

Then seven Dall porpoises, half ebony and ivory striped (like killer whales), zoomed in unexpectedly, describing fluid half-circle arcs under water and cleanly curling up into the air, completing the circle with a smooth reentry into the water—pantomiming the ancient black-and-white circle symbol of yin and yang. For once they did not shy away while we leaned out over the railing watching them frolic in our bow wake.

Jeff hung upside down and trailed his hand in the water, hoping to touch them. I hung ramrod straight out over the bowsprit, with the video camera at chest level. I filmed porpoises launching out of the water, pirouetting on their sides, spraying me with blasts of bad breath and water.

After half an hour, Jeff went aft to write in his journal and express the wonderment which he kept so carefully contained:

> Feeling a need to reach out and touch a porpoise I hook my knees over the bowsprit and drape my body toward the sea. Why I have this urge I cannot say, it's a very intrusive gesture, going up to a stranger and placing a hand on them. The porpoise captivates me because it's so at home in its surrounding, evident in the way they move, like the mountain goat on a knife edge ridge, or a raven soaring over a talus cone, movements that are intuitive, a way of life, not rehearsed. I'm jealous as they are content and comfortable in their home of water while I am afraid of the medium and travel over it in the clumsiest of ways. Outside of the desire for the physical feel of a porpoise (they appear frictionless), I sense a secret would be told through the touch. An enlightenment, that's going too far,

*Jeff communes
with a porpoise
from the bowsprit.*

but a hint as to how I could become more in tune w/ the salt-
water. I failed to touch but succeeded in getting as close as
possible and had porpoise surfacing, smiling, and breathing on
me. The desire to relax my legs and allow gravity to take me to
the cold water almost overcame my sensibility.

Up at the bow, all but one porpoise departed. This Dall's gentle
ballets, wide eyes, and slender snout seemed distinctly feminine.
She swam on her side to hold eye contact with me. Checking that the
Hollenbaughs were out of earshot, I quietly invited her to come
north with us to Yasetaca.

As they bore closer to St. Elias in their steamer, under the spell of Alaska's midnight sun, the duke's surgeon briefly described the unworldly Courmeyeur guides' amazement about the light. De Filippi wrote about how "a band of tawny crimson still hung, throwing strange reflections on the mountains beneath. The rest of the sky was a pale blue, growing fainter and colder towards the horizon."

For the first time in his narrative, De Filippi indulged his awe:

> Next we enter Prince Frederick Sound, resembling a vast, clear, placid lake. . . . Schools of porpoises disport themselves in the wake of our vessel as she glides through masses of jellyfish and great waving weeds. . . . [The sun disappears and icebergs] emerge suddenly out of the fog, and, drifting with the current, vanish as suddenly as they come. . . .
>
> At 1:30 a.m. the new day began to dawn, while the colours gradually faded away from the west. Our vessel glided on silently—furtively, as it were—in the solemn stillness of this enchanted world.

Sella wrote in his diary: "Those animated scenes, of a kind so different from our own [in Italy], will forever live in my memory as fantastic and emotion-filled."

Snowbanks lined the shore outside of the native settlement of Hoonah, twenty days north of Seattle. Breath rose out of our mouths and hung in the air like caption balloons above cartoon characters' heads. Our latitude and longitude were now a Caribbean yachtsman's worst nightmare.

The farther north we went, the more our journey resembled the duke's. The surrounding wilderness had changed little since the Italians had seen it a century ago. Moose and black bear strolled the waterline. Mountains rose straight out of the sea, and the late-afternoon air held laser clarity. Light such as this moved me with the effect of fine music. I danced a warming jig as the sun crept lower and brought out the pearly smooth texture of the waves, enhanced the blueness of the sea, and enriched dimensions. The light transported me. At that surreal moment, if someone had told me that we had just gone backward in time, it would have fit.

De Filippi's book and its observations continued to match my own: "Against this, all the mountains stood out in their minutest details, with the crude white of their snowfields, and the curious, delicate indentation of their crests."

To the stern, two dozen Dall porpoises tripled our boat speed, jumping half out of the water, zigzagging in rapid synchronization beneath one another, cavorting in the light. They moved up to our bow wake. Jeff acrobatically hung upside down again from the bowsprit, locking his lower legs around the railing, extending his body full length, and poking a hand under water. Then it happened: this powerful mammal—swimming urgently, faster than the forty-horse, five-knots-per-hour trot of our Perkins engine—sidled over. It nudged against Jeff's fingers until he felt its rubber yield. Then it galloped off in a flurry of jumps.

"Help me," Jeff yelled hoarsely—as if he was going to let go. I caught his hand and reeled him up in a paroxysm of shivering. For once he was speechless. He couldn't explain what had passed between him and the porpoise.

As the sun finished its parabola into the nearby Pacific, I felt a barrier go down—the kind of release we all hope for and rarely find. Jeff wasn't going to say it, but you could feel these things; for me, it was the surreal yellow light, the unity with wild mammals, and the realization of existing happily in this place and time. The porpoises had shown us that we *belonged*—past, present, and future; that we shared an indiscernible nucleus. The Captain, Jeff, the Italians, the porpoises, the sea, the mountains, and I. We were all one. You didn't say such things on this boat; I only knew how I wanted us all to feel.

Nothing could stop us. We walked back aft together in silent contemplation, grinning like stoners as I keyed the latitude and longitude of Yasetaca into the loran, heard a few beeps, and within a half minute, got a new readout: "170 miles."

O-five-twenty: the eastern horizon was rubied meringue. I shivered up on the foredeck. Frost chalked the *Heaven Sent*.

The Captain suggested hauling the mainsail. I had adapted to this habit of raising the sail when there was no wind. In addition to exercising *Jeff* by sending him up (*I* avoided scoldings by avoiding the sailboat rigging), the salty philosophy went something like: Why motor in an underpowered boat without the sails it was designed for?

Stinkpots (powerboats), tugs, seiners, trawlers, ocean freighters, ferries, and cruise ships passed us with such frustrating regularity that we began to feel like a Model T on the interstate. These ships overtook us at five and six times our own speed and battered us with oceanic wakes. Having a sail up, even if we weren't sailing, helped justify our ponderousness; sails might also identify us more plainly and keep the freighters from splintering us into fibrous glass pieces. According to the indispensable *Sailing Directions*, all vessels under sail have the right-of-way.

As we rose and fell across the last few miles of Cross Sound, rather than consider the vast Pacific—like a worm crawling across the furrowed fields of Kansas—I turned inward, to my own tidal dilemmas.

A month's worth of competition eating and beer drinking—pitted against the extraordinary metabolisms of the wiry Hollenbaughs, and abetted by the sort of minimal exercise that the statistically average American considers to be healthy—had put me in an entirely new form. I had gained fifteen pounds.

"Looking on the bright side of things," giggled Jeff (still skinny and in a vital eating and growing phase long past for me), "we're going to need all the fat we've got to stay warm up on St. Elias."

Our boat was alone as we bounced around Cape Spencer out into the big Pacific. No one spoke. We mostly just hung on. The lighthouse repeatedly boomed out its plaintive cry, "Ommmmmmm," which resonated inside like the first part of the familiar mantra, but with an entirely opposite and disconcerting effect: silence; then a long "Ommmmmmmm" down in the gut. Another minute of silence; then "Ommmmmmmm."

I nervously listened to the prerecorded Coast Guard radio forecast, and although the steady-handed Hollenbaughs dissected it the first time through, I listened over and over again. After the seventh loop, my short-circuited attention span assembled that a storm was blowing in from Hawaii.

By the time the long-awaited 5 P.M. forecast update was due, we had pulled out of radio range. Even the loran had stopped receiving its radio positioning signal. At 6 P.M. we had to make a decision: take the last safe anchorage until 120-mile-distant Yakutat, or pull an all-nighter to beat tomorrow's storm. We were on the most tempestuous stretch of coastline in North America, where the deep Gulf of Alaska waters rose up onto innumerable shoals, cornered against a vast topography of silt-laden river deltas, crumbling glaciers, and uninhabited shoreline.

The Captain was easy: "Whatever you guys want to do."

Jeff wanted to keep going but said nothing.

I parried: "Prudence might be the better part of valor here." Since no one disagreed, I steered in toward Dixon Harbor. Jeff tried not to look upset, but we had spent enough time together to surmise one another's thoughts, although not with the clarity of father and son. This guesswork, rolled together with my respect for the unique Hollenbaugh style of passivity—manifested as a daunting silence on decks—made me cave in and steer back out into the Pacific. Jeff raised a clenched power fist and whooped with excitement.

Within an hour, it was as if someone had thrown a black curtain over the boat, then punched a few holes through the top for stars to pinprick in. I had drawn a 291-degree course on the chart, which would take us to Yakutat in twenty hours, *if* the Perkins engine didn't quit (the Captain had checked the oil dipstick five times that day). We all agreed to stay out at sea and not deviate from the 291- bearing, on the pain of "hanging twenty to the rails." (De Filippi had written that this "shore lies open, exposed to the full fury of the ocean, and so violent a surf that landing is always very dangerous and often impossible.")

We swapped three-hour watches. Falling up and down in the big Pacific swells in pitch darkness was exhilarating if you were standing at the wheel. Otherwise, there was no recourse but to sleep or give in to the nausea of seasickness. There was always the possibility of running aground, being pulped beneath a Times Square–sized freighter, or plowing into a napping whale—all of which kept the helmsman awake. The Captain steered with eyes flickering from the compass needle–bouncing thirty-five degrees east or west in the swells—to the North Star beyond the mainsail leech (rear edge).

At 9:30 P.M. ("2130" in Captain's Log Time), he drew abeam of the only lights for the next hundred miles: beacons marking the thirty-yard-wide entrance to Lituya Bay. Strong rips in its darkened entrance had foundered dozens of ships and drowned numerous sailors— beginning with twenty-one of J. F. G. de la Pérouse's men in 1786.

A cursory glance at the chart showed the six-mile-long, 720-foot-deep waters of the bay, but smart campers knew that it intersected the Fairweather Faultline—the most seismically active fault in the Americas. A dozen boats had been inundated by the bay's recurrent 50-foot waves.

Somewhere up above was the darkened Mount Fairweather. Sella wrote in his diary that the duke stared at it through the binoculars and was "thrilled" about coming back the following year to attempt it.

I had once attempted the stormy mountain. Climbing beneath huge hanging glaciers in such a seismically active place had unnerved me so badly that I moved out of Alaska and quit climbing for several months.

The Tlingits believe that mountains used to be people, and the woman, Fairweather, had been married to the man, Yasetaca. They fought and separated, and the mountains left between the two are their children.

Navigating by compass along this dark coast was a thrilling psychological ploy, akin to night driving on a highway, turning out the headlights, and playing chicken with oncoming drivers (we saw no boats). Staring at the compass too long had the same effect as being hypnotized by the double yellow line in the headlights. I spent up to fifteen minutes at a time steering off various stars, then going back to the compass and obsessing for anything stationary and lit so I could steer off it and hold our 291-degree course. I resisted following the dark and changing coastline, which would suck us off course.

I was relieved at 1:15 A.M. Jeff stayed awake by pretending that he was playing a video game with the compass, and to win he had to prevent the needle from jumping more than fifteen degrees in either direction. I slept deeply and dreamlessly in the foreberth. Even the Captain managed to hoodwink his recurring seasickness and get some sleep. Since the stars were mostly hidden, and Jeff found himself losing to his video game, he began orienting himself by the shadow of land to starboard. The more he thought about it, the 291 bearing seemed too far out to sea. Jeff unknowingly began steering us into a magnificent set of surf and sand shoals, two miles out from the Alsek and Tatshenshini Rivers.

I woke up with a start, sat up, and banged my head on the cabinets like most mornings. Dressed for action, I stalked up to the helm just as a faint thin strip of light began Band-Aiding the eastern horizon. Then I looked down at the sea. "What's that white stuff in the water, Jeff?"

"Just big swells," he replied sleepily, giving the wheel over to his dad. It was 4:30. I still couldn't pull an accurate latitude and longitude off the malfunctioning loran, so climbing atop the pilothouse (like riding in the saddle of a gimpy, trotting camel), I shined the floodlight out to starboard, saw more white foam, then heard muffled explosions coming from the east: surf breaking less than two hundred feet away.

"Turn west, Gary!" I yelled.

For all I knew we were in the midst of the shoals and being pushed in by the tide, so a westward course was our best bet. Jeff sauntered up to the foreberth, yawning. His dad wore his usual look of drowsy-eyed calmness—I wanted to grab him by the shoulders and shake fear or humility or honesty or a confession out of him. I implored him, "We're in too close, can you go out to sea any more?"

"I've turned us due west, Jonathan, ninety degrees."

"We'll be in big trouble if we get caught inside that surf! Can you give us more power?"

"Well, we're doing five knots." I shook with fear. Jeff shuddered with sleep. The Captain stoically put up with my badgering: "Keep it west, Gary! How fast are we going? Can you hear that surf still? Think we're okay?"

After half an hour of harassment, he shrewdly offered me the wheel and retreated into the pilothouse. The sky's Band-Aid became a gauze pad; then daylight leaked through the big wound above and the swelling in my throat (from adrenaline production) subsided; we had snuck around the shoals. Barely.

Although the nonchalance of the Hollenbaughs was impressive, dropping our 291-degree course could have sunk us. I spread my legs wide and fought off my sleepiness by imagining the *Heaven Sent* surfing inside a big Pacific curl. The ever-prescient Captain came out and spelled me as my eyelids were drooping. I stumbled up to my side of the foreberth. Jeff was out cold. Before drifting into another dreamless sleep of exhaustion, a smile came back to my face: I had become salty without killing anyone, and furthermore, we would probably reach Yakutat.

At midafternoon, ten miles from town, an all-enveloping fog appeared on the northern horizon. Storm darkened the western horizon and since this area had an annual 134 inches of precipitation (the Hollenbaughs' hometown averages 15 inches a year), I pulled on my foul-weather gear. We stared at "the fog" for an hour, wondering how we would navigate into the harbor, until I realized we were looking at the Malaspina Glacier—bigger than the state of Rhode Island. Now that we were virtually safe, Jeff confided that one of my closest friends had bet against us ever reaching Yakutat. Jeff and I high-fived it right there in the cockpit.

On the evening of July 22, the Italians steamed into Yakutat. The *Aggie* was towed behind—jerked relentlessly back and forth by the tow chain and buffeted in the Pacific swells. C. L. Andrews wrote in his diary: "Nearly all the boys were sick. Quite a sea outside and some wind. Fionni very sick. 3 of the guides over the rail. Fionni vomits blood. I am half frozen but not very sick today."

In Yakutat, the Tlingits were "waving pine torches," De Filippi wrote, "and swarmed to the beach, with savage yells, to which the barking of innumerable dogs made an ear-splitting accompaniment." The local missionary, a Swede, came on board to accompany the Italians to their landing site across the bay. De Filippi wrote:

> The teacher told me that the Indians are not hostile, though indifferent to the school, and that several of the children show quickness in learning. The village population is somewhat over three hundred. Like all Thlinkets [*sic*], they spend most of their life on the water, either engaged in salmon-fishing or hunting seal and otter.

Hoping to catch up to Bryant, they left at 2 A.M. Mindful of the surf catastrophe that had befallen Russell's expedition, they took along a Tlingit who had accompanied Bryant's landing party. The duke had closed the Americans' lead by the frenetic pace of the last two weeks, and by paying top dollar to the steamship company. An hour from port, they were forced to heave to (anchor) in fog. "So we passed the whole morning fuming at the delay," De Filippi wrote with competitive undertones.

As the fog cleared, they cautiously probed the shore. The Tlingit "who was to have acted as pilot, remained stupidly inert, and gave no sign of recognizing the coast." De Filippi described these people as "having smooth black hair, yellow faces, high cheek-bones, prominent jaws, slanting eyes, flat noses, and straight thin-lipped mouths. The men had a few bristles on lip and chin; the women's faces were smeared with dark, shining paste, composed of grease turpentine, and lamp-black, to protect their complexions from sunburn."

In 1787, the Englishman Dixon (who discovered Yakutat) sailed into the harbor and counted seventy residents. He badgered a native to wipe the paste off her face and discovered:

> Her countenance had all the cheerful glow of an English milk maid, and the healthy red which flushed her cheeks, was even *beautifully* contrasted with the whiteness of her neck; her eyes were black and sparkling; her eyebrows the same color, and most beautifully arched; her forehead so remarkably clear that the transparent veins were seen meandering even in their minutest branches—in short, she was what would be reckoned as handsome even in England. The symmetry of her features, however, was marred, at least in the eyes of her English admirer, by the habit of wearing a labret in the slit of her lower lip.

(One hundred years later, Professor Russell wrote, "We did not find the native women answering to the glowing description of the voyager who discovered the harbor; but this may be owing to the fact that we did not prevail upon any of them to wash their faces.")

C hatter filled the *Heaven Sent's* radio about a demasted yacht and several beat-up fishing seiners, caught by the storm that we had beat by running all night.

Thousands of geese honked above Yakutat, their wings rustling the air. Half-wild wolves tiptoed around the docks. Bald eagles shrieked from tall cedars as skiff fishermen gaffed coffee-table-sized halibut into pickup trucks.

Jeff and I laid out our climbing gear on the docks, alongside fishermen repairing their nets. We stuffed twenty-five days of food (oatmeal, chocolate, Fig Newtons, freeze-dried dinners, yogurt-covered peanuts, two pounds of coffee, powdered milk, and Pop Tarts) into four nylon bags, *sans* Glenlivet; filled our packs (with down sleeping bags, pile clothing, a tent, climbing rope, two snow shovels, six ice screws, twenty carabiners, two snow pickets, and forty feet of webbing); sharpened two pair of crampons and the picks on four ice axes; rigged drag lines for two plastic sleds; then loaded it all back on the boat.

The Captain was inspecting a munitions cabinet—bear guns, boat guns, bird guns, and a people gun (an Uzi)—aboard an all-black limit seiner. He invited the skipper aboard the *Heaven Sent*, hoping to get some advice about Icy Bay.

Marko wore the requisite Alaskan Carhart pants and a graying goatee which hid a double chin. He didn't appear to be armed except for a five-pack of Miller in one hand and an open bottle in the other. He stopped and laughed as he read the name of our boat; "Fuckin' fairies," he said, then stepped heavily onto our port deck, registering a ten-degree tilt on the inclinometer and spilling two cups of coffee in the galley.

"Icy Bay, no problem," Marko bellowed as he stubbed his thumb on the chart, helpfully showing us where to anchor, what shoals to avoid, and how only steel-hulled icebreakers were equipped to deal with the sort of unpredictable iceberg movement in the bay that we were going to. "You're fiberglass, right?" he reminded us. "You got any survival suits?" he asked.

"No," I replied.

"You're nuts. You got a GPS?"

"No," I replied.

"You guys are real turkeys, ain't ya?" Before I could reply, Marko asked: "Why you guys going into Icy Bay anyway?"

"Jeff and I are going to try and climb Mount St. Elias."

"You what?" Now his eyes narrowed with anger. "You haven't got the *wheels* to climb St. Elias." Marko studied us carefully, but before I could ask what *wheels* he recommended, he launched into us: "It's life or death up there. Do you know it's a world-class mountain?"

I looked into his eyes to show that I was listening, but this drove him half wild: his brown eyes bore into mine and he aimed his loaded beer bottle at me, sloshing some out for effect; then he began yelling as he leaned forward to hold me personally responsible: "Hey *stud*. Do you know that you are getting in over your heads! Do you know how many people have died up there? Do you know—"

"Excuse me, Marko," I asked, "do you mind if I film you?"

He brushed back his hair, slathered a sleeve across his runny nose, then silently waved acquiescence. But as I lifted the camera, he said, "No. It's not a good thing to do!" His eyes flashed. "I don't like being interviewed! It'll steal my being, know what I mean?"

I half nodded, but discreetly flipped the on switch with my thumb (Jeff caught it and flashed a look of horror), then set the camera on a bench, its wide angle taking in the listing port side where Marko sat, karate chopping a hand past his eyes and blinking: "Derecho," he said, slowly staring around the cabin at each of us for effect. "Know what that means?"

"You gotta be *right* on. *Derecho.*" Marko karate chopped in front of his face again, but this time the gesture appeared more of a private vision test than the Buddhist promulgation he probably desired. "This mountain's world-class and you guys are getting in over your heads. It's survival, *studs*, believe me, I been coming here thirty years. What right do you have to tax search-and-rescue capabilities, anyway?" Marko was putting on a fine performance, with little coaxing, and the red light on the camera showed that I was getting it all.

Jeff wagged his eyes worriedly at the camera and drew a line across his neck, mouthing: *Cut.*

"You guys have an extraction point?" Marko asked.

"No," I answered demurely, "we're walking in, no aircraft."

"Stud"—he twisted open another bottle, leaned forward, and breathed fish bones and cigarette butts in my face—"you're dead meat."

"You even bother bringing bear protection?"

The Captain fielded this one: "Remington, Wingmaster."

"What ammo?" Marko squinted as if we were vying to win the final question on *Jeopardy.* "Bird shot and slugs," the Captain answered.

"Ahhhh." Marko pounded the berth and roared with anger: "No, no, *no!* You fairies are never going to make it in bear country. You have to have *buckshot!* You're all goners, believe me!"

Jeff and I walked into town in a drenching rain, looking for ways to boost our morale, and picked up our mail. The Hollenbaughs received several fat letters apiece from their loved ones. I anxiously ripped open my three envelopes. American Family Insurance wrote, "Dear Mr. Waterman, This letter is your notification that a policy is not being reissued." Then there was a bill from Visa showing the ex-wife's continuing albeit unsanctioned activity on my personal credit card. I saved the letter—the usual prescription scrawl on medical stationery—from my doctor confidant, Ralph Bovard, for last:

Dear Jon,

Sorry I'm so slow to get back to you. For your Alaska trip, I recommend you bring a radio or cellular phone (with 911 emblazoned on the key pad), life insurance, snorkel (for proper ventilation when you get avalanched), size 6-0 suture and needles, 2,000 mg Nifedipine (for your predisposition with High Altitude Pulmonary Edema), Diamox (take 250 mg a day and beware diuretic bedwetting), 10,000 mg Demerol, 50 rectal suppositories for the inevitable hemorrhoids/ dehydration (not creme because at high altitude it's often mistaken for toothpaste); two bottles of "bean-o" for the devastating flatus of your freeze-dried diet; and 5,000 mg Dexedrine for those situations requiring a quick pick-me-up. If you contract cystitis (not altogether uncommon at high altitude and diagnosed by the hot poker wagging in your urinary tract upon bladder voiding), carry 10,000 mg of Keflex. Same should work if you survive a mauling with *Arctos ursos,* venereal infections intrinsic to your Alaskan ports of call, and to minimize gangrene if you frostbite your toes again. To prevent "hooterbite," wear a cardigan condom. For altitude headaches, climber's knee, sore back and the many undiagnosable and inherent health issues of cold weather climbing, take a 200 tablet bottle of Advil. Also, consider a prophylactic appendectomy.

Call me if you make it back okay.

[signed] Rapher

P.S. Scripts enclosed. Sorry for telling you stuff you mostly already know.

It seemed this final day of basking in adulation for our bravery had recast us as mere fools, so I talked Jeff into sharing a few pints with me at the Glass Door (recently broken) Bar, with a stenciled sign warning us: "Leave your weapons outside." Waylon Jennings growled out of the jukebox, a table of pissed-off fishermen glowered at us, and the bartender made a polite, albeit circuitous, inquiry to see if the strange-looking waterproof video casing I held at my hip contained a firearm. After getting suitably rehydrated, I made the mistake of letting our climbing plans slip. The bartender shook her head and told us that three other climbers had just been killed over on Mount Fairweather in an avalanche and if we didn't want to end up like them, we should sail back home. We left the Glass Door Bar cold sober, and crossed over to the ranger station, braced for yet another briefing about how poorly prepared we were.

Unlike Denali, registration or fees were not yet required to climb Yasetaca. Wrangell–St. Elias National Park had not yet been overrun by bureaucrats. Ranger Rick Mossman showed us maps, didn't question our decision about not carrying a radio, politely asked when we might return, and commended us for trying to climb it like the duke did. There were no standby rescue helicopters, so this park was sending out a message that climbers should take care of themselves. Rick mentioned that we were the only climbers to attempt Yasetaca for two years.

Most enlightening of all, he showed us a glass-cased exhibit. Its four-and-a-half-foot-long hickory alpenstock was the first ice ax to reach the summit. It had the old-style curved, step-chopping adze, which tends to stick in the snow. The archaic straight pick would pop out after being swung into steep ice—I couldn't imagine climbing with such an inefficient tool. Although the lower shaft's wood was unblemished (where a guide's hand might have worn the surface grain smooth from constant swinging and step chopping), the duke's hand had blued the metal smooth between adze and pick.

Part Two

The Mountain

He stood five feet and ten inches tall. He was described as having a "well knit, compact figure, with squat shoulders and muscular limbs." At the beginning of the trip, his round, boyish face was clean-shaven except for the black down substituting as a mustache on his upper lip. He spoke to everyone—guides, porters, Tlingits, laundry attendants, black servants, and chauffeurs—as equals, addressing them in a soft voice, and gazing into (but not challenging) their eyes with his own deep blue irises. One characteristic (if apocryphal) story described the duke winning a lottery, then handing all of the proceeds to an Italian beggar.

In his mostly skeptical journal, the American porter C. L. Andrews wrote: "The Prince is a gem for a scion of Royalty. He has been well raised in every sense of the word. None of the aristocratic snobbishness about him."

The observant Andrews (later listed in *Who's Who* for his accomplishments as an Alaska historian) chafed at the major's martinetism and mocked his (and De Filippi's) idiosyncrasies. Yet Andrews—who (like Mummery) did not bow and scrape before royalty—was impressed by the duke, judging by various journal entries:

> The Prince and the little Italian doctor, Phillipio [*sic*] went up to the next camp. The Prince looks very much like any ordinary mortal when he is on a Glacier. He is quite pleasant and agreeable—the Dr. is a little short fellow and one morning put on a pointed cap and looked for all the world like a fairy—or a Brownie.

Sella wrote home to his wife Linda:

> This morning he [the Duke] climbed to the 3rd camp with 50#s on his shoulders and he came back with out showing any sign of fatique. After such a walk of 5 hours. . . . While I'm writing I have to fight continuously with my left hand to prevent them [mosquitoes] from biting.

Andrews wrote in his journal that he managed only an hour of sleep between the coffee, the mosquitoes—probing his nose, ears, and every millimeter of netting—and slapping noises:

> Major I. rose up and slapped right and left at the mosquitoes and gnats. It was too much for me. I laughed till the tears ran.

> June 24th—At 5 Alexandro and I got up and started breakfast & had it ready at 7. Flapjacks, bacon, coffee, sugar & mush made up our bill of fare. We [the 11 American porters] ate 6# Bacon, 3# oats, 10# flour, 1# chocolate, 2# raisins, about 3# sugar and some hardtack and coffee. No appetites in this crowd.

Although the major omitted bugs from his own account for *The Mountaineer* journal, De Filippi wrote:

We finished our arrangements amid violent explosions of wrath against the swarms of voracious mosquitoes which had tormented us incessantly from the moment we landed. All sorts of ointments were tried in vain: neither nets nor veils could save us from their stings; the pertinacious insects penetrated our clothes, up our sleeves, down our necks, and completely exhausted our patience. No wonder that writers on Alaska describe them as the scourges of the land! Instances are given of travelers being killed by them, poisoned by thousands of stings, worn out by frantic struggles with the invincible foe; of deer leaping into rivers to escape the mosquito torture (Petroff); while it is asserted that bears have been known to scratch themselves to death, maddened with pain. Even the Indians suffer from the stings, although they get some protection by smearing themselves all over with rancid oil.

Late the second night, the major heard someone outside his tent. He asked what they wanted, and they replied, "Four Indians, hungry!"

One of the American porters, Thorton, referred to these Tlingits as "an intelligent lot of fellows, strong, and reliable." Three spoke English and all laughed uproariously at their companion Peter Lawrence, who had the greatest sense of humor Thorton had ever seen. The Americans dubbed this Tlingit "Peter the Josher." Andrews described him as a "jewel . . . not a fool either."

The Indians were paid ten dollars to move a substantial amount of supplies from the beach up to the moraine of the Malaspina Glacier. It would have cost the Americans a long day, but Peter the Josher and his three friends pulled it off in a half day. The Americans were surprised, and when they asked Peter how it had been done, he laughed, then replied, "Injun get contract; do 'em up quick."

Thorton wrote,

One of the boys, suspecting the truth, went down to the river, and there, sure enough, hidden away was their canoe. Those rogues had brought all of that stuff up in their canoe, one of them staying in the boat to steer it and keep it off the bank, while the others pulled it up stream with a rope. We felt cheap then, to think what time and energy we had wasted during the last two days.

The Tlingits wore sealskin moccasins (Peter the Josher sold a pair to C. L. Andrews for fifty cents), but the white men could not walk in these moccasins without bruising their feet. Andrews in turn sold Peter a pair of socks, but Peter ribbed him relentlessly for selling used and smelly socks. De Filippi (large headed and so short that the sensitive Sella had to photograph him while standing upon a stool, or crop him out to avoid embarrassing him) described these joking men:

> Our four Indians, small, thick-set men, are so exactly alike that they seem turned out of the same mould. The development of arms and chest is exaggerated in comparison with the rest of the body, owing to the constant work at the oars entailed by their life on the water.
>
> They either sit together in a separate group, patching their moccasins, or loaf around the camp with contented, smiling faces, peeping inquisitively into the tents and speaking incomprehensible words to us in their guttural tongue, full of *l*'s and *k*'s. . . . The constant substitution of *l* for *r* and of *p* for *c* gives the dialect a certain infantile stamp.
>
> One honorable trait of the Indians' character is honesty. They steal nothing—not even food; and this verdict is confirmed by every one who has employed them.

Although the four Tlingits were dwarfed by the Americans and all but one Italian, they happily carried seventy-pound loads, roped onto their backs and tumplined over their foreheads without packs. Depending upon how rugged the terrain was, according to De Filippi, the Italian "amateurs" carried twenty- to fifty-pound packs, while the Americans or Italian guides carried forty-four- to fifty-five-pound packs. Thorton claimed that once the American porters were fit, their packs seldom weighed less than sixty pounds.

At night, the Americans sang around their campfires. They named one bivouac "Bean Camp" after the cacophony produced by eating a ten-pound bag of beans. They complained about having to fix "flapjacks three times a day while the Italians have a kind of ship biscuit." Andrews wrote that the Americans "talk about their stomachs and about how they live at home—Ostberg—'I lif just as got as de Prince when I am at home.'"

In the duke's obituary, published in *The American Alpine Journal,* the dean of the Cornell Medical School, William S. Ladd, described an incident (possibly omitted by De Filippi and other writers because it would make the duke appear common) that occurred early in the trip:

> Among [the Americans] was a great bully. He became troublesome. There was only one of the packers who dared stand up to him but the bully refused to fight him stating that he would not fight unless there was a purse in it. Whereupon the Duke handed the bully a purse and also a good thrashing with his own bare fists.

Andrews referred to Ralph Nichols's, aka "the Bear's," bullying tactics. He was infamous for taking more pancakes than the allotted four (a true crime to the ravenous Americans, one which has caused fisticuffs during other expeditions), stepping on feet, and committing "sundry other acts both curious and instructive." Not only did the duke put Nichols in line, but by beating the Bear at his own game, the duke (a practiced pugilist) succeeded where the autocratic major had failed, winning a heightened admiration from the porters and a begrudging respect from the Bear.

The Italian Bonacassa wrote that the duke, "although a stern commander . . . held a special place in men's souls." Throughout dozens of arduous trips, and during his command of the Italian navy in World War I, few under his command complained (except Sella, who was more of a friend than a subject) of the duke's leadership—and men would die under his command (during the North Pole journey and at war). Certainly his guides, the American porters, and the Tlingits did not complain.

It took six days to move all the equipment eight miles from the beach to permanent snow up on the glacier. Thorton described the final few miles:

> Imagine a layer of stones and bowlders overlying an undulating field of ice. These stones were not worn like those in the brooks, but each had sharp points and edges sticking in all directions ready to cut your shoes when you stepped on them, as of course you must. And woe to your hands or other portions of your body when a stone slipped on the smooth ice, and let you down suddenly. None of us escaped such falls, and even the labor of toiling over that expanse of rock and ice, sliding around, turning ankles, and wrenching legs and backs, was something awful to endure.

The Tlingit porters departed. Ten tents remained, and De Filippi described their camp, filled with "a crossfire of shouts and orders to the men," ax blows resounding from the edge of the spruce forest, and "the melancholy cry of a small bird (the *Zonotrichia coronata*)" or golden-crowned sparrow singing, *"Oh dear me,"* as if to warn the expedition of what was to come.

The Americans envied the Italians they were serving. While De Filippi, the duke, Cagni, Gonella, and Sella slept nine inches off the ice, courtesy of the fourteen-pound iron bedsteads (De Filippi described them as "light") freighted on their porters' backs, the Americans and the Italian guides gathered heather for insulation and comfort against the rock-hard glacier. Andrews wrote:

> In our commissary we have too much uncooked provision. It takes 6 hours a day to cook for the men and we take hours to

cook hot cakes and mush for 11 men on a small oil stove is [*sic*] no small job. The bread should be cooked. The Italians use a hard bread called galleta. They also have figs, raisins and pickles and drink tea and rum and smoke cigarettes.

His diary revolved around food (the porters constantly ate "mush" or hot cereal, coffee, and flapjacks), and he listed the daily Italian rations several times without description, as if the contents— marmalade, canned roast beef, salmon—were manna from heaven.

In one of De Filippi's scholarly-styled appendices about the Italians' rations, he suggested that "it would have been better to have had less heat-producing and saccharine aliments, and a larger stock of farinaceous [starchy] food."

The Americans woke up in their puddled linen tents without floors (versus the waterproofed, floored tents used by the Italians), had no nails for traction in their boots, and used wool blankets (while the Italians slept in down sleeping bags)—Andrews dubbed one of their bivouacs "Freeze to Death Camp."

The eleven Americans lugged 990 pounds of their own food and gear, plus a lot of the Italians' 2,156 pounds. Everyone despised one piece of equipment royally. Thorton described the four sledges (popular with polar explorers, who watched their men drop like dogs in tethers) that they assembled upon the Malaspina Glacier:

> We had carried them thus far in pieces—and started out to drag them across the snow-covered glacier. I say "drag," but that only partially expresses the idea. Mr. Entriken [accompanying Bryant's expedition some miles ahead], who planned the sleds, is undoubtedly a man of much experience in Arctic work, having accompanied Peary on two of his expeditions. But he had evidently been misinformed as to the conditions which we could meet. His sleds would have done very well on ice or very hard snow, but on the soft snow with which we had to contend, they were all but useless. The runners were made of oak boards about seven eighths of an inch thick, and a sled loaded with

about seven hundred pounds would cut down into the snow so
that it was almost impossible for five men to drag it. This made
it possible to take only about half of the provisions which we
had advanced to this point, leaving the rest for a subsequent
trip. This was our first piece of bad fortune, and had it not been
for the remarkably good weather during the next few weeks, it
would have been fatal to the success of the expedition.

Cagni took daily barometric, temperature, wind, and general
weather observations every eight hours for fifty days. They left a
barometer with the missionary in Yakutat for the same purposes,
and carried a Fortin barometer (fifteen pounds); a Gay-Lussac
barometer (eight pounds); a case of thermometers and hygrometers
(nine pounds); two aneroid barometers, a thermometer, a sextant,
and a compass (six pounds); and a boiling-point thermometer (two
pounds).

Hauling a 700-pound sledge (the duke is pushing).

Cagni played meteorologist. De Filippi gathered worm, arachnid, and insect specimens. Sella exposed photographs, then puttered inside of the black developing tent, while the duke badgered Sella to stop halting and posing the group for so many photographs.

Sella wrote to Linda:

> But I feel sorry to see in the Prince such a mania to do this [sledging] in order to gain time and to push the provisions with the best speed. These days of nervous agitation I think will have their repercussion and that perhaps he will lack strength up high. But I must say that he is a young man, full of strength, intelligence and moral energy. Even in Cagni I observe a young man with a perfect body. The weakest of the expedition is Gonella and me perhaps. I would like to write you more, but with the continuous torment of the cursed mosquitoes, my mind is not capable.

The duke slept alone in a Mummery tent. Although privacy was a luxury, one of Mummery's colleagues had described the tent: "It was necessary on entering or leaving the tent to adopt that form of locomotion to which the serpent was condemned, to avoid the risk of unconsciously carrying away the whole structure on one's back."

During the day, the duke tied the customary bowline knot around his waist and moved roped together with Gonella or Petigax. Although he could strangle to death if suspended in space (a risk alleviated by modern harnesses), a tight rope would prevent falling into a hidden crevasse to begin with.

The duke took compass bearings in the fog to ensure that they didn't get lost crossing the Malaspina. His guides watched over him protectively, but on this fogbound infinitude of frozen water, the duke was in charge, leading the way forward as if he were navigating at the helm. Cagni, the only other experienced navigator, usually brought up the rear. And the guides wouldn't come into their element until the actual climbing began. The duke was not playing prince—he was simply more adept at navigation and logistics.

(Later, during World War I, a British officer would write that the duke, commanding the Italian navy, was "brilliant.")

On the Malaspina, they left camp at 3 A.M. to take advantage of the frozen snow. De Filippi wrote:

> In dividing the labour, the men naturally fall into groups according to their occupations and tastes. Thus we have one team of guides, one of students, a sailor team, and a mixed team composed of Major Ingraham, Botta, and two Americans. The guides go capitally; being accustomed to snow, they pull together in step. The Americans will, little by little, grow used to the novel task.

The men strained like mules, harnessed two by two in front of the sledges, stopping frequently to lift the prows out of ruts. They hauled over seven hundred pounds in each sledge. One porter described the work as "extremely fatiguing," but twenty-one men gave the Italians an edge that Bryant's handful of men (chewing on albuminoid shoe leather rations and pushing just one sledge with *more* weight than the Italians) would be hard-pressed to compete with. Still, the Italians worried about Bryant's lead.

Sella wrote Linda: "The weather is beautiful for 3 weeks and I consider this fact a fortune for the American [Bryant] that precedes us, but this would be a misfortune for us. But the beautiful weather does not last very long in this country."

Sella and De Filippi usually followed behind the sledges, exposing film or making notes, and occasionally helping to push a stuck sledge or build alpenstock bridges in order to cross glacial streams. By 8 or 9 A.M., when the snow became too slushy to continue, they made camp and sought shelter from the sun in their tents. The duke spent the rest of the mornings and afternoons forging the route ahead with one or two of the guides. It took the entourage three days of heaving, careful compass work, groveling through fog, and splashing in rain to cross twenty-one miles of the Malaspina Glacier.

On the Fourth of July, Nichols raised the Stars and Stripes above their hilltop camp, plainly visible by the Italians. The major walked down for a visit and was greeted by the duke, who gave the Americans Independence Day off. The porters cheered.

The major's obsequious reverence of the duke—whom he called "our peerless leader, the Prince"—is telling because the major (an experienced climber as well as a patriot hoping to advance American honor) wanted to accompany the Italians up the peak—and was spurned by the duke. Nonetheless, the duke's charisma, as well as his honesty and graciousness, won the major's lifelong respect. Twenty-seven years later, the major wrote about catching up to the Italians with his porters: "Upon coming into camp he would say, 'My compliments; you travel very fast.' He would then offer us a pot of tea that he had prepared for us. So thoughtful and democratic, the Prince is a most lovable fellow."

As he led in front, carrying out "the dull and ungrateful task of steering our route by the compass," as De Filippi called it, the duke sent his guides back with notes, characteristically scrawled and barely legible:

> To Major Ingraham—
> Dear ES,
>
> Thanks of your letter. I am at Dome Pass and must move tomorrow. The guides leave a sledge for you tomorrow to cross the Seward. Pay attention in crossing the Seward because there are two or three places not very good for a sledge. I hope the guides are able to find a better way tomorrow for you.
>
> I hope to meet you again after tomorrow at the fan. When did the boys start for the moraine? And when you think they will be back?
>
> [signed] Luigi di Savoia

While half of the porters ferried supplies up from the Malaspina moraine, the other Americans accompanied the Italians up the steepening Seward Glacier toward a pass. From on top, looking across the glaciers, De Filippi commented that "if the Malaspina Glacier resembles a placid lake, the Seward is like a stormy sea." While hauling the sledges up above a steep ramp alongside an ice-fall, De Filippi wrote about how the Americans "soon got used to the steepness, but refrained from imitating the guides in their glissades down the slope to bring up fresh loads."

The American porter Thorton remembered it differently, describing the guides being atop this same steep slope, letting loose a shout after they had finished chopping steps. Thorton wrote:

> Lieutenant Cagni knew from their shout what they were about to do. "Now look," said he. "They will slide. You must not do that. No one in the world except Italian guides dare to slide down such a place."
>
> The guides stood on their feet, braced themselves with their alpenstocks, and in a few seconds had made the almost perpendicular descent of the three hundred and fifty feet.

The Italians on the Seward Glacier.

When we had all reached the top with the first load, the doctor [De Filippi], who was always very solicitous for our welfare, warned us not to slide.

"Only the guides must slide. They have spent their lives in that kind of work."

That was all right, and we should doubtless have heeded their warnings, but those words of Lieutenant Cagni still rankled in our hearts: "No one in the world except Italian guides,"—could any American stand that? The first two of us got perhaps a quarter of the way down, when we could no longer resist the temptation. We got into the furrows made by the feet of the guides, gave a whoop, and away we went. The feeling of exhilaration was wonderful. We decided that it was worth while climbing up that pass, even with a heavy load, just for the pleasure of sliding down. Needless to say, we never again walked down that or any other pass where we could possibly slide.

The open ocean to Icy Bay was bouncy. Five miles out from Yakutat, it got bouncier. I turned to the Captain and tried to engage him in some navigational patois: "Only fifty more miles to go, Gary."

"Thanks."

"We're at a hundred thirty degrees longitude, fifty-nine and thirty degrees latitude."

"Are you sure that's right?"

"I'll double-check. How you feeling about the size of these waves?"

"Okay," he said unrevealingly.

"I'm feeling kind of concerned." This brought no reply, so I plunged on: "How much rougher you think it'll get?"

"I dunno."

"Well, how much rougher you think we can handle?"

"Jonathan," he said, exasperated, "I just don't know."

"When do you think it's too late to turn back?"

"You want the helm again?" he countered.

Ancient timber bristled the shoreline like the beard of the great Abe Lincoln (revered by the Tlingits for freeing the oppressed minorities), surrounding the shining, ghostly face of the Malaspina Glacier.

Then Yasetaca breached the clouds, sudden like, more than three and two-thirds miles above. I put on my sunglasses to minimize squinting; my heart rate increased twenty beats; a peristaltic prompting—which normally began while donning my harness below a big climb—hit my bowels.

Once finished with the bucket, I stood and faced the mountain. My previous sightings had been from jetliners looking down, or from the five-thousand-foot Bagley Ice Field looking at the easier north (crouching lion) side of Yasetaca, or from high altitude on neighboring Mounts Logan or Fairweather looking across as if greeting a friendly colleague. But staring *up* from sea level at more than three miles of mountain, from a sailboat already dwarfed by Pacific swells, was like contemplating a raised tail fluke from a dory.

I strode back into the pilothouse, picked up my journal, and tried to control my pen from leaping across the page by printing in double-wide script:

> April 27 (lost like Vitus Bering near his "volcano")/barometer rising
>
> With the exception of a sore back, a newly won beer gut, an arthritic knee, jock itch, seasickness, a creaky shoulder, lack of fitness, general exhaustion, and anxiousness bordering on paranoia—I feel great. Seeing the mountain changes everything; if I wasn't such a jaded divorcé, I'd say it was like quelling my nervousness by looking at my bride before the altar. It is just drop-dead beautiful, and all the madness of small-boat living suddenly feels worth it when looking up at it.

Sella had written in his diary:

> 23 June . . .
>
> Mt. St. Elias . . . suddenly appears, towering in the western atmosphere at a prodigious height, a great, diaphanous pyramid. I will never forget that sight. Perhaps the height was visually exaggerated due to the atmospheric refraction. This magic or real apparition gave my morale a great lift, at low ebb because of sea-sickness.

Two days later, we could put it off no longer. Ten miles up Icy Bay, Jeff maneuvered the *Heaven Sent* in toward the Ceatani River. It was April 27, we were a month out from Seattle, and we had arrived below the mountain I had avoided for seventeen years.

Twenty yards from shore, on the crest of a gathering wave, I swerved the dinghy around floating ice, then dodged the surf by rushing up into the swift outflow of the Ceatani River, dark as a septic system. While Jeff and the Captain fended ice chunks away from the *Heaven Sent* with boat hooks, I shuttled loads in the dinghy.

Jeff and I took turns embracing the Captain on the shore.

"Be careful," he said.

"We *will* see you by May twenty-third," I assured him. "Any later, and we're in trouble." I handed him my boat boots. Jeff and I scuffed the sand. We all simultaneously turned to see a field of ice chunks surrounding the *Heaven Sent;* the Captain pushed off in the dinghy.

As I walked under a heavy pack tied to a plastic sled dragging in sand behind me, my back snapped as some vertebrae settled. Only forty miles of river crossings, boulder fields, crevassed glacier, and avalanche terrain until we reach the South Face, I thought. My insteps were hot with new blisters. I consoled myself with the notion that it would be hard getting lost because we would merely walk or wade the river until it disappeared into the glacier, and then we would ski across a corner of the Malaspina Glacier until the intersection of the narrow Libbey Glacier, which would lead us up to the South Face. (See map page 3.)

After knocking off the easiest half mile of many more to follow, I called a halt. My four-pound double boots felt like cement blocks. "This is too much, Jeff. We're carrying eighty pounds apiece, easy. And we're probably dragging twenty-five."

We sat down, leaned backward, plopped upside down, and—legs fluttering like upended turtles'—wrenched our arms free of packs and rolled onto the sand. We pulled out food bags and tore into Ziploc bags of Fig Newtons, chocolate, and yogurt-covered peanuts—hoping to lighten our loads.

Jeff began cursing just like his dad: "Dang," he spat as he sorted through the food bag. "Darn it, I can't find that extra milk powder."

We separated out a nylon sack with four days of food and two video batteries, dumped it into a yellow bin, and placed it on top of a high stump. We had now committed ourselves to a three-week climb instead of a twenty-five-day climb. We had lost perhaps four pounds.

Fording one of many river branches, knee deep in ice water, I was pleased that the sleds floated behind, *if* we ran quickly across each stream. We tried to talk, but it was simply too painful under the big packs to carry a discussion beyond monosyllabic references about where to walk, how deep the stream crossings were, or pointing at grizzly tracks.

Jeff's country upbringing, filled with hunting and fishing in the mountains, contrasted sharply with my suburban streets, green lawns, kickball, and tennis. He had never eaten shellfish until this trip; I had never shot a deer. But because we were mountaineers, the wilderness around us had become our common denominator.

We were going to need every bit of synchronicity we had to get up the mountain. Consequently, we tried to accommodate each other.

Of course this might change. Both of us knew that a slight discord at sea level might heighten into a prizefight by the time we had marched in forty miles, then climbed ten thousand feet.

(My last trip to the St. Elias Range had been guiding dogsledders up Mount Logan a half dozen years earlier. One of the mushers had been bossy. By sacrificially assuming the role of whipping boy and allowing his insults to roll off my back—while trying to stop his coercion, his thievery of the lunch food, and his abuse of the sled dogs— I did what I could for group dynamics.

As we climbed higher, he grew sicker. But he had steadfastly refused to descend for days. By the time he begged for a rest stop at 16,500 feet, reeling with acute mountain sickness, I told him he had to go down.

He disagreed, and began berating me.

I told him he could die and he should descend before he endangered the rest of us.

He lit into me anew, tapping his finger on my chest, and accused me of trying to hog all the glory.

I considered my options for a few seconds, then sized up a plan. It was time to act—as the duke was alleged to have stopped the bully porter. At high altitude, sometimes words stopped working, and lunacy became logic: I pushed him into a snowbank, pinned his muscular shoulders effortlessly because he could barely breathe, then sat on him, hoping to talk some sense into him. He tried to yell but with no breath in his lungs his words came out as a falsetto.

I told him he had to go down while he could still walk, before we had to carry him down with his lungs filling with fluid. He protested mightily, but sitting on top of him at thirty below zero brought home a point. I helped him up a few minutes later, we looked at one another abashedly for our foolish wrestling match, and shook hands; then he agreed to descend.)

Coming to blows with Jeff—who was relatively ego-free and selfless—was unlikely, but the magnifying lens of stress can render a partner's humorous eccentricities into perceived aggressions. Friendships are canceled. Letters go unanswered. And the climbing partnership assumes all of the inexplicable tragedy of a divorce. For the next month, no expedition climber would deny that Jeff and I were essentially married to one another.

Our kiddy sleds caught on boulders, and within an hour we were turning around to kick them. Once we were through venting our inevitable male rage, we tied the whole kit and caboodle onto our packs to avoid shredding the sleds in the boulders (and kicking them to pieces), then staggered along under hundred-pound-plus packs.

Fortunately, the sun shone, most of the snow had melted—relegating us to carrying our skis—and the air temperature was fifty degrees.

We quit after five hours of slogging. According to my altimeter, we had gained two hundred feet. "Only seventeen thousand, eight hundred four feet to go," I announced to Jeff.

"Is that all?" he replied optimistically.

The weight of the pack and the pressure of its shoulder straps had so far compressed my vessels that I could no longer clench my fists.

Jeff was staring at his pack. "I'm knackered, out of condition, done in." He looked right out of *Romper Room,* wandering around in his union-suit pajamas, and clarifying why Marko had lectured us in Yakutat.

Since we were camped below the snout of the glacier, we prematurely cached the shotgun in a tree, hoping the bears would remain down in the timber. Anything to trim another ten pounds.

We boiled three cups of water, stirred up a freeze-dried bean enchilada dinner, and cut another pound of weight from our packs. I spooned mine straight out of the aluminum-foil bag since my cup had been used for one too many oil changes on the *Heaven Sent.*

A brown cloud of mosquitoes arrived as the sun sank below the treetops. Applying bug dope, or DEET—that cryptic compound of unpronounceable chemicals reputed to render the user sterile—never seemed smart. So we applied Mary Little's dictum, "If a mosquito bite thee on one hand, give him the other—palm downward." Yet swatting bugs was only a temporary gratification.

By my third swat, I had beaten my all-time previous single-slap record with sixteen mosquitoes squashed. But for every casualty inflicted, it seemed another two reinforcement troops flew in from the cover of the nearby forest and a stagnant breeding pond below. We retreated into the tent.

Once we were zipped safely inside, our mosquito pogrom took another fifteen minutes. Ironic blood spots polka-dotted the yellow walls of our new Garuda tent. It was not mosquito blood, and the otherwise satisfying crunching noises against the nylon wall were marred by the knowledge that we were staining the clean saffron ceiling with our own stolen blood.

Jeff played an extraordinary ruse on the front-door bug netting. By spreading out his fingers and placing his hands a millimeter off the netting, mosquito replicas or *bug angels* of his hands (composed of a thick mat of mosquitoes) aligned themselves on the opposite side of the netting, pushing their proboscises through the holes, one millimeter into our tent space, vying for the bloody warmth of Jeff's palms. We sat stunned, until Jeff broke our reverie: "Bloodthirsty critters, aren't they?"

"Excuse me." I stole Jeff's position and deployed some tweezers. My partner—who used to respect me as an environmentalist, a lover of wildlife, and an owner of puppies—looked appalled as I reached forward with delicate and surgical precision toward the flickering proboscises. Partnership dynamics can take the strangest turns. Already, one night out, and I was wondering if Jeff found me to be cruel. By nightfall, I had detusked over one hundred mosquitoes.

Getting up onto the moraine was a trying combination of taking one step forward and a half step back in loose stones, stepping knee deep into silty mud, falling over, and tottering from one boulder to the next. Golden-crowned sparrows (the same birds that De Filippi and Sella had gladly shot and kept as specimens) taunted us with their call from the periphery of the glacier:

> *Oh dear me*
> *Oh dear me*
> *Oh dear me*

Jon under a one-hundred-pound-plus pack, getting up on the Malaspina Glacier.

We staggered like drunken men under our packs, as the glacial moraine—half ice, half rock—snorted, crackled, sucked, moaned, buckled, and melted beneath our feet. Grizzly tracks dwarfed my size twelve double boots.

After six hours of marching, I reported my altimeter reading— "Three hundred eighty feet of gain from last night's camp!"—keeping the overall gain, 1,290 feet (from wandering up and down eskers and lateral moraines), to myself. Nonetheless, we planned to steadily increase the length of each day's outing. As we lost our sea legs, we hoped to be gaining our mountain legs and lungs. I felt poorly, but knew from previous experience that the rhythm of mountain work always came back to me. For now, I took it one step at a time, resting for a nanosecond before lifting each boot anew.

Heat waves shimmered across the Malaspina. We thought we saw people backpacking down the glacier. After going so far as to flash them with our signal mirror, we decided "they" were distant rocks, wavering into a mirage.

In 1890 at this location, Russell wrote about being

startled by the sight of a vast city, with battlements, towers, minarets, and domes of fantastic architecture, rising where we knew that only the berg-covered waters extended.... Although we knew at once that the ghostly spires were but a trick of the mirage, yet their ever-changing shapes and remarkable mimicry of human habitations were so striking that they never lost their novelty.

In 1897, with the Italians around the other side of the mountain, Thorton wished that he had Sella's lenses instead of his cheap pocket Kodak. He took one photograph, then carefully described it all in his journal, making the four other porters present sign it to certify that he wasn't losing his mind; the "Silent City" lasted thirty-five minutes. He was almost certain it was not a mirage, and called it "one of the grandest sights of the entire trip," describing pillars, Chinese temples, streets, factories, and domed buildings, but no sign of life.

Yasetaca was more compelling than any mirage. It mostly hid behind the Chaix Hills as our nights and days fell into the strange potpourri of expedition life: booting sleds, checking and rechecking my watch in vivid anticipation of each day's lunch break, badgering Jeff to stop for photographs (badly needed rest stops), baking in late-afternoon sun inside the tent, and waking up to Jeff's socks dangling from the tent ceiling in my face. (Sella wrote in his diary about having uncomfortable cold and wet feet and not being able to change socks because "His Highness" was in the tent.)

On the fourth day, we exposed our ski bottoms and strapped on our synthetic climbing skins, which allowed us to slide forward but not backward, as the synthetic "fur"—pointing rearward—gripped the snow, then released after the ski was pushed forward. Wise mountaineers never take such equipment for granted.

By day's end we had finished circling the four-thousand-foot-high Chaix Hills, which would be *mountains* most other places in the world, except for Yasetaca towering fourteen thousand feet above their summits. We were now drawn straight toward its great South

*Jeff on the Malaspina Glacier, with the great south
face of St. Elias in the distance.*

Face as two specks of dust are pulled, inexorably, into an industrial-sized vacuum.

If you dream big, as I sometimes clumsily do, it is not always easy to come face-to-face with your goal. My former therapist would label it being "frightened of my unrealistic phallic fantasies." Climbers call it being "gripped" (overtensing your muscles is undesirable because it causes you to lose your grip and fall off). I frequently caught myself shivering while looking up at the mountain under hot sunshine. It was the immensity of things that unhinged me: the volume of roaring avalanches, the amount of time it took for clattering rockfalls to end, the extensive crevassing, and the enormous mountain itself.

Fortunately, I had felt this way before (on the first day of grade school, on my wedding day, at my grandmother's funeral, and beneath other mountains), and I knew it would pass. Climbing is a game of great psychological cunning. Say you're scared, and you will be. Nor would it have been wise to share this sort of revelation with Jeff. Tell your partner you're concerned, and, in all probability, he'll become scared because your (perceived) confidence might have been the only thing previously sustaining him.

As the Pacific turned into a distant blue stripe, the mountain grew in front of us. To allay my fears, I began memorizing every detail: glimmers of blue ice, huge crevassed areas resembling jaws, the tawny granite rock buttress's weaknesses, and the frequency of avalanches sweeping the entire face. Familiarity with a mountain always helps. It is like cramming for a test—the more you study the better your chances of passing.

I was also acutely aware of a vital piece of gear that I had forgotten on the boat: mittens. Jeff tried to make light of it by suggesting I could wear an extra pair of socks on my hands.

As my ski bindings creaked, I worried the route-finding problem out. Route finding on mountains is an art taken for granted by practiced mountaineers, and requires an eye for direct and logical lines that avoid obvious danger (avalanche zones, crevasses, rotten rock) but not necessarily difficulty. Like fine wine, exemplary writing, or a clever point of sail, the craft of route finding takes years to master and its subtleties remain inexplicable. Good route finding demands near perfect eyesight, acute depth perception, a healthy fear of crevasses, intuition, brashness, and a hyperactive sensory awareness. Map and compass and altimeter skills help too. Route finding is also taught, but not really learned, from mountaineering textbooks and climbing guides.

We were interested in an unclimbed South Face route because we wanted to climb on untrammeled ground, as the duke had done to the north. As his mentor, Mummery, had written, "The true alpinist is the man who attempts new ascents."

The big concave South Face held a lot of snow that periodically released as huge avalanches—not particularly hazardous unless we should blunder beneath the huge face during a snowstorm and the concave slopes above would become overloaded. There were also numerous hanging glaciers—nonalpinists often perceive photographs of still hangers as moving avalanches, frozen in place by a fast shutter speed. These unpredictable swords of Damocles demand that you either avoid their run-out zone entirely, run very quickly beneath them, or take out a fat life-insurance policy before walking below them.

No sense coming this far, to such a grand wilderness, then settling for a route already climbed (the Abruzzi Ridge was too distant, too crevassed, too technically uninteresting, and too strafed by hanging glacier avalanches). We knew that we could probably climb the Abruzzi Ridge, but we did not know if we could climb a new route on the South Face.

Climbing or even walking on untouched ground, on our crowded planet, might be the most uncommon experience a biped can attain, particularly on the eve of the ever-accessible twenty-first century. It's not just about "being first" either. On an unclimbed mountainside, it is not unusual to be holding your breath in suspense (or your sphincter in fear) while tiptoeing up ice or dancing over rock. On new routes, you never really know what lies up and around the next corner. The only other physical paths where modern-day explorers can experience the untrammeled is under the sea or in outer space. These sacred places—without footsteps, telltale yellow stains, or leftover human detritus—allow us to behold the original splendor of our once wild and wonderful planet. These untracked wilds, for me at least, are burgeoning with mystery. Up on the South Face of Yasetaca, barren of formal religious instruction, but still open to possibility, I sought whatever gods might speak inside of me. I wanted to try and touch the face of the Creator.

Open crevasses and presumably hidden bridged crevasses lined the Malaspina at its buckled juncture with the Libbey Glacier. Having more experience navigating through crevasses than I had in rush-hour traffic, I knew that injurious falls usually had to do with traveling unroped, poor route selection up a glacier, or soft snow that wouldn't support your weight while crossing snow bridges. I also knew that those teams who thought they had all the answers often let

Jeff breaking trail up the Libbey Glacier beneath St. Elias.

down their guard and fell into "holes." The difference between crashing in rush-hour traffic and out here was that no ambulances stood by to carry you out of the St. Elias Range.

Unfortunately, the intellectually bereft nature of hauling heavy loads up freezing or scorching glaciers demands that you disappear into the intricacies of your own mind (while not disappearing into a hole). I was not thinking about crevasses, let alone the cold mountain, while lost in a fantasy about sailing after the sunset into the warm waters of the South Pacific. As I followed dumbly in Jeff's tracks, his yell brought me back to earth: he had plunged thigh deep into a crevasse bridge. I ran up to give him a hand, but adrenaline propelled him out of the hole as if he had sprung off the parallel bars.

Since glaciers flow and then split apart during their constant and inexorable slow motion toward the sea, crevasses can be found anywhere, usually hidden by a veneer of snow, not altogether different from a hidden trapdoor I had once fallen through in a barn. Instead of hay landings, crevasses usually offer narrowing glass-hard walls that stopper you like a cork in a bottle.

"Boy, wish I had the camera out for that one," was all I could think of saying. Jeff was stonily silent. I considered apologizing, but instead peered carefully down into the ultraviolet depths: it looked like an Alaskan's empty meat freezer under moonlight, long overdue for a good defrost. The bridge itself was indiscernible; no sagging appeared on the otherwise flat glacier, just Jeff's leg holes. For all we knew the area was riddled with hidden crevasses.

"Guess it's time to rope up, huh?" I said.

"Yeah," Jeff replied, "otherwise Dad would never forgive me."

I put my harness on, and immediately after I tied in the peristaltic prompting began.

That night in the tent, after turkey Stroganoff washed down with powdered Gatorade, I pulled out the journal and gave my nightly confessional:

The crevasse that almost swallowed Jeff
(note his leg holes).

4/30/ Left 6:38 stop 4:15/ Elevation 2,280', gain 1830'/ Barometer steady JH apologizes for his sox smell—when was the last time an expedition partner did that for me? (And JH's sox don't even stink—they're in my face: neutral.)

I can remember telling [a friend] that I wouldn't know how to carry on if I failed on Logan, implying *that* particular failure would drive me over the edge. Am I still even nearly that driven? Or do I have more of a safety governor? Certainly I want Yasetaca badly, it has been my dream peak since '78, but if I fail, I could simply come back to it—an idea hard to fathom because somewhere in my mind I see this as the final expedition, my swan song.

Yasetaca is to be a circle closed within my life, the end of an era, a completion of all things mountainous—not to say I wouldn't embark on other adventures, even a small mt, but no more mt expeditions. No more suffering. And Yasetaca is basically the biggest—in my mind & in terms of this sailing approach—so it is the logical one to end it on. In effect, I have been saving it all these years.

I want to try marriage again, have kids. Succeed in that which eluded me in the previous debacle.

Got to be careful about no mitts. Can't lose fingers here.

Jeff wrote in his journal:

As I [ski] skin [across the glacier] I recall the things I miss: Melissa, climbing rock in the sun w/ no shirt on, Sheaf Stouts, my espresso maker, Tevas, the paraglider, my mountain bike. . . .

I get a real uninvited feeling as we near the base of the face. It is immense, there's a diamond shaped wall of rock that is at least 4000' in height framing the main part of the face. Hanging ice falls everywhere. I also get the feeling I am treading on the remains of something ancient. . . .

Despite all the objective hazards there appears to be a sane route up. There is a continuous thunder of ice and rock falling off the face.

I n 1897, C. L. Andrews wrote in his:

A hard day's tramp but only had about 600 # and 6 men.

Major not pulling on the sled. Not much to see, think about or say. Once in a while I wonder how [my children] Pitty Pat and Tippy Joe are getting along and the wife at home. . . .

I can get to Seattle sooner and perhaps get a position while the Klondyke excitement lasts and everyone is going mining—and at least see my family sooner.

As the duke's expedition began to circle and climb around toward the north of St. Elias, it seemed to shrink in comparison with the vast glaciers surrounding them. They now questioned whether the mountain was eighteen thousand feet high. Sella thought St. Elias appeared no higher than Mont Blanc, or fifteen thousand feet.

At three thousand feet, to avoid sleeping on glacial ice, the porters pitched their flimsy A-frame tents on the dirt for their twelfth bivouac (of twenty-two Italian camps) and found a rusty iron fork and a tent floor belonging to Russell. When they climbed up above the legions of blue melt ponds, they lowered buckets down into crevasses to collect water in order to save cooking oil required for melting snow. Temperatures barely dropped below freezing and everyone got soaked by rain and wet snow.

The Italian guides met Bryant on the Newton Glacier. Moving supplies through one quarter-mile section of broken glacier had taken him two days. Bryant was demoralized. He told the Italians that he could not continue because of the stomach illness of their teammate, Hicks.

Sella wrote in his journal:

> One must admit that he [Bryant] is very unlucky. Thus His
> Highness's expedition has no competitors. Wouldn't it have

*The Italians contemplate their sledges, while the duke
(center) supervises.*

been more interesting, even more desirable if other circumstances had deterred the American colleague from challenging the great mountain?

Later, in a letter to the *New York World,* Bryant wrote:

> Nevertheless, we were prepared to undertake the task,
> providing we had the field to ourselves and time enough to
> compensate for the smallness of our numbers, but at this junc-
> ture we learned of the presence of the Italian party. We imme-
> diately visited their camp, at the entrance of Newton glacier,
> with the purpose of calling on Prince Luigi of Savoy. We found
> four guides encamped, who informed me that the Prince had
> already gone ahead. Deeming it unwise to enter on a race with
> a superbly equipped Italian expedition of 21 members, or to
> pose as leader of an American party with chances so much
> against me, I reluctantly decided to abandon the attempt to
> climb the mountain.

Since Bryant had long known about the duke's presence, claiming
to have retreated because it had been "unwise to enter a race" was
disingenuous—he had thrown in the towel, stymied by crevasses,
avalanches, trail breaking, and lack of manpower. It took him a week
to retreat across the Malaspina.

As the Italian party pushed on, they began exposing themselves
to more convoluted glaciers and bigger mountainsides. Risks
increased. Personality differences became readily apparent.

De Filippi never addressed such tensions in the book, but he
later spoke (to the Alpine Club) of the concurrent "sensation of mysterious energy, a force of disintegration, a slow but unceasing con-
vulsion of Nature, while all looks calm and immovable in the huge
coherent mass, and no sign betrays the enormous strain of the millions of tons of ice gliding slowly down."

The guides tiptoed over insecure snow bridges, breaking trail up
to their waists, "patiently seeking our route among a labyrinth of ice

blocks . . . amid the deafening roar of the avalanches and the crash of falling stones that resounded almost incessantly on the edges of the glacier."

While the hobnail-booted and experienced Italians practiced shrewd rope handling in the Newton Icefall, the heavily loaded porters, with smooth-soled boots, slipped and slid and took egg-beater falls. Andrews's journal reads:

> Today was the most dangerous day I have had on the trip. I fell in coming down the icecliffs and slid about 30 ft toward a crevice, skinning my hand and bruising a hip—Major Ingra-ham saved me the fall by hauling on the rope and stopping me. Tomorrow we will lay in camp and rest.

Porters fell two more times at the crossing, and twice the major thrust out his alpenstock so that the "unfortunates" caught it and checked their slides before falling into the crevasse. Thorton wrote, "It is almost certain that they would have been killed." The third time, he fell thirty feet into the crevasse as he was chopping steps. "It seems almost a miracle," Thorton wrote, "that, coming down that distance with forty pounds on my back, I was able to alight on my feet on the hard ice, and escape with only a jar which revealed to me a few millions of stars, and left me a headache which lasted several hours."

As the American porters climbed higher around the mountain, following the Italians onto the Newton Glacier, Thorton described the scenery: "We were amid the continuous boom of avalanches. The valley through which the glacier flows is quite narrow, and the mountains bounding it heavily laden with snow, ready to start upon the slightest provocation. There was something solemn and awful in the grandeur of this roar of nature's artillery."

The glacier leading to the broken icefall was an undulating plain of waves, as if the ocean had been flash frozen in midswell. Between waves, we skied over crevasses and around turquoise pools. Jeff led for the first hour of our fourth day out, poking darkened cracks with a ski pole, testing for solid crevasse bridges. We kept the rope tight in case one of us should break through and fall in. Both of us knew that a team of two (versus three) has limited options if one falls deep and is too injured to climb out. For the first few hours, as poles or skis plunged more than a foot deep into the snow, the hair rose on the back of my neck. After half of the day was gone, it no longer mattered—I became apathetically tired. The slogging often grew monotonous in the rear without route-finding decisions to make.

I stopped in the middle of one crevasse by spanning the two-foot-wide gap with my ski tails and tips—staring down into blue plummeting to black and hearing the howling of a vast, under-glacier river.

"How's it going Jeff?" I shouted up.

"We need Alaska glasses," he shouted, referring to the scale. "Everything's so big here. We've been going for hours and we haven't gotten any closer. We haven't moved!"

"Let's break!"

He reeled me in, his legs braced in the snow, with the rope running through a belay plate (that would check my fall if I broke into a hole) on his harness. For the next couple of weeks we would never move without being attached to tight ropes. As a mere two climbers (instead of three) on a crevassed glacier, we didn't want to reduce our safety margin any more than we had already. We knew of too many experienced alpinists who had been hurt or killed in crevasse falls. So we traveled with eighty feet of rope between us, with another forty feet coiled on our harnesses, in case we needed extra rope to get each other out of a crevasse. We had each rigged two mechanical ascenders for quick deployment, so that if we fell in we would climb the rope with our ascenders to get out. But crevasse extrication is always messy, particularly if you get banged up while falling in, or if you're wearing only a T-shirt before plunging into the icebox, or if you land in ice-cold water (or a fast-moving stream), or if a large snow bridge falls in on top of you.

We sat on our packs. "What do you think of the route, Jeff?" I waved toward it.

"It's kind of contrived and dangerous."

I looked up at the face. The sailboat journey had foiled our Colorado fitness and acclimatization, diminishing lung-respiratory advantages and oxygen-rich red blood cells. In light of this, we had tentatively agreed to cut across a ramp beneath the three-mile-high face, then climb up a two-thousand-foot ice face to the eleven-thousand-foot Haydon Col. The ramp was laced with crevasses and covered with dirty avalanche debris, but we lacked the acclimatization to speedily climb straight up the face.

"I agree," I said, "but do we have any other choice?" Jeff didn't answer—it was the ramp or back to the sailboat.

We sipped lemon Gatorade from our water bottles, discussed how the saline and color content of the ingoing matched our outgoing stains on the snow, and swallowed a few more peanuts. Then I squirmed into the pack and led out. For two days, we bobbed and wove up and down, east and west, back and forth toward the shining, grumbling South Face.

One morning Jeff yelled out, "We're being followed!" He pointed at what appeared to be a raven flying over the glacial waves: the dark form was undulating, appearing and disappearing, until I made out four legs and a hump of fat and muscle on its back. The grizzly was leaping crevasses like it was playing hopscotch. It appeared that we were being stalked; our shouting probably scared it away for a sneak attack.

I slung off my pack and pulled out a food bag, in hopes that a few four-man servings of freeze-dried food would give the grizzly enough indigestion to leave us alone. Jeff reeled me in. I sat waiting to chuck the bag, but after twenty minutes—holding our breath to hear the bear stalking through the crevasses—it never came.

We resumed route finding through the maze of crevasses. The safest route was following the bear tracks, which appeared another hundred yards beyond where we had stopped. *Ursus arctos* neatly avoided the weak bridges, jumped the narrow cracks, and generally navigated the icefall with more directness than any mountaineer. One particularly big jump gave the bear enough pause to stop, sniff the bridge, and let loose a horse-sized bank of feces. Apparently, we had surprised the bear, who had circled around us, heading out for the coast to grow fat on fish for the summer.

The most popular Tlingit legend of all, described by Yakutat residents to the anthropologist Frederica de Laguna, tells how their God, Raven the trickster, was hungry for a brown bear, so

> Raven and old papa Bear were out halibut fishing. Raven was catching; Bear was catching nothing. The old Bear said: What are you using for bait? . . .
>
> Then the Raven cut off the Bear's pecker. The Bear was jumping around in the canoe. Then the Bear died.

The convention of modern alpinism is to climb fast and light, with no fixed camps, and no porters. I had tried this "alpine style" climbing and—with the exception of contracting acute mountain sickness—I had gotten away with it. Getting the climb over quickly meant lessening your exposure to avalanches and storms too. But climbing quickly, according to many physicians, often means that climbers will not build adequate acclimatization to high altitude. Hard-core alpinists counter that they can outrace snowstorms, dash through avalanche areas, travel with lighter packs, even race back down before they became debilitated by their own altitude sickness. This is what Jeff and I hoped to do.

At the turn of the century, as climbing became popular, the father of high-altitude physiology complained that climbers weren't documenting their episodes of altitude illness. "Most of the tourists whose narratives fill the *Alpine Journal* have hardly any scientific interest in their ascents," Paul Bert wrote; "they climb for the sake of climbing. . . . They are almost as afraid of being ridiculed for mountain sickness as they are for seasickness."

De Filippi was more scientist than tourist. In one of the appendices of *The Ascent of Mount St. Elias,* he concurred with Bert:

> I was the first to be attacked with mountain sickness. At a height of between 14,700 and 15,700 feet, on starting afresh after a short rest, I suddenly felt my legs as heavy as lead, a difficulty in breathing, a sense of suffocation, palpitations, throbbing of the temples and headache, with the sensation of having a tight band round the brows. Without feeling actual nausea, I could neither eat nor drink, and took absolutely nothing the whole day, until we had descended to the *col.* However, I did not suffer from thirst. I was aware of no disturbance of the power of vision, and had no buzzing in the ears.
>
> When we halted, I found it easier to rest standing; after involuntarily drawing four or five deep breaths, my breathing soon became more normal. One seemingly paradoxical fact [was] that smoking a cigarette while at rest aided me to breathe more regularly, and was almost the best means of combating the heavy somnolence which came over me whenever I came to a standstill.

Jeff and I began dosing ourselves with 250 milligrams of Diamox a day. Although the drug is purported to speed the process of acclimatization by acting as a respiratory stimulant, there were some adverse effects. Diamox causes increased sensitivity to sunburn, so I wore a curtained billball cap shading my face and neck. More noticeably, the Diamox caused a tingling in our fingers and toes that felt remarkably similar to the sensation of "capillary shunt" that takes place as circulation stops and frostbite begins. We just had to assume it wasn't cold enough yet to be freezing fingers and toes. The drug also makes beer taste awful. And Diamox is a diuretic, which caused us to stop frequently and water the snow. It is a little-known fact that frostbite and altitude illness can be staved off by proper hydration—

affirmed by clear and copious urination—so in this regard, Diamox's side effects threw us off. (Jeff began dealing with our racehorse bathroom habits by utilizing my second water bottle inside the tent.)

Climbers are more aware of medical information than of history. Mention the duke of Abruzzi to most climbers and they'll snort about "servants carrying his iron bedsteads." As if today's feather-weight equipment, medicines, breathable yet waterproof Gore-Tex fabric, airplanes, radios, modern maps, and GPSs aren't similar lux-uries. If our equipment had comprised ten-pound sleeping bags (ours were four pounds), a fifteen-pound tent (ours was five pounds), and tweed wool jackets (ours were polyester Gore-Tex suits), Jeff and I would have happily taken a retinue of porters, established fixed camps, carried real beer, and imitated the duke's expedition-style tactics.

I frequently consulted a well-thumbed copy of Walt Gove's epic on the South Face from the *American Alpine Journal* (*AAJ*). Because the *AAJ* usually avoided lurid accident stories, the art of its understated expedition narratives allowed you to believe that the authors were describing weekend hikes. But Gove's climb was the basis for one of those rare *AAJ* reports that sounded more like an accident account, effectively deterring readers from attempting Yasetaca.

Gove had been here in 1979, motoring up into Icy Bay in a dory with three partners. Disheartened by the avalanche activity on the South Face, they attempted the left-trending ramp to the Haydon Col that Jeff and I were bound for, but the snow was too slushy and dangerous, so they abandoned the constant roar of avalanches.

Gove, forty-five, came back in 1984 with the twenty-four-year-old Andy Polluck, flew in under the face, and clambered over ice blocks and avalanche debris to the right side of the face. On their second day, an avalanche stole their chosen route, so they detoured behind some rock towers. After a week's climbing, they reached the summit ridge. While Polluck went to the top, Gove grew hypothermic, lost his eyesight, became delirious, then started hallucinating with the most deadly form of AMS, high-altitude cerebral edema, which caused his brain to swell with fluids. He concluded the *AAJ* article:

> By the time [we] were halfway down the chute, I was no longer troubled by edema. Once down, I was shocked by the frostbite as I had no memory of it.
>
> [Polluck walked out alone to get a rescue.] On June 1, in very marginal weather, a Hughes helicopter picked me up. . . . On June 27 I was operated on. I lost five toes, including both big toes, part of one finger on my left hand and part of three fingers on my right hand. . . . It is clear that objective hazards will frequently make major sections of the route impassable. Given the typical weather on St. Elias, an alpine ascent is much more likely to succeed than the traditional siege approach. Furthermore, by moving quickly an alpine ascent will minimize the exposure to objective hazards. . . .
>
> Much as I wanted to do the climb, it is now clear to me that without a great deal of luck, the physical demands of such a climb surpass my capabilities. One of the lessons to be learned from our climb is that serious alpine ascents are for the physically elite, and even then one is treading a fine line.

As first light colored the yellow tent walls, clouds gathered ominously. I used the prospect of crippling ourselves to convince Jeff to take a rest day. As I slept, he wrote in his journal:

> How did I end up on this trip, it all seems so rushed. I thought I swore I'd never do another trip w/o Mike [from the Peru shooting] oh Mike where are you? . . . One main reason this trip appeared so perfect was because I could do it w/ Dad, we had not done a trip in a while and I felt I needed to, he has the time I should enjoy it w/ him. There were and are so many agendas: for Jon a job and book contract, the fucking video (I'll never do another trip w/ one), for me a sail and a climb and

more which I'll probably babble about later, and for Dad simply getting to sail a boat, his boat, a beautiful boat.

He and Jon don't see eye to eye on many things or ways of doing things. Dad is very gentle, methodical, mechanical, well thought out and experienced. Jon the opposite, forceful, jumping to conclusions, compulsive, trial by error style. They shouldn't spend a lot of time together on a 30′ boat.

Similar personality discrepancies plagued the duke's expedition. Sella wrote to his wife:

> The Prince is not at all an artist and the beauty of the view does not interest him. What draws his attention are distances, heights, measures of nature that we explore. In conclusion, he's a mathematician alpinist and his feelings toward mountains are purely and simply those of glory and topographic curiousity [*sic*]. This is not a simpatico aspect of his character. Besides, he's a Prince in all the extension of the term.

Jeff woke me up at noon dangling a package of freeze-dried beer in front of my face. It was a cruel offering. I dumped the powder in my cup and poured half of my first bottle's water in as I read the instructions: "This refreshing drink will help revitalize the weary by providing carbohydrates necessary to lift the spirit and move the body."

I took a sip: flat and obscure thanks to the Diamox. But by reading on, we learned that grain alcohol or vodka could be added. I read the rest aloud to Jeff: " 'Please do not drive or undertake activities requiring sharp mental acuity.' "

"No problem this trip," he replied.

"What else can we add?"

We dug out a bottle of prescription-strength cough syrup from the medical kit. I read aloud from its label, " 'Do not exceed recommended dosage because at higher dosages, nervousness, dizziness, or sleeplessness may occur.' "

"Just what we need," Jeff added.

I poured in a healthy dose, jiggled the cup, then swished some into my mouth, passing the cup to Jeff, who drank freely. "Sheaf stout it ain't," he said.

"Well," I hedged optimistically, "the Robitussin gives it an interesting fruity taste."

Jeff tinkered with the stove out in the vestibule. To quell the foul cough-beer I grabbed my second water bottle, which Jeff had thoughtfully filled with lemon Gatorade, and sipped some down: it sank like an acid salt bomb into my stomach. It couldn't be, I thought, but I was too embarrassed to inquire. Then I loosed a prolonged gaseous belch that burned my throat. As I sat crosslegged in the tent—the horror flooding into me like a depressed toilet lever—the burp's aftertaste and odor were unmistakable.

I had swallowed Jeff's urine.

Sella complained in a letter to his wife that the duke wanted everyone working toward moving their equipment, thereby demanding

In camp, Jeff tinkers with the stove.

that Sella (rather than his assistant, Botta), lug the glass plates and five-by-eight camera. He wrote in his diary:

> As usual, the Prince nervously and immediately orders the sled and the whole expedition to start moving up the glacier. I was very sorry not to have had my camera with me yesterday; today I regret and deplore the total lack of interest in the good outcome of the photography work which, it seems to me, I was formally instructed to undertake. Today the Prince made it quite clear to me that it annoys him to see the efforts of a bearer (E. Botta) expended for a few minutes for any purpose whatsoever, scientific, artistic, or other, which is not advantageous to the rapid advance of the caravan towards Dome Pass.

My video camera kept blinking off; Jeff reacted with a sly smile as if this was good news. I filmed everything as a matter of course, and although Jeff had originally agreed to help me make a movie of the trip, asking him to repeat interesting statements or hang upside down over the bowsprit "one more time" to try and touch the porpoises had his enthusiasm dwindling.

Our trail-breaking contortions wrenched skins off our skis—sliding us backward and necessitating excavations in order to recover the missing skins. The kiddie sleds were loaded with forty to fifty pounds and continually flipped, became stuck, rolled, spilled gear, and relentlessly yanked against our shoulders, causing an anguish that was depleting the Advil bottle. Jeff had kicked a hole in his, so pieces of plastic scraped the snow like airplane wing flaps, braking his progress and filling his sled with heavy slush.

I called him "Ani-mule" because he broke trail as fast as I could follow. As he sidehilled up my tracks around a steep glacial hummock, I turned to watch his progress so that I wouldn't pull him off with the rope (I was on a flat ridge). His hat appeared, so I took two strides, looked back to see his face, then took two more strides. When I felt his weight yank the rope, I swiveled my head in time to see him disappear. "Ani-mule?" I shouted.

"*Fuck!*" he replied. Although he was merely regurgitating my favorite stressing-out idiom, hearing it from Jeff was akin to seeing the duke flip off his king, as well as verification that it had taken one week (versus my one day) for Jeff's degenerative descent.

"You in a hole?" I shouted, unslinging an ax from a holster and getting ready to anchor the rope so he could climb out.

"No, my sled just pulled me off!" Then he came tumbling into view, tangled with his sled and whipping it with a ski pole before trying to stand up in the slush. He stood up, brushed off the snow, and yelled: "Thank you!"

We had it easy. The duke's four-man teams had dragged up to one thousand pounds in their sledges. As the snow softened under the heat of the sun, the runners sank in and broke, necessitating frequent repairs. No account mentioned any sledge-related cursing, but Andrews wrote about the lean, ruddy-complexioned major (forty) spending hours in front of the ponderous Nansen stove: "S. swore 'he would break the ———— old stove if it took that long to cook a meal.' "

Throughout his diary, Sella described the duke's moods or weaker moments: "The Prince was in the lead with the compass and, a bit irritable as he tends to be when things are not going according to his plans, he took our suggestions badly."

Or: "Stopping for any reason would displease the Prince."

My relationship with Jeff was similarly imbalanced, albeit entirely democratic. For starters, I now had the sense that his parents had wrongly expected that he was in *my* care. I was also steamed about Jeff's perception of danger being colored by not breaking a promise to his father about climbing a *safe* route—as if I was the wolf leading him astray.

As a younger climber, Jeff might have been deferring to my wider experiences in Alaskan mountains. I tried to offset this unacknowledged deference by respecting his strength: being the first to ask for rest stops, telling him how quickly he broke trail, and warning him that it was *my* lack of altitude acclimatization (rather than *ours*) that would debilitate us if we tried to speedily climb a route up the steepest section of the South Face. I hoped that these things gave him confidence—something I didn't lack, because I had hard experience, even if the mountain did scare me.

Like his father on the sailboat, however, Jeff might have been having a hard time accepting our differences. It was annoying to hear him prompting me about how I should use my ski poles to more quickly elevate my ski bindings (I couldn't help thinking that I started backcountry skiing while he was still learning to walk). This was the closest he came to criticizing me aloud, which I didn't entirely mind, because I expected this sort of anal-mastery behavior to be passed from father to son, and I had already experienced similar tutelage aboard the sailboat. He seemed to be seething with other knowledge, but he couldn't express it, or his emotions—manifesting the same outwardly passive silences I had endured from him and his dad on the sailboat.

I could see our closeness slipping away amid the stress of what we were launching into. There was no question in either of our minds that we were preparing to undertake a greater risk than ever before because of the hanging glacier avalanches menacing our ramp route. My obduracy and acceptance of the hanging glaciers was part of the problem—because I had never been the type of person who folded the picnic and went home due to rain. Although I still respected him in more ways than I could count, this no longer felt mutual. Worst of all, for the same reasons that we kept our fears bottled up inside (so as not to unsettle one another's confidence), we did not dare broach this new petty and unspoken chasm between us. Nor did I *know* for certain that his father had warned him about not doing something dangerous because of my prompting, I only *felt* it. If asked, Jeff would only deny it. There was nothing wrong with a climbing partner who prioritized his relationship with his father, but I had never climbed with a son whose father waited for us below. Still, I knew Jeff could handle most anything the mountain dumped on us if he would just let loose and trust me.

We stopped in the lee of a six-thousand-foot snow dome—the only avalanche shelter for miles. We sat on top of our packs, brewed tea, and shoveled snow on a black trash bag, which absorbed ultra-violet radiation, grew hot, and melted snow into gallons of water, saving our limited stove fuel. Sweating all day had left my body brinier than the rim of a margarita glass. After pitching the tent, we shut off the jetlike roar of the stove—which required shouting conversations for the five minutes it took to boil a quart of water.

Jeff wrote in his journal:

> Sitting in the afternoon sun writing again, t-shirt on this time, it's only about 85 degrees F tonight, incense blowing in my face, socks not as bad, I put on a fresh pair this morning. . . .
>
> The ramp is guarded by ice falls to the north (very active), a chaotic glacier to the west and ice cliffs to the south, another ice fall to the east (it is the most benign). This was a feeling I've had all along, it's a known fact ice falls don't make good routes. But it was the logical option given the condition of the Tyndall and our desire to climb the mountain from the ocean. It's still, my God it's still. Despite the fact there are thousands of tons of ice moving under and around me it is still. . . . Just yesterday, hell this morning, I wanted to climb this mountain so bad, then one little section goes sour and I feel lost. At loss for the time away from people, places, and things I love.

We strolled to the side of the snow dome to consider an alternate route, also unclimbed. The lack of safe options and the anticipation of dashing beneath hanging glaciers was playing havoc on our emotions. I was game to attempt Jeff's new route *until* the access came into view: a mile of overhanging ice crackled, groaned, heaved, ran with water, and collapsed piece by piece. On the face leading to the ridge, a distant clatter of rocks pirouetted down runnels—pock-marking the ice.

"Well," Jeff clarified, "guess we forgot our helmets anyway."

We turned to reconfront Option A: our dreaded ramp to Haydon Col.

"What do you think of the route?" I asked (a daily routine now).

"Like I said before," he said sincerely, "it's contrived and dangerous."

"You know, Jeff," I countered, "I'm sure it's not as bad as it looks." Just then a vibratory rumbling came from the largest hanging glacier ("Big Bertha") on the South Face—dumping down toward the ramp; at least the dome above us hid the visuals.

"Jonathan." Jeff then asked in an unusually polite tone: "Do you think our sponsorship is dangerous?" He chopped at the snow wearing the borrowed Patagonia suit and the glasses Bucci had given us. Two years earlier, I had helped him obtain a small grant for another Alaskan trip. I was glad that he could finally spit out something that was bugging him.

Even with what amounted to limited sponsorship, coming to this mountain had plunged me (but not Jeff) into debt because of the sailboat. Unlike the duke, I felt no obligations to anyone other than Jeff (and now his parents). I told him: "No, not really Jeff. It's more complicated than that. The *route* might be dangerous, not the *sponsorship*. We just have to figure out how to outfox the avalanches. There are three obvious debris piles, and when we get to them, we just move quick. What are the chances one actually lets loose while we're in the run-out zone anyway?"

No reply, but Big Bertha, emanating from some two miles above, was roaring closer: tumbling down toward the slope we had earlier traversed, simultaneously and slowly mushrooming over toward our present position with remarkably similar shape and color to an atom-bomb fallout. "Besides," I told Jeff, "it's not dangerous because we can always come back another time if we don't like what we see tomorrow morning."

Jeff looked up from the snow he'd been worrying with his ax as the cloud hit, chilling the air forty degrees, occluding the sun, fogging our sunglasses, and refrigerating our lungs. "Yeah," Jeff added, coughing up ice crystals, tiring of my logic. He didn't believe me. So I decided then and there to let him call the shots tomorrow.

"Don't worry," I concluded, "I'm too old to try and kill myself."

Before going to sleep, Jeff wrote in his journal: "Just watched the grandest ice fall collapse I have ever seen, right across the path we will travel tomorrow. The only thing I like about this route is that if I get crushed by the ice it isn't a bad place to check out."

I shook Jeff awake at 3:30 on May 5, nine days out from the sailboat. The darkened sky twinkled with distant constellations. Mars glowed red as a stoplight. The face above sparkled phosphorescently, and for once it was silent. But as Jeff torched the noisy stove to roaring life, I jumped, thinking the face had let loose again.

I shoveled over our cache—four days of food, kiddie sleds, expired video camera batteries, the heavy items from the medical and repair kits, and a bag of trash—then marked it with bamboo wands. We would retrieve it on our way back down. Our stomachs would be quite shrunken, since our packs held only eight days of fuel and food (half of the dinners were ramen soup packages) that, theoretically, could be stretched into eleven days.

After Jeff finished his morning tithing into the snowpit, I took my turn. I couldn't help but notice how watery his donation was. An inconsiderate wind whipped toilet paper out of the pit and into my face, but before I could wrench it away, the paper flew away like a runaway brown-and-white flag toward the tent. Burning toilet paper this particular windy dawn would have been like torching a billowing Kevlar storm sail under a gale.

Full-body suits with zippered butt trapdoors made these frigid mornings less of an ordeal, but I shivered thinking of the indignities suffered by the pioneers while dropping their wool knickers, clutching their tweed jackets, and praying for the sanctity of their family jewels. Worse is this same injustice suffered by women alpinists, who frost themselves every time they have to simply urinate.

Anyway, I had considered positioning the signal mirror beside the pit in order to monitor clearance because one can never be too careful about aligning the inside layers with the suit's trapdoor.

No climbing manual or self-respecting outdoor magazine dares to describe subarctic bowel-movement techniques. In addition to fearing that this will be perceived as too graphic, the uninitiated believe that the exercise is all too banal, no different from that same unmentionable chore that the reader attends to at home. This is not true. Furthermore, while plenty of accounts are devoted to avalanches, crevasses, high-altitude illness, and medical emergencies, writers have not explained the one peril that expedition climbers hate most: pinching a loaf in a blizzard.

Once, during a February climb of Denali, I was frostbitten, my partner had been hurt in a crevasse fall, basketball-sized rocks whizzed within inches of my head, and I nearly died from pulmonary edema. Yet the worst experience of that trip, by far, was undershooting the trapdoor in a hundred-below-zero wind chill with mittened hands—forever ostracizing myself from future expedition invitations from my two partners. Dodging a rock or recovering from altitude illness lasts anywhere from a half minute to several days, and then the terror is supplanted with a giddy rush of adrenaline, but dumping in your suit might be worse than dying. In addition to the social stigma (no climber can resist entertaining others later with the story of your bathroom antics), and fouling the air of tents and snow caves, Alaskan peaks lack cleaning facilities. The onus of sullying your suit will stick to you forever.

Before Yasetaca, I had practiced with the new suit at home by opening the window during a cold spell and, once the bathroom was chilled down to vodka-serving temperature, practicing the mitten technique, peeling down the zippered trapdoor while fully suited and perched cormorantlike on my rocker-soled double boots atop the porcelain. I was taking no chances on Yasetaca.

Hence my elation upon completing the most onerous task of the day. Hence expedition climbers' heretofore undescribed fascination with the shape, regularity, size, and firmness of one another's stools. As I helped Jeff disassemble the Garuda tent, I nodded back toward the pit and said sotto voce: "Looking a little loose there, Jeff."

Without further conversation, we inhaled our oatmeal and packed away the stove. We stepped into our strapless crampons— the twelve anodized steel points cupping my double-boot welts as securely as a jockstrap; I clicked up the heel levers.

We duckwalked up the dome, painfully flexing our soles parallel to the thirty-degree slope and applying the crampon spikes like clog dancers gently stomping a newly varnished floor. At a soft-looking crevasse bridge, I pulled out the rope, tied in, then punched my leg into blackness once, then twice, before clambering over in an undignified yet functional quadruped crawl (also not shown in any climbing manual).

After an hour's work, we passed over the crest of the dome just as two ravens bickered out of the sky and dropped straight onto our cache. The ramp still looked crossable, albeit more complex than I had imagined. After Big Bertha's massive debris pile—dirty brown ice blocks laid down as neat as a pile of volcanic scree—a twisting passage led up through some ice towers. Up above, a series of large crevasses looked complicated. But that was only the visible half of the route. If Jeff wasn't up for it, I wasn't going to argue—it was too dangerous a place to resort to coercion. On another level, I hoped he would respond to the route as a challenge and as a creative route-finding dilemma. "What's your gut tell you?" I asked.

"How about if we just go check it out and if we don't like it, we can leave a cache and come back?"

I was stunned that he was up for it. "Yeah, particularly if it starts snowing or gets whited out."

We trotted downhill, hearts in our throats as we moved into the bombardment zone. It took a half hour to reach the debris from the avalanche that had dusted us last night. I stopped to admire the cinnamoned blocks of ice, arranged into an orderly, football-field-sized semicircle, as if it had been swept there by a giant broom to be dustbinned up later. The neatness of it all dazed me; it looked somehow planned.

Jeff yanked on the rope from behind and yelled like a drill sergeant: "C'mon, let's go!"

A layer of clouds hung five hundred feet below us and the world as I knew it shone in a soft white ethereal texture that occluded everything else in my life and lifted me to a higher plane of being. It was just us, the clouds, and Yasetaca, so high above I had to lay my head back on the pack to see its summit. I had waited for this moment for nearly two decades. We were committed and nothing could stop us: not fear, not avalanches, not any mere crevasses. I felt omnipotent. This was the power of sheer wilderness mountains—you respond to their overwhelming indestructible magnitude in kind, by feeling similarly invincible. This was my church if only because I was indestructible here: if the mountain buried me, I was soaring so high that my spirit—the spirit of the duke, of Jeff, of countless other adventurers—would never die, even if the *American Alpine Journal* obituary did mention my susceptibility to balmy risk taking.

I yelled back: "We can do this, Jeff, I know we can!"

I couldn't see his face. He *had* to be smiling, he *had* to feel the same way.

The main debris pile stretched a square mile and carpeted the glacier as much as a hundred feet deep. We jumped on board warily and catlike, as if catching a train from an overpass, and balanced across at a sweaty five miles an hour, skipping, then jumping to get our crampons to pierce ice blocks hard as petrified wood. Jeff was mute behind me, so I announced the obvious good news about saving time in the danger zone: "Nice that the avalanche filled in all the crevasses!"

We were off the pile and up the opposite hillside in less than twenty minutes. Jeff took over the lead, jumped two crevasses, and started weaving through ice-serac towers. We crossed a filmy bridge over a seemingly bottomless hole, then another—both would be impassable once the sun softened the icefall. I gave the bridges maybe a week, just long enough so that they would disappear before our descent.

De Filippi wrote about similar encounters:

> The passage effected, we made our way over masses of ice connected by shaky bridges of almost loose snow, most of which

were either broken or incomplete. All of us broke through more than once, but by careful use of the rope no accident occurred. Through the great holes with jagged margins produced by these stumbles, we saw mysterious azure caverns deep below, of the most marvelous blue ever created by snow, with a sheen like watered silk, and brilliant, almost metallic reflections.

Jeff and I stopped as the clouds finally rolled up to us on the lip of an enormous crevasse, shutting down all visibility. Jeff stopped talking: a bad sign. He took a wrong turn—inevitable for this sort of blind route finding—but his voice sounded too soft and timid when he shouted to me, so I took over.

In two hours, I got dead-ended by a half dozen chasms. By following tight compass bearings in the whiteout, and constantly consulting my altimeter, I was determined to wriggle through. Jeff was concerned that an avalanche would smash into us like an oncoming snowplow in the wrong lane—but I argued that the crevasses would swallow an avalanche before it hit us.

The Italians had similar obstacles in the Newton Icefall. "We walked like somnambulists," De Filippi wrote,

> mistaking shallow depressions for bottomless gulfs, and scraping elbows and packs against walls of snow close beside us which we thought to be flat! Climbing seracs or marching along their edges, we appeared to one another as shadowy giants on giddy heights and impossible slopes, plunging apparently into space at every step. One curious phenomenon caused by refraction was that while we could fairly distinguish the outlines of seracs about 150 feet distant, we could see nothing that was close to us; and the illusion was so complete that the leading guide occasionally sounded with his axe to ascertain if his next step would fall on the snow or into empty space.

After several hours, Jeff and I had made small progress, and in desperation, I swung southwest, ninety degrees off our intended destination. An avalanche roared somewhere nearby, deep and mysterious, like an operatic bassist bellowing from a hidden radio. I kept going as fast as I could move, partly from fear and partly knowing that the concentration needed for such boogying would suppress the retreat in our minds. We were cloud blundering, our nerves strung so tight that if we stopped, the conversation would naturally turn to retreat. Things kept rushing and booming and rustling above. I frequently tripped, not being able to tell up from down in the whiteout. I swung my ski poles in front of me like a blind man so that I could gauge how high to lift my feet.

At another dead end, I balanced along the lip of a crevasse, and in forty yards, forward progress was pinched off everywhere but up a thirty-foot crevasse wall; I asked Jeff for a tight belay and swam up crotch deep through the tenuous snow. I blasphemed its rottenness, scared to bladder looseness of plunging into a hidden hole or being avalanched backward, employing the language my former therapist would have tried to wean me from, as if it empowered me.

On top, the clouds miraculously began lifting and I took a deep breath of relief, until I discerned another maze of crevasses. I corked my fear, sucked in my stomach, then walked down to the narrowest gap on the first one, where, hesitating only long enough to determine a solid landing, I took the sort of running crevasse jump that I had done only once before (in front of a television camera). Space plunged wider and deeper and bluer than any crevasses I had ever seen—I had given up trying to sight bottom. Peering down into so many deep crevasses at such close range was invoking my fear of heights: my voice rose a half an octave as I shouted rope commands to Jeff, my sphincter muscles tightened, and my bladder finally loosened: I rim-painted every third hole's jumping platform with unmistakable glow-in-the-dark Gatorade for Jeff to follow. I left my crotch suit zipper down for handy access.

As the clouds lifted, I spied a way around the last batch of holes. (De Filippi wrote of a similar escape: "At last we emerged from this labyrinth of ice-blocks at the head of the ice-fall in the great upper basin.")

Within five minutes, Jeff and I were sweating in hot sunshine, peeling off our suits, and raising our water bottles to the sky for a toast—just as the sun triggered the itchy Big Bertha, a mile eastward. I filmed through the zoom, admiring the billowing chameleonesque quality of airborne snow mimicking a cumulus cloud and roaring with thunder. "Beautiful, huh Jeff?"

His shout—"*Look!*"—made me lower the video camera. "We're dead meat," he said calmly, verifying Marko's prophecy. I followed the subject of his finger, straight above our heads: another avalanche, bigger than Big Bertha, was billowing out a half mile wide and oddly silent.

"*Run!*" I yelled; Jeff moaned dubiously but followed anyway as the roaring sound of the avalanche finally reached us. I tried to force away the panic and adrenaline that would seize all cognition from my brain—*think, think, think; don't look up; don't stop running*—and just as it seemed my lungs would collapse from sprinting, I saw our salvation: a semi-truck-sized ice serac with a crevasse on the lee of the oncoming avalanche.

"Jeff, there, I've got it!" I checked before jumping in: only eight feet deep; Jeff jumped in beside me.

"Let's put our suits on."

"Fuck, fuck, fuck," was all Jeff replied, which, considering the source, seemed indicative of catastrophe.

"We're going to be okay," I pronounced as confidently as possible, given that my voice now sounded an entire octave higher. I pulled into my suit, ran a checklist through my mind, and fumbled my gloves and hat on. It bothered me that I might be buried alive like the stuff of my nightmares, so I yelled, "Grab your shovel and if we have to, we'll dig our way out, okay?"

He ripped it off his pack as a sign of consent. And that was it. No last embrace. No thank-yous. No I'm sorrys. It's funny how cool your thinking becomes amid the heat of conflagration—Catholicism implies that this is to make proper atonement before checking out. I figured that Jeff must be mad for not saying what his gut really told him that morning.

I tried to take the optimistic view: "We're *really* going to be okay Jeff, I just know it."

He said nothing, and visibly trembled. I locked my arm against the side of the crevasse. We both took deep breaths, like pearl divers getting ready to set a new record. The waiting was awful.

Suddenly the sky went dark and the roaring came over us. I pulled my hood up and practiced a few shoveling moves as we were engulfed by a blizzard. It turned to night, the way you were supposed to go. I repeated my earlier remark like a mantra, as if saying it aloud and clapping Jeff on the shoulder would make him believe it too: "We're going to be okay." Neither of us spoke again as a wind reached down into every nook and cranny of our crevasse and up into our clothing, spackling behind our sunglasses, licking our eyelids, and retracting my testicles up into my groin as surely as if I had been kicked, stealing all of the morning's wrongly perceived omnipotence. Then it stopped as suddenly as it had begun.

The last few minutes had passed like hours. The sun swung through it all again and brightened us back into daytime.

We were both panting.

I poked my head up and looked around into a cloud of ice vapor: safe. Quiet too. I couldn't see where the avalanche debris had landed. I clambered out, took a few tentative steps, and turned on the video inside of its waterproof housing, pointing it at Jeff. His snowy white hair (formerly black) was plastered straight up. His eyes were fluttering, but he had not yet spoken. "How do you feel?" I asked, figuring that Jeff was too amped not to reply to his least favorite camera question.

"I've had bullets go by within inches of my head but this was closer!" He was venting a combination of euphoria and anger: "God-damn it!" He threw his gloves down. "You kid around about that kind of stuff and it catches up to you."

"Sun's out anyway," I said. "I'd be curious to see where the debris pile is."

"We were running from it, like it was going to help!"

"Well the upper face is clean now," I said as consolation. (I couldn't help but agree with De Filippi, who wrote, "The snow-avalanches are the most beautiful of all.")

"Well let's get outta here," Jeff said, nodding upward, and except for the words, I was struck by the fact that his tone of voice sounded more like he was thanking Melissa for the best evening of his life.

I was calm inside. We had made all the right moves, deep into stark and ominous wonderment, where no person had ever visited, where my coveted mystery might reveal itself—although I was aware, as Voltaire had written, that if God didn't exist, I would be tempted to invent him. Sun glistened on the hanging glaciers above. A rock bounced and clacked for thousands of feet with the clarity of an approaching cowbell. Certainly, the big concave face above us was dangerous for the unpredictable hanging glaciers, as well as all of the snow it held (and would eventually release again as an avalanche). It was also a startling insight into giant earth-shaping forces, mountain-sculpting meetings of continent-sized plates that gnashed to the surface with a deafening, seismic roar, then collapsed, leaving two vertical miles of this face in its wake—the world's greatest tsunami, ancient rocks and bugs and water frozen in mid-froth before it could collapse into the sea.

This place surely bore witness to the ultimate mystery. Plate tectonics or an act of God? I might never know, but only here in this untrammeled arena—no longer feeling indestructible, only fearful of my own fat-chested, skinny-legged mortality in the face of such a Creation—could I mount the question.

Jeff was primed to keep moving until he dropped. I had never seen him break trail with such fury. But the snow was softening by the hour, sapping our strength, and plunging us belly deep when steep headwalls forced us to remove our skis. If there were any hidden crevasses around, this soft snow would help us find them. At another overhanging cottage-sized wall of ice that looked like a suitable avalanche bunker, I called a halt, although it was hard to convince Jeff.

He listened carefully when I explained that we would be forced to break trail up to our hips, agonizingly slowly, as the hanging glacier above drooled and burped. By dawn the glacier surface (and the hanging glacier) would freeze hard again, and we would be fresh enough to run if necessary. Our fight-or-flight instincts tempted us both to go now, but this was high-stakes chess, and we had to anticipate the mountain's every move.

It was only a few hundred yards to the debris pile. The final (or so we hoped) hanging glacier perched a mile above—Jeff dubbed it "the Gatekeeper" with our sudden renewed interest in religion. I explained to Jeff several times that the Gatekeeper's avalanches would shoot over the overhanging serac-avalanche bunker immediately over our heads. He made a good point about the serac-avalanche bunker simply collapsing on our heads, but I argued that it was unlikely and I had camped quite happily beneath such ten-ton Bessies before.

We hid in the tent and retreated to our journals as the water bottles filled beneath dripping icicles. I agreed immediately when Jeff suggested that we not descend the avalanche- and crevasse-ridden ramp that we had struggled up all day. Although I felt that we had skillfully attended to all the weak snow bridges and the surprise avalanche, it was just too dangerous to repeat. The problem was that the ramp offered the only return to the four days of food that we had cached. The prospect of climbing up in order to descend the unfamiliar South Ridge route, then beating back out to the sailboat through an unknown route in the Chaix Hills (read *Mountains*) was a bit unsettling. But first we had to summit.

5/5, El. 7,590 feet/ Off 6:35am stop 2pm/ 2 miles progress?

We're now nine days out, a mile and a half of vertical above the *Heaven Sent*, and perhaps 40 miles distant. For all this progress, the summit is still a long way off.

Jeff is mad that he told his Dad that this route was safe; he was mad because he thought he had lied to him and because he thought he knew better all along.

Pondering our next move, from our camp at the avalanche bunker.

What good karma, in retrospect, that I found a route in that whiteout! Fun (how quickly I forget) routefinding through seracs above B Bertha debris, weaving & endrunning & stepping gingerly across rough textured snow bridges above great voids. I felt in control, plying the options w/out getting upset, and employing a sense of direction which I had little right to believe in.

After the avalanche, JH said "he hadn't felt like this, like he did in Peru, that he was going to die for certain & no one would even know where." That bothered him to match those feelings from Peru.

Breathing hard. Feeling altitude already. Took 3 advil for headache this afternoon. And now I can barely get enough O2. [I thought twice, reached up and unzipped our supposedly "breathable" tent door.] Otherwise, I felt stronger than ever before, knowing exactly what had to be done and performing the most difficult & high pressure route finding of my life. Maybe I only shine when the world appears to be ending?

How do we climb peak and get out to our pickup by 5/23 w/ only 11 days of food? (I'm hoping for old abandoned caches at Haydon Col.)

Descending this avalanche prone ramp is no longer an option—perhaps we took that debris pile too lightly. When I suggested we descend the South Ridge (after summiting) and wait at landing strip until 5/24, JH chided that as irresponsible.

I could only surmise that Jeff was writing about my lack of *respect* for the mountain, a word he had mouthed several times that afternoon. Any denial would only strengthen my indictment. I tried to catch a glimpse of Jeff's journal and he looked at me askance, not speaking, as if I were trying to kill us both with my heinous route selection, but he would never point a finger at me.

S ella wrote in his journal about a similar safety disagreement on the Newton Glacier:

As the baggage is carried across the passage impassable by the sleds, a little altercation arises. His Highness wants to risk crossing an unsafe bridge and we try to dissuade him. A discussion ensues about the danger and the rashness Mummery attributed to his Highness (Mummery accompanied him on the Matterhorn climb up the Zmutt Wall). Ideas contrary to ours.

The duke was a visionary alpinist partly because he believed in climbs that involved risk—even though his guides tried to protect him. The guides preferred that their prince did not cross untested crevasse bridges, or lead the rope. The climb on the Matterhorn, without guides and on a seldom-climbed, rotten-rock ridge, was considered a sketchy undertaking by the more conventional Italian alpinists.

Since the beginning of alpinism, one climber's justifiable risks have always been perceived as another's death trap. One tenet of mountain safety is vaguely defined as avoiding *objective dangers* (storms, hanging glaciers, or active icefalls), places where acts of God would kill a climber, rather than *subjective dangers* (climbing above your ability, being improperly equipped, or being inexperienced). The game gets even vaguer when you introduce alpine-style climbing, which theoretically allows climbers to sprint beneath hanging glaciers or cross icefalls quickly and safely (it is vague because Jeff and I had disagreed on the safety of the icefall ramp). Although the duke's climb was being conducted in expedition style—with fixed camps, shuttling loads back and forth—his Zmutt Ridge climb had been in alpine style (like ours). So as the summit of St. Elias loomed closer, he and the guide Antonio Maquignaz proposed switching to alpine style, in order to minimize their exposure to storms.

On July 19, Sella wrote in his diary:

> Anxious to take advantage of the weather and seeing the mountain so close (an optical illusion) His Highness, with youthful ardor plans to lighten the camp and push on in a reduced group as far as the foot of the divide (Russell Hill) at the head of the glacier in order to attempt the ascent as early as possible. He had been spurred to make this decision in part by the bold, reckless guide [Maquignaz] who believed it was possible to carry out this plan.
>
> When the Duke consulted us we declared ourselves opposed to this plan. We believed it to be practically impossible because of the distance and the difficulties we would probably encounter on the 3rd cascade, not yet crossed, as well as the negligible altitude we had so far reached [5,082 feet]. There is some ill-humor, and His Highness is obviously annoyed by our reluctance and momentarily discouraged, perhaps even demoralized by the fact that his idea could not prevail without our approval. He remained silent for several hours, then gathered us together to say that he left the direction of our moves up to me.

(It was the same sort of democratic leadership decision Jeff and I implemented before entering the icefall ramp.) Sella continued:

> My difficulties! Far too explicit words and inconsiderate opinions from some among us. Our responsibility [toward protecting the duke] is brought up. Unpleasant moments.

The next day, Sella took Petigax up into the crevassed labyrinth of the third icefall and made precious little progress. Still, the duke and company welcomed them back into camp courteously.

The next day, Sella forced a route through.

> In the evening we are all settled higher up on the mountainside. I accompany His Highness in this second trip up the 3rd cascade; his mood has changed. He no doubt recognizes the folly of carrying out his plan. The weather shows obvious signs of impending serious disturbance.

Jeff and I crammed gear into our packs before dawn. Between the mercury dropping, the cadaver-pallored sky, and an eerie stillness, we had to escape, or the coming snowstorm and its avalanches would bury us. Even the avalanche bunker above our heads would be no protection from a major storm.

We were moving by 6:30. The temperature was twenty degrees, and the sloppy slush of yesterday was now more akin to concrete, admitting only the tips of our sharpened crampons.

Jeff and I quickly mounted the dirt brown debris, sewer line for the upper mountain. The "Gatekeeper" hanging glacier jutted out into space a mile above our heads—several thousand tons of cocked, overhanging, ancient, compressed sky blue ice, hard and dense as a rock, and impenetrable by any ice ax.

We strode briskly, trying to remain calm, not talking. The philosophy among most mountaineers is that any vibrations from below a delicately balanced hanging glacier might bring it all down upon yourself. Although most sensible climbers try to avoid selecting a route beneath "hangers," the next best thing is to avoid being cavalier—"respecting the mountain" as Jeff put it—and to maximize your odds by crossing at a time when the mountain is frozen "quiet." No sense in running, either; it was better saving our ligaments and our breath in case it snorted to life—then we would make the bull runners of Pamplona look like slow-motion joggers.

It felt like returning to the thinly frozen ponds of my childhood: shuffling across and adopting a pins-and-needles alert for the sound of breaking ice. We entered a state of kinetic, extrasensory awareness. No movement escaped my vision, my nostrils flared as if I could smell trouble, and if Jeff had even burped, I would have broken into a sprint. The next half hour was going to be the longest of my life. I wished we had had the good sense to bring avalanche beacons.

I remembered Charlie Campbell's story about trying to outski an "explosive" hanging glacier avalanche on the Abruzzi Ridge route in 1981. It steamrollered him from behind, knocked him unconscious, and buried him. He woke up, saw blue, and tried to breathe, but the ice was pressing so tightly against his chest that he passed out again. His partners found him because of his avalanche transceiver signal and dug him out with their ice axes; shovels wouldn't penetrate the icy debris. Campbell had stopped breathing, but suddenly coughed up some ice, vomited, and experienced a few minutes of delirium. Aside from bruises, cuts, and hypothermia, he was uninjured. They beat a hasty retreat off the mountain.

I had also met the soft-spoken Toby Wheeler, who wore a turban (but denied the rumor that his conversion to a Middle Eastern theology had anything to do with his accident on the Abruzzi Ridge). On August 11, 1971, an avalanche roared down from two thousand feet above Russell Col. Wheeler and his team dug into the snow, braced themselves, and were engulfed and then swept away by a wall of snow. When it all stopped Wheeler was the only one remaining on the surface. He dug with his hands, searched the area, but couldn't find his girlfriend or three other companions. He spent two long days beating out to a radio on the Seward Glacier; his friends' bodies were never recovered.

In 1897, Sella carefully photographed two of the guides climbing beneath these huge hanging glaciers. De Filippi wrote about the dangerous nine-thousand-foot run-out zone: "We pitched our camp within a mile of the outlet of the basin, out of reach of the avalanches threatening to fall on every side." De Filippi expressed concern about this northeastern face, which was "rocky at the steeper parts, but showed almost everywhere a coating of ice overlapping its precipices that threatened us with formidable avalanches."

The duke was not going to retreat after crossing fifty miles of chaotic glaciers and spending thousands of the House of Savoy's lire. Better a quick burial than turning around and admitting defeat to the king and queen when he sailed home. It was the reaction of a proud twenty-four-year-old prince, and a decision over which the older and more responsible Sella and Gonella agonized. It was decided to leave early in the morning, when the mountainside was more securely frozen. European climbers often crossed under hanging glaciers because *le Alpi* are smaller, drier mountains that have been in glacial retreat for hundreds of years and hanging glaciers rarely avalanche there.

As a disciple of Mummery (who was probably buried alive beneath a Nanga Parbat avalanche), the duke had read the 1895 *Alpine Journal* obituary: "Once he [Mummery] had accepted nature's challenge at a certain point he went forward avoiding by care and skill all dangers personal to himself, but accepting without reluctance or regret the other elements of risk which no skill could avoid." Just the sort of vainglory that Sella and Gonella (and to a lesser extent, the guides) tried to protect the duke from.

We ran off the last clattering piece of ice debris and up onto steepening snow toward a bergschrund that resembled any old ordinary crevasse, except for the steepening snow on the far side. We yelled out quick rope signals, moving above the Gatekeeper's firing zone with all haste.

Jeff belayed me over the bergschrund's snowbridge onto a forty-five-degree headwall. To keep from punching into the mysterious void below, I used an old "lightening" trick on the hollow-sounding snowbridge, swinging my axes limp-wristed and mincing my crampon kicks as if I were a 120-pound alpinista instead of a 190-pound mountain man.

One hundred and fifty feet up, feeling euphorically safe, I plunged in both axes, clipped them into my harness, and belayed Jeff up. He had been tense and brooding for days, so I asked, "How goes it?"

"Much better now," he said.

"Why?"

"We don't *think* we have things hanging over our head." Then he qualified: "We might."

"Let me tighten the rope for you."

He suggested untying; I promised to keep it from tangling with his drag bag (holding clothing and a sleeping bag). Most strong young climbers pooh-pooh roped belays on moderate-angled snow slopes, but if Jeff disappeared into a crevasse while unroped, I would be forced into a week's worth of crawling over unstable crevasse bridges to exit the range, to say nothing of the guilt I would feel, or the angst introduced to his father.

"That debris pile I thought would never end," Jeff said.

"Staying warm?" I asked, thinking about my numbed fingertips, thankful that Jeff had loaned me his spare overgloves.

"Now I am, yeah." He cramponed up, front-pointing one foot, splaying the other, eventually crunching up and out of sight.

At nine thousand feet, atop a small spur that was our safest avalanche shelter below the Haydon Col, two thousand feet higher, I called a halt between two huge crevasses. It was difficult stopping only three hours after breaking camp, but clouds had "whited us out" and robbed depth perception. Again, I had to talk Jeff into staying, but this time the decision was not as easy. He wanted to get as far away from hanging glaciers as possible. Wind ruffled our suits.

Big snowflakes swirled leafily around us. Jeff wanted to continue, but the ice face up to the col was guarded with yet another hanging glacier (he dubbed it "the Terminator"), and without the visibility to dodge avalanches, it wasn't worth the risk. I felt bad for constantly reining him in and hoped he wouldn't hold this unfathomable conservatism against me.

We set up the tent and prepared ourselves for one of Yasetaca's famous snowstorms. By early afternoon, avalanches began roaring everywhere; now I felt vindicated, but Jeff could have been right too—we *might* have been able to beat the storm up to the col above.

As the avalanche volume increased, with all the vibratory menace of a bustling munitions factory, I repeatedly assured Jeff that our camp was safe. He squinted his eyes at me, but said nothing.

I craved for him to express himself or loose some anger. But he held it all inside and turned silently to his journal. Asking him how he felt only seemed to irritate him.

In between pages of *Candide* and *One Hundred Years of Solitude*, we thumped the snow off the tent walls and listened. The avalanches started like crunching crampon steps approaching the tent, getting closer and closer until the crunching rolled into a continuous roar and the avalanche tally got another hash mark in my journal. In the last week we had heard over a hundred avalanches.

Our five-and-a-half-pound nylon tent was pincushioned to the top of an icefall, shaped like an alligator's snout, and cleaving the South Face's avalanches from the South Ridge's avalanches (and theoretically protecting us). In geology-speak, we were flowing down to the Malaspina Glacier, almost imperceptibly.

Almost until the pressures of gravity forcing billions of pounds of ice down unmoving bedrock caused some freighter-sized shard of glacier to shift a few inches and produce a localized quake, transmitted throughout the icefall and absorbed into the foam pads we were reclining on. It was reminiscent of being gently rear-ended by a pickup truck: the car hopped forward while your neck jumped backward. Even the crunching noises matched.

Jeff's eyes went wide with terror. "What was that?" he asked.

"Icefall's just moving," I said with a shrug. "Happens all the time. I've felt it before."

My imagination conveniently substituted other experiences, which was one way of coping with tent fever and the bewilderments of expedition life. Yasetaca, like most big mountains, was so full of strange new sensory-overload material that if you couldn't liken it to some other more tangible part of your life or a previous expedition experience, it would drive you to distraction—which it was doing to Jeff. I listened to snow pattering (not altogether different from waves caressing the foreberth of the *Heaven Sent*) on the tent walls: swishing, waving, brushing, pounding to a crescendo, then going quiet between sets. Sometime after midnight it occurred to me, as the tent walls billowed in and out, that we could be encased inside the accordion of Nirvana's Krist Novoselic, and with that thought, I finally fell into a rhythmic sleep.

Dreams are perhaps the best recreation when you're stormed in. Aside from their entertainment value, they put you in touch with your desires and vulnerabilities. The first night's dream had me kicking steps up the South Face in time to our musical wind tent, then burrowing through the final cornice:

> While unzipping to leave the traditional summit snow flower, I discover that I have frozen one of my digits. Something clicks hard against my still-pink fingernails, so when I bend over trying to figure out what the excitement is all about, I discover that my penis is the size and color of a Cajun fried jumbo prawn.

I awoke at first light to the sagging tent wall, badly overloaded, and pressing cold against my abdomen and genitals with its load of frozen snow. I kicked Jeff through my sleeping bag. "Think we probably got a few feet of snow."

He sounded wide awake, yet similarly pinned. For once, his reply seemed relaxed: "Back home if this happened, we'd be jumping for joy about the skiing."

In the ever-changing chemistry-dynamic of our team, someone had to play the skeptic, so I took my turn: "If this keeps up, we'll be digging for our lives." I forearmed the tent wall and its load of snow off me, and while trying to remember where we left the shovels, said, "I'll do the first shift."

I zipped out of my bag, grabbed my suit from its pillow position, and submerged my hand in a milky white puddle—Jeff had inadvertently copped a buzz while painting on the waterproofing glue and forgotten to seam-seal both sides of the tent. It also irked me that he had put half of the tent's ribbon zipper pulls on his clothing zippers rather than on the tent. In the interest of maintaining harmony, these petty tent-fever observations did not warrant complaining. I buried them in my journal. Surely Jeff had more than a few complaints about me.

While similarly trapped on the Newton Glacier, Cagni measured thirty inches of snow falling in twelve hours, "surrounding us," Sella wrote, "like a pile of flour." The duke and his guides were pinned down for three days, "in the most obstinately bad weather it is possible to conceive," De Filippi wrote.

The resolutely hostile mountain was meeting its invaders in a manner worthy of its fame. Snow began to fall heavily on the night of our arrival, and leaving our tents early the next morning (21st July), we found that the drifts had completely buried stoves, utensils, instruments, and numerous miscellaneous objects, left out on the previous evening. After a long and patient search, we succeeded in recovering all our belongings, and carefully gathered them together to avoid losses which might entail serious inconvenience.

The appearance of our camp was now entirely changed. The sides of the tents had caved in under the weight of the snow, the very pegs were capped with big white heaps, and even the ropes were covered with a thick layer of frost.

Notwithstanding the waterproof qualities claimed for our canvas roofs, the water was dripping through inside, and we had to clear off the snow and tighten the ropes, to try and put a stop to this very inconvenient leakage. Armed with axes and cooking utensils, we set to work to dig trenches round the tents, and get rid of the accumulated snow. But it was falling so fast and so thickly, that almost incessant labour was needed to prevent everything from being buried.

I dug the tent out as slowly and carefully as possible (a decade ago I had shoveled our snow-laden tent too zealously, sliced it open, and frosted my ranger-colleagues inside), then piled back inside. Jeff went out in another hour, and we continued shoveling all day to prevent our tent from collapsing.

One of the most treasured traditions for first ascensionists is to name their new routes (or peaks). The duke's ridge was named "the Abruzzi" (he named another ship-shaped mountain after their Atlantic steamer, the *Lucania*). Jeff and I indulged ourselves by discussing our new route's potential names: "Alive!," "Dusted," or "Avoiding the Skunk" (Jeff had been slaughtering me in cribbage card games). We settled on "Dumber than the Duke."

The next few days could make or break our already tenuous partnership—Jeff had made oblique references to my route choice being as sane as the trajectory of a Japanese World War II Zero pilot. What bothered me most was that he might be right.

Periods of listlessness on the thirty-foot *Heaven Sent* had been mere training for our internment in a 3½-by-6½-foot tent. Space is always the most precious commodity during expedition storms, and space is easily violated by any act impinging upon your partner's territory: fouling the air, hogging more than your carefully delineated half of the tent, or even talking too much can turn the sweet soul of your partner into a raging bull.

Reading books is one way to subdue the storm outside and quell the beast within. No one knew this better than the Alaskan veteran Boyd Everett. Avalanches scared him off Yasetaca in 1963, but he returned and summited in 1965 (performing the world's longest golf drive—10,500 feet off the mountainside); but in 1967, Everett was killed with six teammates in a Himalayan avalanche.

Everett had also authored *The Organization of an Alaskan Expedition,* which dispensed insight into climbers' literary tastes:

> Since Alaskan climbing almost always entails lots of bad weather, reading material becomes quite popular. Each book carried should be of general interest. It is questionable whether poetry in the German language or physics textbooks qualify as general interest reading. While the writer makes no moral judgment of the practice, books emphasizing sex and violence are always popular.

Jeff and I wiled away the day by reading, napping, discussing the proximity of each avalanche, playing cards, and writing in our journals. Jeff wrote:

> I still get terrified even though I convinced myself we were in the safest place possible yesterday. I can't relax, every thought, everything I do has the fear of these ice falls behind it. I give them as much respect as I can and talk to them. I have begun to observe all superstitions and do all I can to live the right path while I am here. In a way I've been praying to the spirit of this mountain and asked forgiveness for my trespass on this beautiful and powerful South Face, it is not a place for humans.

I was dreaming of mountain biking with my dog riding the handlebars when the sound of a cannon being discharged across the tent vestibule catapulted me up into a crouch. I checked my watch: 4:45 A.M.

Jeff bolted up: "Oh, no, not again!"

Snow started hitting the tent wall, so I leaned into it, expecting the debris to hit at any minute. "Jeff, help me!"

He jumped on top of me and together we braced the wall—Jeff's arms and my back—as wind-driven snow pushed us backward, straining the nylon. I braced my legs behind to keep my balance and support the wall. If the avalanche hit us, it would wash us down the icefall and into an enormous crevasse below. In two minutes, my pulse shot up from sixty to over one hundred beats per minute, constricting my throat. Running out was not an option, and there was nothing to do but brace the tent, so I consoled myself with the notion that one way or another, I was going to plunge right back into a blissful sleep where I wouldn't have to cope with all of this nonsense.

The roaring stopped as suddenly as it had begun, so I lay down, closed my eyes, and returned to dreamland as if the mountain had thrown me a roundhouse. It was clear that we were going to be trapped for several days.

De Filippi wrote about the area on the Newton Glacier where they had been snowed in:

> A guide made the valley echo with the typical, long-drawn mountain cry. His voice had the strangest effect, breaking the silence of the peaks. An answering cry came from Sella . . . ; and although we were well over 45 minutes' march from him, his voice was as strong and distinct as though he were only fifty paces off.

Sella was undergoing that bane of most expedition photographers. By trying to capture some art—posing the duke, the guides, and the porters in every imaginable position—he was isolating himself and incurring their silent wrath for impeding the group's forward progress. Unlike Cagni, De Filippi, and Gonella, Sella had both his own separate and invaluable function as the photographer, as well as his climbing prowess. From 1883 to 1885, Sella made the first winter ascents of the Matterhorn, Monte Rosa, and the Lyskamm. By 1897, climbing became the means to further craft his mountain photography. Sella was only twenty-eight, but he had become renowned throughout Europe for his photographs of the Alps and the Caucasus Mountains. His photographs were sought after because he juxtaposed climbers into the picture as a means of accentuating the mountains; he had impeccable technique and photographic expertise (learned indirectly from his photographer father); and he combined this technique with an artist's eye.

On St. Elias, he had taken only one photograph with the forty-five-pound, twelve-by-sixteen-inch brass Dallmeyer camera (which the duke had convinced him was too heavy to drag up the Malaspina Glacier). Up on the Newton Glacier, he was lugging his ten-by-eight-inch Ross camera, lenses, and glass plates, along with a backup seven-by-five-inch folding Kodak—the same model that the duke was photographing with.

Unbeknownst to Sella, while inside his black tent, packing away glass plates by sandwiching them with gelatin paper, moisture (possibly from his breath) was absorbed by the gelatin. Dozens of photographs were destroyed.

The duke drove his companions hard, particularly Sella, whose work with slow-shutter-speed lenses demanded that the climbers hold their breath while the photographer trailed behind seeking out proper composition. In De Filippi's words, "As the ascent of Mount St. Elias was the main object of our journey, all else was made subordinate to it." If the team failed to summit, it was a failure for Italy, which would reflect badly upon the duke. Ultimately, all of the men understood this, and while none complained about His Royal Highness's forcefulness, Sella's photography work and his more conservative mountaineering philosophy compromised the duke's agenda.

On July 29, Sella wrote again in his diary about opposing the guides' "senseless plan to climb Mt. St. Elias immediately." The duke agreed with the plan, however, and they left the next day with light loads for Russell Col. Sella did not complain.

The duke's seven-by-five-inch folding camera.

(On January 6, 1909, the duke wrote and invited Sella to be the photographer for his K2 expedition. In his characteristic scrawl, the duke alluded to his previous behavior:

Dear Sella

Have you had enough of my character and of my not too easy disposition during the journeys? . . .

To you aff[ectionately]
[signed] Luigi

Sella accepted. In his flowing calligraphic letters to the duke and others, he came across as insecure, constantly apologetic for his past behavior, and as a deeply sensitive artist. For instance, responding to the duke's invitation to be the photographer for the 1906 Ruwenzori expedition, he vacillated back and forth, alluding to botching the photography and slowing everyone down on St. Elias, then writing: "The unforgettable memory of the ascent of St. Elias encourages me to accept for the pleasure of doing another journey under the dear leadership and companionship of HH [His Highness]." He was not just patronizing royalty—he wrote kind letters to everyone.)

Although there were over a hundred of his photographs—some retouched—used in *The Ascent of Mount St. Elias*, Sella salvaged the other moisture-spoiled photographs into thirty-four ink-enhanced photogravures. The duke's photographs were also used, although this wasn't widely known.

The *New York Times* book review of October 6, 1900, called it a "sumptuous volume and a splendid specimen of English bookmaking . . . and the illustrations, which include several superb photogravures and other reproductions from photographs taken by members of the party [the duke and Gonella], are equal to the splendid ones which adorn the records of the mountain expeditions of Conway, Fitzgerald, and Whymper."

A few years before his death, Sella wrote about ruining his plates: "After nearly fifty years, the memory of that sorrowful and unexpected misfortune which could have been avoided, causes me to weep."

The Italian photographer, Vittorio Sella, fiddling
with his 10″ × 8″ camera on Mount St. Elias.

S een through the lens a half mile above camp, our tent was a yellow speck alongside the rumbling South Face, the blue-gilled glaciers, and the sea—a great shimmering mirror for the evening sun. But there was no way to compose this scene; it was too vast, the glaciers too bright, the scale too large. I needed Sella's panoramic camera.

Jeff wrote in his journal:

> <u>5/8/95</u> Awakened at 0445 by the rifle report of a serac breaking loose. Less than a minute later we are hit by the strongest and heaviest blast yet at this camp. All the terror returned as I was sure at any moment the blast would turn into a wall of ice and snow and then all would be forgotten, blackness. It was hard getting back to sleep, but I managed to doze. . . . I am so paranoid here that I wanted to run for the col as soon as possible. . . . The sky is blue like the melt ponds and Melissa's eyes, the evening light enhancing the monotone

The 9,000-foot camp, where we were trapped for five days; Malaspina Glacier in rear.

black and white of the peaks w/ shadows. W/out the sun the temp. drops fast, it's after 1800. I look to Icy Bay w/ a great ring of floating ice. I see Moraine Bay where Dad is anchored and I feel lonely, I wish I were w/ him. This route has made me a wreck. We re-set camp in the dropping temps and jump in to fire up the stove for heat.

Although it had stopped snowing and we spent the afternoon breaking a trail through five feet of new snow up to the bergschrund, we decided to give the snow a day to settle (rather than becoming the human avalanche triggers) off the Haydon Col ice face. Over the roaring stove inside the tent, I heard another avalanche blasting above. I jumped over the stove, shouted to Jeff to kill it, grabbed the drying sleeping bags off our skis, flung them into the tent, and jumped back in, zipping the door shut.

Jeff resignedly passed me the video camera. He looked at the tent floor, his mouth tight, hiding his dilated pupils.

"Here it comes," I said, putting a finger to my lips as the stream loudened into a river.

"You really think it's just a blast?" Jeff asked.

"Yeah, I'm sure."

"Did you see where it set off?"

"It came from way high. Boy, I grabbed those sleeping bags just in time." The river's side-eddy of wind and snow hit the tent and buffeted us back and forth like the accordion of my dreams.

"Everything says it can't travel that ridge," Jeff said, looking for confirmation.

"Yup, money's on it."

"Lovely campsite," Jeff concluded.

"Boy, every day," I said as the blast relented and the main river faded on down the mountain.

"Lot better when you're wide awake," he said.

Then he added, sounding just like his dad: "Well, the more it happens the more that new snow will be gone. These last six days have been the six most unnerving days of my life. I feel like a wreck. I've aged twenty years."

"Wish we had some Valium in the first aid kit," I said, trying to get him smiling.

"Or the Robitussin," he parried.

"Yeah, even that's gone." I flicked the Sony off and turned to my journal, lamenting that the hanging glacier avalanches would prevent us from trying to recross our kamikaze ascent ramp beneath the South Face:

> JH hates being filmed.
>
> It's decided: we can't go back down the ramp. Too danger-ous. But it creates a problem, because now we don't have a food cache for getting back out to the sailboat, let alone descending a strange route (the South Ridge) and beating back out via the convoluted, canyony Taan Fiord. . . .
>
> My body smells like sour vinegar. Disgusts me.
>
> Missed vestibule loo corner & hit snow-drinking water area while emptying gravy [pee] bottle; just a little bit. Didn't tell JH. . . .
>
> This game we play is all about patience, or so I tell myself on this 4th day of waiting for avalanche slopes or snowfall to subside. I do know that, once at the col, moving up will be completely different, w/ a new sense of purpose, directly toward the summit, and best of all lightened packs—no skis, no poles, no drag bag, minimal food/fuel and w/ the end always in sight.
>
> Gulf Air skiplane flew by today & circled, wagged wings. Did Gary send them? Took away some of the great feeling of isolation. Also, opens an option for catching a flight out, now that it seems likely they will be checking up on us by air.

Jeff wrote with a completely different perspective about the route we had climbed:

W/ luck we will find a cache at the col. At this rate our fuel will outlast our food. Jon is still talking summit if we find food at the col. My priority is working on a way out. If there's no food at the col and we can't see anyone on the route then I think we have to start down and find our way to Dad and the *Heaven Sent*. I will feel very fortunate to reach the col, I will not deserve the summit after this stunt. Out of respect I'd be happy not to even make an attempt. . . . Time to sip a cup of tea and nibble some chocolate ginger. If only Melissa knew the comforts (of body and mind) that her package has provided, and the memories they have triggered.

"How goes it, Jeff?" He was fifty feet up, dangling from his ice axes and tenuous crampon-kicked steps. Ice screws jangled from his waist.

"Getting soft all of a sudden."

I checked my belay: solid, but if he peeled I hoped it would be a safe air-fall straight into the darkened bergschrund-crevasse. I zoomed the video in on him, spread-eagled and gasping under his pack, perversely glad to be freed from our avalanche camp. "Looks like it gets better a little higher," I offered.

Aside from a few audible hiccoughs, the Terminator had only avalanched once in the last four days of being trapped, but we had now risen out of its line of fire. Sunlight broke through the clouds, hitting the col 1,500 feet above. Rocks clattered somewhere close by. The Libbey Glacier fell below us in a jumbled mass of crevasses and teetering ice towers, rolling out into the vast Malaspina, with an eye-shadowing of Prussian blue Pacific and faint brown haze around its borders. Cold air bit my lungs and I speed-polkaed on my platform to stay warm, cowering beneath my pack (in lieu of a helmet) for protection against falling rocks, ice, or one 170-pound-plus-70-pound-packed partner fastened to twenty-six razor-sharp points. I panned over him at the crux, a vertical lip of dubious-looking snow that demanded high stepping and levering up onto his wobbly axes. "Snow firm?" I shouted up, trying to stimulate more dramatic footage.

"Kinda in between," he replied. He smashed in a picket above his head, clipped the rope into a carabiner and effortlessly cranked his foot up to his chest, then kicked it into the lip. "Would you watch me here?" (Climberspeak for *Pay attention!*) and without looking down, he said, "Fuck that camera."

I punched it off, put both hands on the rope, and paid attention to Jeff pirouetting over the lip, as close as one could come to ballet while lugging a seventy-pound monkey and a week's worth of avalanche-ready adrenaline.

After Jeff hauled up the skis, I swarmed up to the lip, plunged in my axes as high as I could reach—and before contorting my right crampon placement up above my waist, I complimented Jeff on his lead. He explained that his earlier profanity about the camera was an attempt to spice up the film and that I shouldn't take it personally.

"Whatever," I replied, knowing he was so nice it forced him to lie.

I gave a samurai grunt, closed my eyes, and launched myself over the lip without having to confront the gloomy depths of the bergschrund. A beam of sunlight lit my face; if this had been the final overhang at the North American Sport Climbing Championships, the crowd would have jumped to their feet applauding. I turned, looking down for acknowledgments, fantasizing about a quick *sayonara* bow, and the crystalline, incalculable gulf of the bergschrund's depths made my knees wobble and my stomach flip-flop.

I raced past Jeff at breakneck speed, then began breaking through to my hips in unconsolidated snow. After half an hour of swimming a mere several hundred feet—contemplating how much more weight the newly fallen snow crystals could bear before the entire slope avalanched and took us on the Great Sled Ride—rocks began zinging by me. As the sun peeked fully out of the clouds, the melting above increased—and the rockfall came pulsing down in waves, speckling the air with shale. Jeff yelled from below when to duck as I broke trail in nightmarish slow motion toward a sheltered overhang, rocks *whoomf*ing into the snow all around me.

We were back in trouble again.

He joined me beneath the second snow overhang, bug-eyed, wavery-voiced, and wearing the same look of fear that must have been wrinkling my own face. No question that one of these rocks could alter our hat sizes.

Any remaining vestige of courage let go as I imagined my subscription to one certain rock melting out of the snow above, labeled with my name, express air delivery. If I took a head injury or got killed, Jeff would be hard-pressed to get out—with uncertain down-climbing, innumerable crevasses, more avalanches, roaming bears, and river crossings.

He began flailing upward, throwing his arms in an attempt to give himself more momentum through the snow. I screamed up to him at each new barrage: "Rock!"

It seemed completely fair that if either of us had to die, better me than him. This mess was my own doing and Jeff had merely followed me here, so there seemed a certain justice to his surviving—I would make him survive. I was determined to see him through this as he confronted the tenuous-looking crevasse bridge above. I shouted up descriptions of each rock size and asked each time if he was okay.

I gripped the rope so tightly he screamed down for slack. He bowed over and crouched beneath his big pack, and took no hits, although the pack and strapped-on skis were getting dinged. Each of the hits against his pack sounded like crotch seams splitting tight jeans, and if the pack survived surely it would win Jeff a lifetime sponsorship from MountainSmith packs, but this lone note of opportunistic optimism was negated by a sick curiosity that I couldn't suppress: How will a rock sound bursting bones?

Suddenly with no warning a watermelon-sized rock blurred past within a foot and a half of his head; I suppressed a whimper—which would have spooked Jeff worse than seeing the rock.

He pulled out his skis and started thrusting them like giant cake skewers into the wall above, several feet down into loose snow, as he slowly pulled himself up and across the aerated snow bridge. His breathing went alternately ragged as he scuttled up over the bottom-less-looking crevasse, repeatedly punching his legs into snow that became space, pulling back up, and kicking away all but a sliver of bridge for me—twenty pounds heavier—to follow. He bobbed left and right as if dodging an agitated colony of spitting gulls, step-kicking out of sight up to a sheltered spur. Since I couldn't hear any screams, he was probably unhurt, but I shouted up anyway: "You okay?"

Suddenly my skin started crawling: We were talking (and thinking) in questions because when your ship is sinking it's bad form to make declarative statements.

"Yeah, you're on." His voice fell down tiny, yet confident—good. But then he shouted down: "Will you be careful?"

I didn't want to go up—the rockfall had cranked up its whistling-*whoomf*ing volume level. So I pulled out the video camera, wondering how one dodges a rain of rocks while looking through a zoom lens, and realized that I was shaking too hard to get clean footage; I stuffed the Sony hand cam back into my pack. With my luck, a rock would have bull's-eyed the lens.

Then I procrastinated further by moving the foam sleeping pad under the pack lid, just above my frontal lobe. Now maybe the risks of a head injury—if I wasn't brain-damaged already—would be lessened.

A rock caromed in sideways off the snow slope, showing the illusory nature of my "sheltered" overhang, missing my right hip only by virtue of a quick dive into cold snow. I stood up, brushed off, and unzipped (after carefully looking for more errant rocks), then painted the snow yellow for the second time in five minutes. As if I didn't have enough problems, I accidentally caught the business end of myself with the climbing suit crotch zipper, then spent a long minute trying to free things without causing any more damage than necessary. Finally, I decided to simply yank the zipper down and get out of the danger zone—promoting a quick involuntary scream.

Jeff, out of sight above, shouted down with obvious concern in his voice: "Are you okay?"

Somehow I lost my nerve and convinced myself that one of the rocks above had my name on it. If I got beaned, Jeff would be screwed; I had to get up intact. Up was survival. Down, through that pit of avalanche iniquity below, was no longer an option.

Convincing myself that indiscretion was the better part of valor, I began floundering up, resigned to my fate, looking for the rock of my fears because Jeff's position hid him from view and he couldn't warn me when rocks were coming. A few feet below the bridge, an ascending-frequency whistle approached, so I jerked right and watched a hand-sized rock sing through air where my left ear had been a half second earlier. I sped straight onto the gauzy bridge—my Neanderthal crampon work broke the last snow pedestal off, and I watched it luff down into the darkened crevasse. *"Fuck me!"* I screamed, and in a lather of sweat, grunting over the three-foot gap, I thrust my skis down to their bindings and hauled myself, legs fluttering, over the blackened hole.

Twenty seconds, two steps higher, a boulder swished cleanly into the hole for two points. "Boy," I said, looking up at Jeff under his sheltered overhang, knowing that if I couldn't joke about it I might break down and cry, "that was fun, huh?"

No reply.

We cramponed up forty-five-degree ice and out of the deluge. After running out two rope lengths (I insisted we belay one another in case one of us took a rock in the face), we stayed roped up and moved together without placing ice screws—if one of us fell, he would pull the other off and both of us would plunge the length of the face. Those who do not place protection (ice screws, rock cams, pickets) move faster, but when they fall, they fall far. It was too cold, or maybe too low-angled for a young climber of Jeff's caliber to stop and place ice screws. I wanted to untie, which would have prevented one of us from pulling the other off in the event of a fall, but it seemed like a breach of trust, so I moved up as soon as the rope came tight. Jeff was forced to front-point and strain his calves for the last several hundred feet of brittle ice. Having filed off his ax ferrules (the bottom spikes) like most hotshot steep-ice climbers, he had to face forward and swing his ax picks in as if the angle were much steeper than fifty degrees. This slowed him down.

With functional, traditional ice axes, I foxtrotted up with the rhythmic, ankle-swiveling method known as French technique. I

*Jeff following Jon up to Hayden Col, climbing out of
the rockfall bombardment.*

stood sideways, flicked in my ax ferrules, aimed crampon spikes into
marbled ice, and compensated for wind gusts by careening in
another few degrees.

I stopped to catch my breath. Up here it was sheer dance, unen-
cumbered movement, the freedom that crystallized my motivation for
climbing mountains. If we had been climbing at the turn of the century, we would have spent all day chopping steps for our quarter-inch
nails (instead of one-inch crampon spikes) beneath our boots. Below
was the most avalanche-prone, crevasse-laden, rock-peppered, serac-
tottering, unobvious, and objectively unjustifiable route that I had
ever survived. The last five thousand feet had never before been traveled, and if I had any say, no one would ever step in it again.

The duke and his nine companions arose at 1 A.M. on
July 30 to move a final camp up on the col. The six-
thousand-foot ridge to the summit looked straightforward and low-
angled. De Filippi wrote, "So confident were we now of success that
hope amounted almost to certainty."

They divided into three rope teams and moved quickly up to the avalanche debris, following the guide Petigax, who had chopped steps up toward the col in his hobnailed boots the previous day. Prior to the invention of front-point crampons, stiff-soled boots, and French technique, chopping a ladder of steps was the only technique by which the Italians could climb steep snow or ice. Over a mile's worth of avalanche debris "crackled under the nails of [their] shoes, and was thickly sprinkled with serac fragments fallen from a height of over 3,000 feet."

De Filippi wrote that (unlike the snow that Jeff and I had waded through to the ice face) "the accumulated snow had already come down during the past three days of fine weather, and the rest of it had time to harden a little; but what chiefly served to keep the ice safely bound to the precipitous rocks was the intense cold of early morning."

They reached the steeper slopes in an hour, and relieved to be out of range of the hanging glacier avalanches, they confronted a series of crevasse-bergschrunds, separating each of the snow slopes above. Since the guides had been up the day before, and since all of the climbers had tackled steeper slopes in the Alps, no one was particularly ruffled. De Filippi wrote:

> We zigzagged up these snow-slopes, the surface of which was pretty good. . . . The first crevasse immediately beneath the isolated rock that projects from the middle of the wall cost us some trouble, and nearly half an hour's labour. The first two caravans crossed it easily enough by a snow-bridge, but this broke down when attempted by Sella, the leader of the third rope [who took a header into the hole and was yanked out by the guides behind him.]
>
> After searching vainly for some solid foothold on the snow-vault, the third party finally managed to reach the other side by leaping boldly across the gap in the bridge. But the last guide unluckily dropped his jacket as he jumped, and had to be let down to a good depth in the fissure to recover it.

Keeping to the left of the rocks, we then mounted to the second crevasse, which cuts straight across the steep incline in such a way that its upper edge overlaps the lower one like a roof, leaving an interval of about seven feet. At a short distance, however, along the lower side, we discovered a point where the edges drew a little closer together. By mounting on a guide's shoulders, we managed to get safely across, and our loads were hauled up after us.

They hauled the last guide up and crossed one more bergschrund. At 10 A.M., after six hours of climbing, they pitched camp on the 12,280-foot col. The duke named it after Russell, who first climbed it.

De Filippi snatched up his leather-bound journal:

> Northward all is cold shade under a steel blue sky, but the rest of the horizon is orange red. Little by little, Mount Augusta crimsons like a fiery volcano. The thermometer is at 18 [degrees] Fahr., and a chill north-west wind drives us into our tents. Lying down closely packed in these narrow shelters, we try to get some rest to fit us for the last and most serious effort; but most of us are too excited by the thought of the morrow's task to be able to sleep.

Jeff and I laced the tent down to skis, pickets, and ice axes, behind a partially sheltered ridge. Rock flecks flew through the air like snow, stinging our faces. Every few minutes the wind was pushy enough to coerce us down onto our axes for balance. We piled inside.

"You took some pack hits down there," I said.

"Pack, fingers, anything that wasn't beneath the pack." Jeff pointed at his heart.

"One missed your head by about two feet."

He nodded and looked down. "I'm glad it missed my head." Then he confessed, "I couldn't sleep last night."

I asked, "What's our food situation?"

"Six days."

"Stretched?"

"Real stretched."

It would take us at least a week to get back to the sailboat. Talk wasn't cutting it, so we both turned anxiously to our journals:

> Nearly unroped today while 3rd classing up final 4–500′ of snow-ice. JH put nothing in & was frontpointing instead of frenching, so he was going terribly slow; I didn't have the heart to untie, but by the time he got to a place to belay me up I was already there. JH clearly lacks routefinding skills & climbed perhaps 300′ higher than he needed to; also I've seen other instances of false perception about getting round crevasses & not understanding avalanches (be it hangers or powder) so it's best to try and *steer* him. All of this (basically a lack of many diff. experiences on big mts) is easily made up for by his easy-going nature & leading (steep ice/bergschrund) abilities.
>
> I sense that he's ready to go down, maybe the route beneath the dangerous S. Face has worn him out. Nonetheless, he's right: if we can't find any abandoned food caches, we have to go down. . . .
>
> I am upset at the world tonight. At my ex-wife and all the legal morass she contrived (which I haven't thought about for weeks now); at GH, for his impatience w/ me (the landlubber) and his lack of teaching ability, and even JH and his inability to *talk* to me. I am upset at the world mostly, however, because it seems pretty certain that we won't make the top.

Jeff had turned away. I couldn't see what he was entering in his eight-by-twelve spiral notebook (and again, I felt criminal for looking, but any form of communication was better than none). He wrote in his journal:

About a thousand times I wondered what the hell I was doing here. . . . I felt relief, I kissed the col, a relaxed feeling came over me despite the constant 40 mph wind and gusts up to 60 mph. . . . The new view to north was as fantastic as that to the south, a change of scenery was nice. The nicest change was that the hanging glaciers you could see weren't above you. It took about a half dozen serac collapses for me not to get panicked, and when I'd hear them, I still got that tight feeling in my throat. It would be admirable to give the summit a shot from the col. As Tim Wilson would say, "I admire your courage but question your judgment." It would be a foolish attempt and I feel lucky enough to have arrived here w/ the opportunity to descend.

The sun fell behind Mount Huxley and poured hot light into the sky, warming the mountainside. Going for alpine-style broke, as a mere pair of unsupported climbers on North America's most difficult big peak, we had performed well. I felt proud. As Jeff's face blushed with the light, a thunderous roar arose, and now that we were perched out of the line of fire, poking our torsos from the tent vestibule, we cheered as a hanging glacier avalanche raced down a face, shot into a runnel, then exploded out into rosy space, billowing out into the sky like a great mushroom cloud, then disappearing as the light blued and the avalanche dissipated into cold dry air.

As an approaching gust audibly cycloned down toward us, we zipped up the tent before more spindrift dumped onto our sleeping bags. I knew that Jeff had a different take on the events of the last week, so now that we were relatively safe, it was time to hold forth, even if he would never see it my way:

"Jeff, I've got something to say. I don't believe in luck and with one or two exceptions on mountaineering expeditions, luck has not been a part of my survival. And that includes this trip."

Judging from the blank and tight expression on his face, I knew that he wouldn't be taking notes. I plunged on anyway, determined that this, my last of a score of Alaskan climbing expeditions, should give me the final say:

"This trip was the most dangerous experience I've undergone in the mountains, but we are not alive because we're lucky. We're alive because we moved properly, camped in the proper places, left when the snow was frozen, and ran and hid in the right serac crevasse.

"We're alive because we did not attempt the col when the storm blew in, and because we found the way through that maze of crevasses because I knew there *was* a way. Luck *would have been* great weather, or no avalanches, or camping in the wrong place and *not* being avalanched, or finding some route that we didn't know about. This was *not* a cribbage game like the ones you've been skunking me in."

At a clear and still midnight, with Venus shining above Mount Newton, the Italians gulped down cups of hot coffee. According to the duke's biographer, Gigi Speroni, Cagni exclaimed about the good weather, "A stroke of luck!"

The duke immediately replied: "But it is also true that everyone is tricked by his own luck." Then his rope led out, skirting an ice cliff, and searching for firm snow.

De Filippi wrote that they were "too excited to talk." Every half hour, Petigax and Maquignaz traded step cutting, and by 5 A.M. they passed Russell's 14,500-foot high point.

The duke called their first cigarette break at 6:30, when "some of our party began to feel the diminished pressure in the shape of palpitation and difficult breathing," De Filippi wrote, "which although too slight to impede progress, yet sufficed to suggest that some of us might be prevented from reaching the summit." De Filippi's legs felt leaden, he could not eat or drink, and he felt a tightness around his temples.

At 8 A.M., the team stopped as Cagni pulled the fifteen-pound Fortin barometer out of his pack, then carefully lifted it out of the straw-lined wooden box. After making some corrections, he calculated their elevation at 16,509 feet, noting that the sky was foggy, and the temperature was 16.88 degrees Fahrenheit.

Maquignaz could not chop steps or break trail with the efficiency he would display at higher elevations in the Andes. Because of "troposphere depression," the thinner atmosphere of the subarctic is physiologically several thousand feet higher than a matching elevation in the nondepressed Andean or Himalayan atmosphere.

De Filippi wrote:

> Almost all of us are suffering more or less from the rarefaction of the air, some being attacked by headache, others by serious difficulty of breathing and general exhaustion. H.R.H. slackens the pace of his caravan, and sometimes calls a halt, to wait for those who have fallen in the rear. He is determined to keep us all together, knowing the sense of discouragement felt by any one left behind by the rest of the party. The ascent is very monotonous on the whole and perfectly easy.

As the least experienced alpinist, De Filippi's appraisal of the summit ridge was an accurate team consensus. More than sixty years later, the second and third ascents of this ridge underscored the Italian achievement. In 1964 and 1968, experienced alpinists from Japan and America avoided the Newton Icefall and the hanging glaciers by climbing a knife-edged ridge over Mount Newton. From Russell Col up to the summit, both parties took longer than the duke (although both parties were more acclimated than the Italians); an American climber rode an avalanche below the summit; then Japanese and Americans were forced to spend the night sitting up in a bivouac before returning to the col.

While latter-day climbers rarely mention the effects of altitude, the Italians were hurting. Cooking inside their unventilated tents may have given them carbon monoxide poisoning. They would stop every ten minutes, De Fillipi wrote,

> while some sit or crouch, while others take their rest standing, and lean on the ice-axes. H.R.H., Sella, and two of the guides are the only persons showing no signs of distress.

Gonella suffers from headache; Cagni, myself, and Botta have to fight against the drowsiness which comes over us at every halt. . . .

Every step requires a distinct effort of the will, and we get on by dint of certain devices familiar to all who have made ascents when tired out—leaning both hands on the knees, or planting the ax in the snow ahead and dragging the body up by it, while at every step we pause for breath. Still, we manage to climb somehow; we are spurred on by excitement, and our nerves are strung to the highest pitch.

Sella wrote in his diary:

When we stopped at about 9 o'clock to eat, almost all of us were convinced that our struggle was soon to end. I take advantage of the brief stop to photograph the view. It was only 11 o'clock, however, when some of us were almost completely exhausted physically, that the slope facing us flattened and became almost horizontal.

Petigax and Maquignaz stepped aside to let the duke take the first summit steps at 11:45 A.M., July 31, 1897. It had taken them thirty-eight days to negotiate the previous fifty miles of glacier (the same time it had taken to travel the eight thousand miles from Italy).

"His Highness reached it in excellent shape," Sella wrote in his diary.

De Filippi wrote in the book:

We hastened breathlessly to join in his triumphant hurrah! H.R.H. hoisted our little tricolour flag on an ice-axe, and we nine gathered round him to join in his hearty shout for Italy and the king. Then all pressed the hand of the Prince, who had so skillfully led the expedition, and had maintained our courage and strength to the last by the force of his inspiring example.

*The duke (seated at right) and his companions, with
the Italian flag at the summit of Mount St. Elias.*

Sella set up his camera for a summit photo. He exposed five glass
plates. Most of the men were sick, and similarly stung by the anticli-
max of achieving a goal so long sought after, they slumped in apa-
thetic indifference. The duke—unaffected by the altitude, carrying
a forty-pound pack—named one mountain Bona (after his cousin)
and a large tributary glacier Quintino Sella (after Vittorio's alpinist
uncle). He physically shook Cagni and De Filippi, telling them to get
up and make their observations.

Cagni measured the summit elevation as 18,090 feet, noted that
the temperature was 10.40 degrees Fahrenheit and that the sky was
completely clear and windless. Then he stopped and gawked at the
sea of ice. He later told a reporter:

> When we reached the summit we were amply repaid, how-
> ever, for all of our trouble. The weird grandeur of the scenery,
> embracing miles upon miles of glaciers, broken here and there
> by fissures, the ragged edges of which glistened like many
> thousands of little diamonds in a noon-day sun, was a sight we
> shall never forget. It may not be as picturesque as the scenery

close to our homes in the Apennines and Swiss Alps, but the very dreariness of it, the fact that one can go for miles and miles without coming across a living being of any description, makes the vista much more impressive.

De Filippi wrote,

No words can express the desolation of this immeasurable waste of ice, which Russell has compared with the ice-sheet that covers Greenland. No smallest trace of vegetation can be discerned on it, no running water, no lake. It might be a tract of primitive chaos untouched by the harmonizing forces of nature. . . .

But sheer physical weariness soon unfits the mind for contemplation of so much supernatural grandeur. We felt vaguely crushed by the immensity; a desolating sense of isolation comes to us from those infinite wastes of ice, and from the solemn, oppressive silence of nature.

They also felt blinded by the high-altitude brightness, caused by the lack of atmosphere to block ultraviolet light. After an hour and a half on the summit, they leaned against their long alpenstocks and began glissading down. Gusts of wind blew ice in their faces. Above Russell Col they plowed through knee-deep snow. Since altitude hypoxia dimmed De Filippi's memory, he would borrow from the others' diaries in order to compile the day's events: "Nevertheless, we got on fast, slipping, falling, regaining our feet, plastered with snow from head to foot, but eager to reach camp, to hide from all that blinding, white glare, into the comforting shade of our tents."

Although the high altitude (or carbon monoxide poisoning) had played havoc on the Italians, no one was too tired to eat. "We had only a little broken sleep that night," De Filippi wrote about their bivouac on the col, referring to their irregular, periodic breathing and altitude headaches, "and awoke early on the 1st of August in a very battered, aching, and stiffened condition."

On Haydon Col, Jeff and I spent most of the blustery day vainly searching for food caches abandoned by previous climbers. The summit was obscured by a fearsome lens cloud, and as we turned back to our tent, empty-handed, trudging through shale-blackened snow, descent seemed our only option. We simply did not have enough food to try for the summit, come back down the ridge, then out to the sailboat. In a last-ditch effort, I suggested to Jeff, "I'm tempted to do something foolhardy, even though going down is the *right* thing to do."

He wasn't having any of it. He countered: "The trip isn't over by a long shot." He was referring to the long and unknown descent down the ridge and out to the sailboat, but I knew if we had climbed through the storm, or if we had not been exposed to all the avalanches, he would have agreed to try the summit with little food. Since I couldn't go up without him, and since he was inherently right, I began rationalizing in my journal:

> Isn't one's dream peak all the more elusive, all the more alluring and beautiful because you can't climb it? . . . Surely I don't have the wherewithal to try it again from the ocean. And I will not ruminate over "what ifs" when I'm an old man.
>
> I am through with Yasetaca.

In the media hoopla preceding the 1897 climb, a reporter from *New York Journal* stabbed at the duke's motivations:

> St. Elias has a fascination for mountain climbers because no one has perched as yet upon its topmost ridge. To the joys of stumbling among rocks, hanging over the edges of precipices, slipping and falling upon ice and snow, and freezing between times, it promises to add the ecstasy of pioneering. Relatively considered this is certainly something. If the ambition to stumble and fall and freeze is incomprehensible to most people, everyone will understand the desire to do what

has never been done before, even if it excites no very great sympathy.

The duke also wanted to climb the unclimbed mountain to promote Italy, but he was further motivated because he had nothing to lose. His mother and father were dead, and the king and queen (although they supported his mountain climbing) maintained a royal aloofness, so Luigi gave himself totally to St. Elias. The mountain, and his companions on it, became his family. Because his companions knew these reasons for his "melancholia," they followed him closely and made sure to protect the duke from himself.

In our latent drive for *why* we undertook risks in climbing, and nothing else, the duke and I could have been brothers. We both had nothing to lose.

I preferred being on the mountain (versus participating in the other sedentary events of my life) because the small things—the acrid coffee crystals, yet another sunset vista, even the privation of freeze-dried food—were alchemistically altered on expeditions into events that I appreciated. More importantly, in the last two weeks, I had relearned that dying on the mountain was a fate far preferable to getting hit by an ice-cream truck or any number of "natural causes" that kill most people. Anything less would mean that I was dishonest, uncommitted, or ready to quit climbing. But like most long-in-the-tooth climbers, I believed that the protracted habit of surviving indisposes you to dying.

These were my thoughts while tiptoeing down around the avalanche-prone Haydon Peak traverse on thirty-degree windslab, eight hundred feet above a gaping crevasse. As a diversionary tactic, I was thinking that there were probably better causes to devote myself to and I would give up the why-less crusade of standing atop mountains. More than anything, I was flat-out disappointed to have come so far and risked so much, only to run out of food.

At nine thousand feet we missed a crucial turn on the South Ridge route and descended too far. We cut down a fifty-degree couloir to return to the climbing route two thousand feet below. The snow was underlaid with ice, so we used the rope for five hundred feet, front-pointing carefully, setting off wet snowslides, and concentrating so hard that there was no time to regret our shortcut. Halfway down, I stopped and cupped my hands to slurp out of the first snowmelt trickle we had seen in a week.

Suddenly Jeff yelled: "Rocks! Move!" Head-sized stones came crashing down, and in three strides I sprinted out of the rock gully, taking only one glancing yet painful hip hit, while another rock dinged the video camera housing lens—Jeff was not at all sympathetic. We worked our way down rotten, steep shale slopes. I slipped and recovered from one potentially long fall by deliberately cartwheeling onto my knees.

At 8 P.M. Jeff and I arrived above the infamous Shale Ridge, wriggled out of our packs, and turned back north to the summit, completely clear and taunting us as a steep pink siren, 11,000 feet above. I could not look at it without feeling like a failure. So I turned to consider the next morning's work: 2,600 feet of decomposing shale stacked upon rotting snow. A score of other parties had grappled with the Shale Ridge since its first ascent. Harold Topham wrote about his 1888 contest with the ridge:

> This formation renders climbing very tiring work. No step is quite safe. Whole masses of rocks become dislodged and fall thundering down the mountain side, and so thick was the cloud of dust which enveloped us on our descent, that the last man had great difficulty to see where to walk. . . . As we approached the mountain from the Tyndall Glacier, we had been under the impression that the pillar of dust was smoke or steam due to volcanic agency.

To take our minds off the Shale Ridge, Jeff and I considered our shrinking stomachs—neither of us had moved our bowels that day, the instant coffee was gone, tea bags were being recycled, and I couldn't get my pack belt and climbing harness tight around my diminishing waist. By chopping around in the snow and lifting up rocks, we scavenged mummified turds, toilet paper, a 1930s novel, scattered Valiums (which we debated ingesting), freeze-dried food wrappers, and three eight-ounce cans—dented, rusted brown, unmarked, and best of all, *unopened.*

I tapped my ax into one and recoiled as the can let out a long hiss of rancid air, reminiscent of a summer sled-dog yard—it was cantaloupe-hued salmon.

Jeff shook his head dubiously. "Could be botulism."

I wasn't listening, because, as one Roman statesman said, "It is a difficult matter to argue with the belly since it has no ears." So I replied, "That hissing might be the pressure difference between here and where it was canned at sea level."

"How old do you think it is?" Jeff asked.

"Maybe ten years." We needed the calories, so I plunged my finger into the mealy orange flesh, bones, and withered-looking skin, then licked it—Jeff looked at me as if I had just stepped unroped into a crevasse. "It's settled then," I announced. "If I don't drop in the next hour, it's probably okay."

We boiled it another hour in a quart of water, mixed in a package of soup noodles, and inhaled our two ten-ounce portions of watery fish swill (with what looked like roundworm topping). We fell asleep to our bellies gurgling in gastric distress.

Jeff got up in the middle of the night, and later wrote about "one of the eeriest and most tranquil sights" he had ever seen. "The full moon was over Icy Bay with the thin layer of clouds creating a yellow light, illuminating a lower layer of the clouds. I had a hard time placing myself for several minutes."

As the weather deteriorated during the Italians' descent, De Filippi wrote, "Great banks of violet-hued clouds obscured the eastern sky; the Augusta chain was suffused with a pale, livid light, as one summit after another disappeared; while Mount Augusta itself was swathed in thick clouds, until gradually the whole prospect was blotted out. Mount St. Elias was the last peak to vanish."

They slogged through knee-deep snow, under heavy loads, tediously probing out a safe route through the melting and ever-changing icefalls. Despite having to find a new route down the melting crevasses, the Italians all but flew down the Newton Glacier.

They would bivouac at only nine of the twenty-two camps that they had established on the ascent. At their 6,400-foot camp, De Filippi discerned the American porters through the mist:

> Standing outside the tents, we watched with strange emotion the approach of shadowy forms struggling slowly up through the heavily falling snow. At a hundred paces from us, their leader, Ingraham, halted, shouting out, "Did you reach the top?"
>
> "Yes."
>
> "All of you?"
>
> "All of us!"
>
> Their loud hurrahs echoed through the valley, and we again felt the exultation of that moment of victory as though it had been scarcely realized before.

C. L. Andrews was sulking. Half of the porters were relaxing on the shore, while he and five others had been subsisting on flapjacks and mush, huddled beneath blankets in sodden tents on the glacier while waiting for the overdue Italians. The duke remedied everything by tossing them a blue bag of Italian food—the American porters feasted on marmalade and roast beef. Andrews jubilantly asked the duke to autograph his (Andrews's) tin plate.

A t 9 A.M., I started down the backbone of the beast. Every dozen steps I stopped to spit out flecks of vintage salmon that had come unglued in our cooking pot while making tea. The snow was crotch deep for nine hundred feet. My first step onto the Shale Ridge levered off a five-foot rock, which threw up a tremendous ruckus of dust and noise as it accelerated into the void.

After a half hour of entropy through rotten rock and avalanche-prone snow, I stopped and pulled out the mirror in order to make a cursory attempt to signal the Captain out in Moraine Bay. After five minutes of worthless flashing, I checked out my own image: the uncontrolled Fu Manchu would have scared off small children, while my thinning hair stood straight up, glued in place by the combination of sweat and rock dust. I looked like a cross between an Iroquois and Wolfman Jack.

Jeff caught up, so I popped up from behind a boulder and goggled at him cross-eyed—he jumped back in unfeigned horror and continued down the disintegrating ridge. I gave him a fifteen-minute lead.

Previous expeditions had fixed ropes on some of the steepest sections—but the ropes were so frayed from rockfall that Jeff didn't touch them. The first one I weighted promptly broke away in my hands; I dropped five feet, caught a wobbly boulder, then flipped the rotted rope off the ridge.

Several hundred feet down, I cut off the ridge by butt glissading down steep snow and flying over a bergschrund. I tried to stand up, but the snow was bottomless, so I lay back, deployed skis from my pack like snatching arrows from a quiver, and buckled my boots in. Sucking in my breath, I schussed over yet another deep-looking crevasse, carving a wobbly stem christie turn in ligament-tearing snow. I continued schussing three crevasses, slalom style—theoretically preventing me from weighting the waterlogged snowbridges any more than it would take for them to collapse. Jeff sat waiting below, commenting dryly that he would never again set foot on the crumbling South Ridge of Yasetaca, let alone recommend it to anyone.

We dropped our sixty-pound packs to the ground with a muffled *whumf* just as the fog rolled in at 4,200 feet, a flat expanse where ski-planes habitually dropped off and picked up climbers. Jeff would be eternally mortified if his dad had to come looking for us. He reluctantly gave in to my optimism that we could catch a ride out with a passing plane by signaling it with our mirror (and by pulling in our belts even more) before the Captain would be forced to the embarrassment of rescuing us, ten days from now, on our due-out date of May 23.

The next day, our eighteenth day out, we took signaling watches on top of a hill above camp. I propped my red climbing suit up like a scarecrow climber—no low-flying pilot could miss it, even though Jeff reminded me that we had seen only one airplane in three weeks. Since fog occluded Moraine Bay, some thirty miles (fifty walking miles) off, I aimed the bright sight of the signal mirror into the corner of the bay that we presumed the *Heaven Sent* to be anchored in.

Thus began the hungriest days of our life. Snow and fog blanketed our tent and we gave up signaling. On the third dawn, I woke up to the Captain shouting my name outside of the tent—but it was only ptarmigan, taunting and calling us, then flying off faster than we could throw our ski-pole spears. All day, every day, our faces would suddenly go blank in the middle of reading or playing cribbage as we imagined the approaching whine of propellers.

Jeff wrote in his journal:

> Wake up to snow w/ a growling stomach. Try to sleep in as late as possible to ignore the hunger. It's good to go light on food, especially after our gross excess of the sail north, although now I'm glad I ate as much as I did.

We lay back on our sleeping bags, tormented by our growling stomachs. Without meaning to, we eyed one another ladling out each morning's quarter cup of oatmeal, cutting the 1 P.M. Snickers bar in half, and serving out each night's cup of salmon-rancid gruel—the fairest course seemed to be trading places as the server.

It had now been five days since either of us had peeled down the useful trapdoors on our underwear and Gore-Tex climbing suits. For the last two mornings, I had loosened lone musical notes of flatulence—which caused Jeff to look up with expectation—but our bowels remained unmoved.

Jeff stamped a fifty-foot OUT in the snow for passing pilots to read. I spelled out the same word up on the ridge with our multicolored skis and the fuchsia climbing rope.

It was a shabby way to finish. After all of our good intentions about doing it on our own, without airplanes and in pioneer style, I had thrown my ethics out the window. I felt too "stretched" by the mountain to take any more risks, too gripped to cope with grizzlies, crotch-deep slush, impenetrable alder thickets, and decaying cliffs on the unexplored Taan Fjord and the Chaix Hills. In the end, fear and hunger were in danger of stripping all our well-intentioned plans.

But there was something else that I still wanted from the mountain—I couldn't explain this to Jeff because I didn't fully understand it. I wasn't through with Yasetaca yet—as if our failure to climb it obligated me not to leave. Ever since I had been a sixteen-year-old Outward Bound student, I had developed the habit of spending several days of fasting and solitude after intense experiences. I did it after relationships ended, after expeditions, and anytime when I wanted perspective on where to go next. Jeff and I had run out of conversation anyway, and although we spent long hours together in the tent, I spent equal time alone on top of the ridge, staring out into the ocean, or writing in my journal.

I wanted the answers to my life now that the obstacles of the peak and our slim rations seemed to have cleared out my head. I was in no rush to go anywhere, Yasetaca had spat us out unharmed, and everything appeared in front of me with new clarity.

For lack of a better word, I had come to Yasetaca for *therapy*, and as a sort of preparation for growing old gracefully. But now it all felt hollow. Jeff and I had formed a functional and efficient partnership, but our actual relationship was barren. He would probably not be accepting any future trip invitations from me, lacking one very important reason—camaraderie—to go climbing in the first place. I had probably bossed him around too much in the interest of survival.

The last two weeks of jumping crevasses and dodging avalanches had also invoked whatever remnants of intuition and awareness I still possessed—I had become acutely conscious of my body. My resting pulse, normally sixty, had inexplicably dropped to thirty-five. I measured my pulse without palpating by watching the second hand of my altimeter-watch and *listening* to my heartbeats. I could also close my eyes and smell my outgoing urine for acidity to tell if I was dehydrated.

For several startling moments each day—and I would have called them hallucinations except for their absolute clarity and texture—I could interpret Jeff's thoughts as if he were speaking.

I still admired and respected him. He was so kind and thoughtful he would have given me his half of the Snickers bar ration if I had only asked. He would carry anything I didn't want to carry. It occurred to me that he might even have climbed a route he didn't want to climb, simply to indulge me. Once, during an insecure moment during the approach march, I found myself wishing that I was as levelheaded and selfless as he. But I lacked the courage to tell him any of this. It seemed certain that he had given up on my self-absorption, my impatience, my videoing compulsion, and my intractable conviction on subjects in general. If there was any one thought I imagined him clinging to like a security blanket, it was how much he looked forward to flying home and getting away from me. Even stranger still, I couldn't begrudge him for distancing himself from me; to the contrary, he had simply misread me through the stress of the last seven weeks. And I didn't know how to set him straight.

It might take the time and distance of these words for him to learn the truths I hold as pure. Then he will know how much I looked up to him, that I respected the mountain as I have no other, and I would have sacrificed myself for him—during the rockfall—if that's what it would have taken to get him out safely to his dad and Melissa. Then he will also know that I owe him, big-time, because this trip had been my dream, not his, and he had taken profound risks to accommodate me.

I grappled for perspective on the life and "the real world" that I had abandoned. Although I didn't entirely trust these sentiments, since I had made similar promises after previous expeditions, I wrote them down anyway:

> So much of these trips are about allowing me to reenter the rest of my life with a fresh appreciation and along with the usual wonders of thanks that I will now give (to a cup of cocoa undiluted, a full meal eaten slowly and thankfully, a stroll through a flower garden), I am now looking for love in its proper manifestations, with a woman, with my own family (Rick, Jerry, Mom, Dad, Erna, Tasha), as well as the family I hope to raise.

By the fifth day of waiting for an airplane to pass by, further progress in my journal became impossible. I had thoroughly dissected my motivations, and, light-headed from hunger, Jeff and I contemplated dying from starvation. We would eventually drop to our weakened knees and hallucinate into a permanent and peaceful sleep, higher than migrating geese, higher, perhaps, than the Demerol we had robbed from the first aid kit and ingested in lieu of the previous night's half rations. (For lunch, the sore-throat lozenges had supplied us with nearly fifty calories.) This new clarity of mind became intriguing—was it celibacy, starvation, or the Demerol clearing out my head?

(It was probably ketolysis, the beginning stage of starvation. After all of your fatty tissue burns off, your muscle tissue is metabolized and ketones are released, signaling the heart to slow down—explaining my lowered pulse—and inducing a state of confusion or heightened awareness. There is evidence that this state is achieved as a self-defense mechanism for survival situations.)

When Jeff asked for the map, I knew his thoughts: We had to leave while we could still walk. Late that afternoon, after a quick power nap, we cached a shovel, ice screws, carabiners, and pickets, burned the two books, then left the South Ridge with lightened packs toward a mess of crevasses, a maze of alders, and a cliffed fjord.

From the same latitude, nine miles east, De Filippi wrote, "The south ridge of Mount St. Elias stood out clearly, merging into the long chain of the Chaix Hills." The Italians were virtually running out the Malaspina. De Filippi boasted (again) of the "remarkable skill and strength" that the Italian guides displayed descending with the sledges, "without removing the baggage, now checking their pace with ropes, now executing brilliant glissades, while propping up and supporting their cumbersome loads; thereby exciting the earnest admiration of the Americans." While topping a glacial esker, De Filippi spied the sea:

> We clearly distinguished the white sails of the yacht *Aggie*,
> that was waiting for us off the coast. . . . We felt as joyful and
> excited as mariners on sighting land after a long voyage, and
> not in the least discouraged by the fact that several miles had
> to be traversed before reaching the moraine. . . . The guides
> were as merry as boys, and flew down steep slopes clinging to
> the sledges.

Now that the end was in sight, the duke could finally relax and allow the full magnitude of his accomplishment to wash over him. The duke's nationalistic pride and motivation were summed up by one of his Italian biographers, Professor Giotto Dainelli, a geologist, who concluded his own "St. Elias" chapter:

> It was, from the period of "the Great Explorations," the
> first great enterprise led by Italians and only by Italians. It

The Italian team descending with a sledge.

marked the start of great mountaineering explorations, until then almost completely unknown. It represented a clear success to the competition, interested in the proper conquest of those Alaskan peaks, by explorers of various nationalities, especially of the nationality holding the dominion of those regions. Italian exploration was newly descended in the field, and they came out victors.

But the initiative and the organization and the management had not been sponsored by public Institutes of culture or of politics, but came only from the firm will of a young Prince, who wanted Italy to make a name for itself in the world of competitive athletics—a powerful, civilized and modern State—as well as for the ever greater knowledge of our Earth. These are all circumstances and deeds that Italians should not forget.

The snow turned to slush underfoot; then the duke steered out on compass bearings through the fog. They reached the beach on the same day—August 10—that the duke had asked the skipper of the *Aggie* to return. Cagni said:

Prince Luigi was a model leader. Never on the whole trip was he impatient or irritable. Often was he to be found, pack upon back, working as hard or harder than any others of the party. No opportunity passed for giving praise to guide or packer that he employed.

The most famous mountaineer of the nineteenth century, Edward Whymper, wrote about the duke's American porters: "It used to be said on the Pacific Coast of North America that the meanest thing any white man had ever done was taking home washing for a Chinaman; but what is that compared with a professor of Greek and a Poet carrying up soap, candles, and petroleum for a party of Alpinists?"

The duke presented each of the long-suffering porters with a fifty-dollar bonus, and one hundred dollars to the *Aggie*'s skipper.

Jeff and I got dead-ended in an icefall by a slew of crevasses blocking our route like an impassable defensive line. By quarterback sweeping sideways to a lateral moraine, I found a safe route off the glacier and down a frothing river. Snow was melting in torrents and rushing down out of the Chaix Hills. We inhaled white sulfurous seeps, tiptoed around steaming mires chartreuse with summer grasses, and spied tracks where a romping grizzly had splattered its muddy size nineteens, rolled on its back, and ripped up grass. After plodding for five hours in the rain, we dumped our packs at a stream six hundred feet above the sea.

At the edge of a moraine we peered down at Taan Fjord: the cliff dropped sheer to the sea, just as we suspected—we would have to walk around two ten-mile canyons before we could begin bushwhacking along the shore out toward the sailboat.

I turned on the video camera and pointed it at Jeff. "How's it feel to finally be looking down at the ocean?"

"It's a long way off," he said distantly.

Taan Fiord with toe of Tyndall Glacier and Chaix
Hills canyons.

"We're kinda rat-fucked here," I commiserated.

We trudged down to the tent. Jeff wrote in his journal: "I want to get to the bay and see Dad. . . . The going is not easy and there are several deep side gullies to bypass, just a taste of the bigger ones we know are yet to come."

I wrote: "Before we left, I lay asleep in the cold sun imagining starving to death; certainly you'd get dizzy and eventually go to sleep from lack of food, not a terrible way to die, but now I'm too hungry to continue contemplating such an end."

We were merely in the first euphoric stage of starvation. After the grim metabolization of more fat and muscle tissue, we would descend into a torpor of agony, fatigue, and helplessness. We had to get out, fast.

In the morning I tried another camera interview. Jeff granted me patented one-sentence replies. My partner, normally the most energetic and enthusiastic companion imaginable, was close to the end of his rope with me now.

I was certain that I could plod another week on only soup vapors, but when I got ready to drop, I would probably start acting similarly irritable. It also seemed likely—by his gloomy silences—that Jeff was holding me responsible for our present situation. Judging by his frequent and taciturn requests to see the map, he no longer trusted my route finding. Given the avalanche-rockfall-hunger gauntlet I had devised thus far, most beginning Alaskan mountaineers would feel the same way. Again, I didn't hold it against him, I just tried to empathize with him. He was the only partner I had, and if he was estranged from me, I needed to take whatever responsibility was deserved.

We plunged into the alder thickets and began circling the first and largest canyon. Branches swung in our faces and ripped at our clothes. We yelled out obscenities to scare off any lurking bears.

By midday, we dropped into the canyon and emerged onto a side cut that would lead us around the next canyon. Although our 1:250,000 scale map vaguely indicated that we might have to gain a thousand feet, the going looked smooth, the snow was firm, and it had stopped raining.

I felt wasted. As a means of disassociating myself from my own misery, I turned the camera on and filmed Jeff coming up one of the Chaix "Hills." By now Jeff might have been frustrated that I could so easily remove myself from suffering by "playing" with my camera. Nonetheless, he was too tired, and as a young point-and-shoot photographer new to the art of composition, he lacked the years staring through camera lenses to have much use for my video camera—even though I constantly encouraged him to use it.

"No other comment," he said, throwing his pack down angrily.

"I feel the same way if it makes you feel any better."

He was looking at the precipitous canyon end and entertaining a different route from the course that I was on. I suggested, "Looks like a dead end up there."

Jeff gave me the silent treatment. A long moment passed. I knew what he was thinking; he knew that I knew: accepting my judgments had only got him into trouble. We didn't need talk.

As confirmation of this thought, he asked, "Where's that map?"

I broke it out, along with our lunch: three Fig Newtons and a half a Snickers bar. He ate his facing away from me. I felt so full when I finished lunch thirty seconds later that I fell into a nap, but Jeff shook me onward.

By midafternoon, we had been forced up onto the crest of the Chaix Hills to get around the second canyon. My sweat still ran freely—dripping off my nose, fogging my sunglasses, soaking my crotch—but now I could have squeezed my Capilene T-shirt over my mouth and recycled the sweat: tepid yet salt-free as Perrier. I had, as the holistics say, sweated all the poisons out of my body.

At 6 P.M., we stopped for a quick blister patching. I closed my eyes. My stomach sent forth its gnawing reminder (reminiscent of an infected tooth rooting down deep and buzzing like a stuck doorbell). I dug out some emergency rations: two unwrapped hard candies sweat-glued to the bottom of a pack pocket from two years ago. Jeff popped one into his mouth and thanked me profusely.

Yasetaca flung its white tail fluke into a limpid blue sky, and we sat fidgeting like Ahab and Ishmael, antagonized by our breaching whale. I was as stunned by its form as I had been seventeen years ago. Whether or not I ever managed to climb the final seven thousand feet, I would always fear Yasetaca—I had made it into some sort of symbol. Making it to the top of most mountains usually lessened my fear. I had returned to Denali a dozen times, abstaining from standing on the summit and beating my chest a second time, but continuing to slog up and down the various glaciers, skiing, climbing smaller peaks, and kayaking its rivers. Although I respected that mountain, I didn't fear it like Yasetaca.

Ever since abandoning therapy, I found it amusing to consider how my former therapist would analyze me: Denali would represent my mother, ex-wife, and all women—whom I hold at arm's length. And Yasetaca, she would add with timeless Freudian logic, was a climb I would always subconsciously abort so that I would not have to concede my descent into old age.

Trying to climb the mountain as the duke of Abruzzi had did in fact allow me a certain intimacy with Yasetaca. Although we wanted a ski-plane to deliver us from our hunger, employing airplanes on

Alaskan peaks is equivalent to a one-night stand: you never really get to know the mountain.

Great mountains also have a way of wringing confession out of you—a form of emotional bloodletting. In the shadow of this peak that had demanded all of our tricks just to escape, Jeff finally spoke his emotions: "This trip," he said, with hesitancy, "has made me take a serious look at mountaineering."

I didn't want to push him. Most climbers allow a few months, or a year—depending on how many times they think they almost died—to go by and rob their memories before they can talk about, let alone tackle, another expedition.

"I'm not sure it's all worth it," he concluded.

"You might feel differently when you get home," I suggested. Then, riding a sugar rush that temporarily quelled my stomach's churning and knowing that my pancreas's energy would soon crash from the ancient candy, I pulled on my pack.

"I don't know," Jeff said as he finished lacing up his boot.

I had seen and admired (and experienced) this "internal sanity debate" numerous times. No less than a dozen of my partners lost their resolve—if they lasted through the climb, bushwhacking out always offered the coup de grâce. Climbers often joke about their short memories. We swear we won't forget, we swear that we're through with expedition climbing. This time, of course, it was different for me because I was pulling off a long-held promise about ending it all with Yasetaca.

In Alaska, it was easy to outfit yourself with the specialized expedition gear of those who sold off their tools dirt cheap after "seeing God" and swearing off subarctic mountaineering. But few serious mountaineers ever fully quit. No matter how bad the trip, it always assumes a soft and luminous quality back at the pub, out on some sunny crag, or while daydreaming at work. Climbing mountains is like robbing banks, finding religion, falling in love, or being an alcoholic. You *have* to return; one more heist, one last prayer, one loftier affair, one last drink.

Suddenly I was distracted by some unlikely geology: a dozen marble boulders perched on a knife-edged ridge above the gulf of the third canyon. They were the furriest boulders I had ever seen. Drawing closer, I looked up and the boulders began rolling adroitly down the scree. I blinked my eyes: they transformed into a flock of mountain goats, grazing down the ridge.

I needed food. Badly.

Jeff and I stepped into our ski bindings at the top of a huge ravine. There was no sense further debating the route. We were going to the sea, and as long as we pointed downhill, we were on the right route, as long as we didn't hit cliffs (we were so weak we had abandoned the rope several hours ago). As I sideslipped down onto a steep avalanche slope, I was thinking about how expeditionary mountaineering is a dying art in the world of modern climbing. Commitment is the cornerstone of expeditions, and in isolated mountains if there is a chink in your resolve, it is only a matter of time before heavy packs, trailbreaking, and the bicolor drudgery of glacial living bore you to a stump. Add a bit of objective danger and expeditions can seem insane.

For a month and a half of approach time, Jeff had led only one moderately challenging ice pitch (with the added titillation of a massive pack and the possibility of getting lobotomized by flying slate). If he had spent a similar amount of time at City of Rocks, Yosemite, or the Schwanagunks, he would have cranked scores of multipitch routes, buffed out his body, upped his ability a grade or two, partied with the tribe, slept with Melissa, grooved to some good tunes, and drunk countless cups of singed espresso. An expedition partner as gifted in climbing and as committed as Jeff is rare, and he was right to question what he was doing on the most difficult and dangerous big mountain in North America.

I schussed down into the water-primed snow basin, cutting off a continuous snowslide and weighting my downhill ski edge, keeping my speed up so that I wouldn't get caught in the small avalanche fanning along in my wake. It wasn't big enough to kill me, but it might break my leg; Jeff had given me a good head start in case the whole basin let go. I knew my partner's head was okay, but what worried me was that nothing seemed out of the ordinary to *me*. If the next outing manifested the same escalating pattern of humming rocks and sublime avalanches, I was likely to fall victim to the very Nietzsche platitude I had always tried to avoid: "He who fights with monsters might take care lest he thereby become a monster. And if you gaze for long into an abyss, the abyss gazes also into you."

This time, I am not going to forget, I told myself, my eyes tearing in the wind, snow ripping down in a wet wave beneath my left ski. As I steered my hips toward a safe-looking bench, I recited a mantra to keep cool:

> "I am through with Yasetaca.
> I am through with Yasetaca.
> I am through with Yasetaca."

Down in the alders, we took off our skis and hand carried them down a steep streambed. Tired of catching his skis like moose tines in the alder canopy, his arms numbed from the weight of his pack, Jeff started trying to unscrew his ski bindings from the heavy skis. I reconnoitered the route to the fjord, slipping down past a waterfall and Batmanning down alder branches until the scent and sight of green brine showed that we could make it to the sea. When I climbed back up, Jeff had given up blunting my screwdriver-knife and reluctantly strapped the fifteen-pound skis back onto his pack.

"It goes," I said.

He looked at me dubiously.

"It definitely goes," I said with more firmness.

Several hundred feet above the shore, fiddlehead ferns poked up out of the leafy forest floor. "Roughage," I told Jeff. His trust had disintegrated so far that everything I did or said was suspect. I weeded out a fern, plopped it in my mouth, and chewed freely as he watched. "Just like asparagus," I assured him, "and high in vitamin C and A."

He looked more skittish than he did with the salmon cans, but I continued stuffing my mouth and pockets. When I turned the video camera on, he allowed me to film him taking a tentative bite.

We set up the tent on lumpy rocks above the high-tide line. Jeff would have nothing to do with my hale "congratulations" about reaching the sea—muttering something about it being over when the fat lady sings. We jumped inside to escape the mosquitoes. After the drama on the mountain above, a cloud of mosquitoes seemed relatively tame—avoiding bugs was only a matter of walking briskly or sheltering inside the tent. Again, this was yet another coveted part of mountaineering: upon your descent, everything seemed so pleasant, so tame in comparison to the coldhearted mountain above.

A pot bubbled on the stove with the last of half a ramen soup noodle package and several pounds of curled fiddleheads. "After this meal," I shouted to Jeff, sitting directly behind me, "we should be able to figure out if our bowels still work." Sweat poured off our foreheads from the stove.

Jeff grimaced as I plopped two cups of what looked like green cat intestines into his bowl. I was so grateful to be down intact that I could no sooner detusk the horde of mosquitoes on the bug-netting door than I could shoot a porpoise. Between mouthfuls, I told Jeff, "If we leave the mosquitoes alone perhaps they'll leave us alone." His eyebrows raised slightly in disbelief. Then we both passed out with the still steaming and empty bowls in our hands.

In the morning, it bent me double like a lower torso migraine as soon as I stood up. Panic gripped me.

Jeff was back in form, raving about how much he liked fiddleheads, and clicking on the video camera to reciprocate our team filmmaking effort. "How do you feel?" Jeff had resumed his "in my face" sportscaster voice.

"Rushed," I got around him.

"Where you going?" he asked, peering through the lens.

I tried to hide the soggy toilet paper that we were carrying as a gesture of optimism. "First time in eight days." I smiled wanly.

In the windless shelter of alders the cloud of mosquitoes descended just as I finished kicking out a hole. In all probability Jeff was also hovering nearby with the zoom lens behind a camouflaged blind. This was not going to be pleasant. A harbor seal's shiny head crowned up above the water amid the ice floes, splashing after salmon. As I pushed my drop flap open and bared my flesh, *Anopheles earlei* landed upon my private area as I contemplated the dirt under my fingernails and tried to shorten the longest bowel movement of my life.

Just above the beach, one of the American porters was inexplicably struck down with a 104-degree fever and profuse sweating. De Filippi shrewdly dosed the man with quinine and cut the fever short. The porter had been bitten by a malarial mosquito—the only illness of the entire trip.

De Filippi wrote:

> Before we had been an hour on the beach, we were driven wild by the mosquitoes, which were more numerous, more voracious, and more tormenting than in June. They swarmed about us in dense clouds, got in our noses, mouths, eyes, and ears, crawled up our sleeves and down our collars. Before long our faces were like masks, all swollen and bloodstained by the innumerable stings, and the vain slaps and scratchings by which we sought protection or cure. . . .
>
> Meanwhile the surf, slight enough at first, had grown rather violent, and just as Gonella was pushing off, a big breaker turned the boat bottom up; but luckily no one was hurt. [Sella's five-by-seven camera was soaked.] His next attempt was perfectly successful. Then came my turn and

Sella's; and we got off all right at the cost of a good ducking from the spray. H.R.H., Cagni, the guides, and six porters remained on shore, where they passed a sleepless and most wretched night incessantly tortured by their insect foes.

The duke was the last to leave the shore, at 8 A.M. His and his companions' faces were "so disfigured by venomous bites as to be totally unrecognisable." The skipper on the *Aggie* shouted at Andrews to haul the halyards and they luffed across the eighteen-mile-wide bay at four and a half knots an hour.

Henry Bryant was bear hunting around Yakutat. Gigi Speroni claimed that the duke slapped Bryant on the back and told him he was waiting to make sure the Italians had completed the climb.

Bryant shared his own version of the encounter at the next American Alpine Club meeting. This oral history has been passed down as meticulously as a Tlingit legend, from one tribe of climbers to the next. The duke was reclining in his stateroom below decks, his face terribly sunburned and swollen. He did not stand up when Bryant entered, so his exhaustion spoke for itself.

Bryant congratulated him.

The duke replied, "Mr. Bryant, I have conquaired zee mountain St. Elias, but zee mosquitoes have conquaired me."

One more long day and we could light the prearranged bonfire, signaling the Captain across the bay to come pick us up. Yasetaca continued to beckon us with a perfect summit day, 18,008 feet above our heads and less than a dozen (air) miles away.

Jeff said, "I'm thinking real differently about mountaineering now."

"Why?"

"Because of its lack of hard climbing and its danger."

What could I say? I grunted monosyllabically in agreement and let him brood through the day about it alone. He trailed behind me, grunting monosyllabically every time I pulled out the camera.

Taan Fjord stretched on through a complexity of peninsulas and thigh-deep river crossings. Wolf tracks dappled across solid-looking mud mires. Glacial silt sucked at our boots as our stomachs made similar churning noises beneath our mouths.

We slipped and slid and forded and bushwhacked and waded and traversed rotten cliffs along the water. Seals swam alongside the shore, curiously poking their heads up to watch our heavy-footed cursing. Two kingfishers rattled above their clear fishing stream. A cow moose galloped into an alder thicket with the grace of its cousin, the deer.

I stooped over the tide flats and started gathering black, three-inch mussels. "Make tonight's soup thicker," I told Jeff. "Protein too." We spent a half hour cleaning out a pot's worth.

Late that afternoon, while marveling at how I was able to bush-whack for seven hours on a stomach shrunken to a peach, I saw a skiff out in the fjord. I shimmied down an alder trunk, then leaped twenty feet off a cliff onto a sandy shore, falling over on my pack like a parachutist. The Tlingit at the tiller instinctively reached for his rifle, surprised about the burst of shaggy-looking life at the cliffed shoreline, then swerved over for a look. I disengaged from my pack and rolled to my feet.

Mike Harry was seal hunting with his girlfriend. He wore a good-luck salmon cap, which he had carved out of alder, and a smile of rare self-possession and calm. We offered him ten gallons of gas from the *Heaven Sent* in return for a ride across the bay. Jeff pre-sented the bare-handed Mike with a pair of neoprene gloves.

As we plunged into a solid line of ice blocking either side of the five-mile-wide bay, he repeatedly rammed his skiff into ice chunks as if his fiberglass boat were composed of a material more dense than ancient shards of floating glacier. His girlfriend was frightened, but Mike had been hunting seals here for forty years and he regularly crossed fifty-five miles of open ocean from Yakutat as if driving to the grocery store. He was living one day at a time. His life was not complex, but I immediately envied its simplicity. Beneath the Mountain at the Head of Icy Bay, Mike Harry was happy. It seemed that there was some message in all of this, but my stomach distracted me from further contemplation of anything but food.

Jeff was too mannerly to mention how hungry we were. But when Mike showed me five gallons of gull eggs, I asked if they tasted better than chicken eggs.

"You hungry?" His graying wispy beard hung down to his sternum like Ghengis Khan's.

"This is our twenty-fourth day on seventeen days of food."

He threw us a jar of salmon, a box of pilot biscuits, and a tub of cream cheese. As I kept a continuous parade of crackers marching toward my mouth, I recalled the words of Oscar Wilde:

> *Whenever cannibals are on the brink of starvation*
> *Heaven in its infinite mercy sends them a nice plump missionary.*

Jeff politely accepted two crackers, but he was obviously being overcome by his own personal demons, and he finally gave in, pointed at the Maxwell House can, and asked, "Is that coffee?"

Mike pulled over to shore, fired up his stove, and dumped two fistfuls of black grounds into a big pot of water. He grinned at me and displayed his missing teeth, wiping his hands on greasy bibs. It had been so long since Jeff smiled that I had forgotten how his whole face lit up like that of a kid beneath the Christmas tree.

Before the duke left Yakutat, he presented their Tlingit porter, Peter Lawrence, with a royal autographed portrait. (Fifty-two years later, when Peter was destitute and near death, this prized photograph was one of his few possessions. He spoke in Tlingit, hiding his English from the anthropologist Frederica de Laguna and revising a well-known tribal legend of their God hiding inside a killer whale by referring to Raven as "the Prince.")

C. L. Andrews wrote about his seasickness en route to Sitka. After a fair sailing wind all the way to Mount Edgecomb, "a strong

SE wind came up—we were again lucky. A lucky trip." He groused at length in his journal about not being a "lackey" again.

> Mt. St.E. passed from our view about 4:30 p.m. at a distance of 175 or 180 m. Good by Eli—A cool winter to you. . . .
> Loafing around Sitka with an appetite like a bear. Have eaten 75 cents worth of fruit since coming ashore—weighed 149 #.

Andrews was the only one to stay on in Alaska. He immediately accepted a job as a customs officer, while the other porters and Italians rode the *Topeka* and the *Aggie* back to Seattle. Andrews's appetite didn't relent for days. He wrote his last journal entry from the trip like a customs officer's list, then ceremoniously sampled all that he had seized:

AUGUST 20

Contents of Italian Tin
2 Doz Galetta
1 garlic
1 Box Bouillon . . . sliced bacon
1 # Butter 1 can salmon
1 can Marmalade
2 cans Evap cream
2 # can Corned beef
2 # can Roast beef
1 can Cauliflower
1 can Apricot Marmalade

In Sitka, the English alpinist Archdeacon Hudson Stuck wrote about the duke's paying a visit to the Alaskan governor. He asked about the duke's sun-blackened and mosquito-bitten face. "When you climbba de mountain, you freeza de nose, eh?" Later, the governor explained that all dagoes looked alike to him.

For all of the graceless behavior he was shown by Americans, the duke remained a gentleman. From Nanaimo, British Columbia, he sent an appreciative telegram to Professor Russell (who had both informed and denigrated the duke):

August 25

Following your direction I had the pleasure to climb St. Elias July 31st. The good results of the expedition was [sic] greatly due to your precious information, and I thank you heartily.

Luigi of Savoy.

In that provocative photograph that Sella exposed of the duke immediately after the climb, he had a sun-bleached beard and white raccoon eyes (shaded by his glacier goggles) set off by a sunburned face. There was a quality in him that cut across the gulf of years separating us. He wore the usual stern regal expression, his eyes lined with exhaustion and puffy white mosquito bites. His sweater was

The duke of Abruzzi after the climb.

obviously stained with stove oil and sweat, while his fedora had been slept on. I was wrong; he was no dandy. He loved the dirty ragged exhausted feeling of accomplishment that followed a hard climb—a sensation that negates the years and speaks to the essence of alpinism—otherwise he would have made Sella take the portrait after he had cleaned up. No doubt he was as hungry and happy as Jeff sitting across from me in Mike Harry's skiff.

It was the only relaxed image of Luigi among hundreds of taciturn, uniformed, or sad-eyed countenances. If a photograph could reveal the emotions of a mute prince, Mount St. Elias must have been the watershed of his life.

Part Three

After

Jeff and the Captain embraced each other out on a multimillion-dollar raft of virgin spruce, chainsawed from around the Malaspina and bound for the Orient. From a distance it was plain that Jeff was apologizing to his dad—his arms rose up then dropped down to signify raining avalanches—for the dangers of our route.

An Icy Bay tugboat pilot uncorked a bottle, filled several glasses, then proposed a toast: "To a safe and successful trip and all of your toes."

"To Neptune," the Captain added.

"Hey," I said, as it burned down my throat, "Glenlivet twelve-year-old, my favorite. I've got a bottle of this on the *Heaven Sent*."

"Not anymore you don't," the pilot said. "Gary gave it to me and said he didn't want it on the boat anymore."

The duke was accosted by newspapermen from British Columbia to New York. A Nanaimo journalist wrote, "It is the most successful expedition ever undertaken." The duke granted no interviews, so the wires recycled stock stories from De Filippi or Cagni—about how easy the climb was, the mountain's elevation, that it was not a volcano, and how the Italians sobbed like children on top.

The *New York World* described the duke as a "pleasant, breezy, manly fellow, with an ingenuous simplicity that is perfectly delightful, and a knack of making friends wherever he goes." Many papers mentioned that he was rushing back to England in order to race his yacht in mid-September.

Edward Whymper wrote that the trip had been pulled off "without a single casualty or hitch of any description. The spirit which impelled this young Prince to travel 15,000 miles to carry out his enterprise, the perseverance and tenacity with which he stuck to his work, and the thorough mastery that he exhibited over every detail, render most memorable the first ascent of Mount St. Elias."

He arrived back in Italy only slightly celebrated; *l'alpinismo* was still the game of rich men and not the stuff of the mainstream. Also, his brother, Vittorio Emanuele, the count of Turin, stole the headlines on August 15 by wounding a Frenchman (Henri d'Orleans had ridiculed the Italian army in print). It was the last noble duel of the nineteenth century, further diminishing the accomplishment on St. Elias—recently determined to be only the second-highest peak in America.

The Hollenbaughs and I skulked back toward Yakutat hoping to avoid an "I told you so" meeting with Marko. We were all seasick, but just looking back at the mountain—and the memory it represented—was enough to let me confront the bouncing ocean with little trepidation.

I took my watch as the Hollenbaughs slept inside the pilothouse. As Point Manby fell away to port I craned back toward the mountain above the clouds. There was no one to wisecrack to, no one to delude but myself about how badly the mountain had gotten to me, how far we had extended ourselves, how many rules we had broken (no radio, traveling as only two on crevassed glaciers, and the objective dangers of our route). I nearly let myself go after holding everything together so tightly for so long. A school of humpbacks passed in a blur, blowing geysers on either side of the boat. Seasickness neatly staves off emotion and affectation—when you're trying to control the urge to vomit, any further sentiment would be unwanted luxury. As the humpbacks faded to the stern, their white vaporous spouts appeared as distant sailboats. The forested shoreline seemed impossibly green; and we were probably going to make it to Yakutat in one piece. Life, as the saying goes, is far too important to ever talk seriously about. Life, versus the only other option I knew of, was indeed sweet.

In Yakutat, nothing could persuade Jeff to accompany me any further. He had confirmed his flight back to the Lower Forty-eight to go rock climbing with Mike (from the Peru trip) before the summer carpentry work began. He pushed the *Heaven Sent* away from the dock.

"Any last words, Jeff?" I aimed the video camera at him.

"Yeah, *stay afloat!*"

"Thanks for everything," I yelled.

I accelerated too quickly, throwing the Captain back aft. He was watching his son shrink into the distance as he said, "I'm getting tired of saying good-bye to him."

We traded shifts across the next 140 miles of open ocean. While he slept through midnight, I inhaled nine sandwiches, seven cups of coffee, and two liters of juice. A crab boat passed, eerily incandescent from twenty miles off with its halogen lights, but otherwise, we were alone on the ocean. As the moon faded to the south, the sun flooded over Mount Fairweather and torched the eastern sky. The water was tranquil enough to set the autopilot, so I took most of my watch braced up on the bow. I wrote in my journal and watched the light fall into the shadowed gullies and icefalls of Yasetaca's wife, Mount Fairweather. As the Captain slept, the sun climbed higher in

the sky, and the mountain reached a point of saturation: the Fairweather Range transformed into a blinding white repository of light.
I slipped on my sunglasses and an hour later, to the Captain's horror,
he came on decks and found me on the foredeck, quietly slumped
up against the mast, drooling down my chin, sound asleep.

In Juneau, I hung eight-by-five cards at the climbing shop, restau-
rants, and marinas:

> Sailing crew wanted: Juneau to Seattle. No pay, all the food
> you can eat & fish you can catch. High adventure guaranteed.
> Apply at the *Heaven Sent*, Auke Bay. No whiners.

I phoned all of my friends. The list was quickly whittled down; I
spent a hundred dollars in long-distance calls. Dr. Bovard asked if I
had any blackened, amputated digits to display in formaldehyde in
his office, but like most of my friends, he expressed reservations
about helping me ride the *Heaven Sent* to Seattle. It was no secret
that I didn't know how to sail.

As I waited with the Captain at the Juneau airport for his board-
ing, I realized that I had misread him. While on shore, he was gentle, considerate, engaging, and open-minded. While under sail, he
was as stubborn and impatient and Ahabian as I am climbing a
mountain. Sitting across from him, it finally dawned on me whom he
reminded me of. He had the same pinched face, gaunt body, and
oversize glasses as Jacques Cousteau (whom I admired). "Thanks for
everything you taught me," I said as we shook hands.

As I walked back to the *Heaven Sent*, it occurred to me that the
Captain must have been in a waking dread that I would sink the boat
taking it back to Seattle, but he had kept all of his advice, his doubts,
and his uncertainty to himself. He knew that I needed to settle some
things, alone. And he trusted me. Just like Jeff. I could do whatever
I wanted with our boat. I then realized not only why I respected his
son, but that the Captain was the source.

Everything has its time. We started in winter. Now it was summer. The Hollenbaughs had left, and although we didn't always see eye to eye, they were honest, hardworking, thoughtful people who read the same books as I, who loved the wonder of a sail curving into the sky, or a crouching lionlike summit finning the wind. They loved the same things that I loved. Sitting alone on the boat, not yet into regret, I wondered if it was too late to have the same relationship with a son that the Captain had. The time might come.

And next time with the Hollenbaughs it would be different. Next time I would not be so obsessed. Next time we would be *compagni*.

B efore leaving for St. Elias, the duke had commissioned a yacht designer, George Watson, to build a racing boat smaller than the Prince of Wales's 122-foot *Brittania* (which had cleaned up in the racing circuit for four years) and Kaiser Wilhelm's *Meteor*—both also built by Watson. The *Bona*, 83 feet long, sailed nearly as fast as its bigger competitors, but also took shrewd advantage of the Yacht Racing Association's handicapping rules— the *Meteor* and *Brittania* had to give the *Bona*, respectively, thirty-five and twenty-two seconds a mile off their final race times. Such a racing machine would allow the duke to assert Italy's rising naval sovereignty by beating both the Germans and the English, who were similarly trying to promote their own navies.

Although the duke could not attend any of the 1897 races, his English skipper, Captain Sycamore, piloted the *Bona* to sixteen wins and two second places over twenty-six spring and fall races. He earned over one thousand pounds for the duke.

His nationalist pride and tongue-in-cheek humor gilded his March 2, 1898, letter to Sella about the *St. Elias* manuscript:

> It's better to do something by ourselves and have the book made in Italy, and not "half and half." If I had the time I would have come to see you in order to plan the book and see the last

photographs. But I couldn't, and I cannot come now. I'm leaving for Cannes to race *Bona* and will ask De Filippi to try to meet again later this month in order to examine this *famous* [italics added] book so that you, De Filippi and I can coordinate the publication. I have seen that in London your photographs have been much admired; De Filippi is going to go to London in a few days to lecture and we shall try to understand from him what the English think of this summit that we did not allow them to deflower.

The duke won nine races in the Mediterranean, sweeping 1,500 lire in prize money. After returning to England in the spring, the *Bona* continued to collect flags.

In June, the duke showed his characteristic humility in a letter to Sella:

I thank you for the kind letters. About the book I will not allow myself to accept your proposal. The photograph was okay, but my [royal] portrait doesn't work alone. The good St. Elias in the frontispiece is what pleases me most.

Finally, at the *Bona*'s helm, he won the prestigious Queen's Cup. That evening at a banquet, he was honored by a toast, to which he replied that he was sorry that the competing *Alisa* couldn't complete the race after losing its topmast rigging. The *Bona* finished the 1898 English racing circuit with four thousand pounds in prize money. Like climbing St. Elias, his motivations had as much to do with promoting the Italian and House of Savoy colors—prominently flying from the *Bona*'s masthead. And like his meticulously executed climb, the boat competed in over a hundred races without injury to crew or damage to the boat (drownings and wrecks were not infrequent in early yacht racing).

He spent much of that year preparing for an expedition to the North Pole by training with dogs in Siberia, corresponding with Dr. Fridtjof Nansen (the polar explorer), and attending to his duties with the Italian navy. In May 1899, the duke sold the *Bona* for four thousand pounds. The new English owner totaled her bowsprit in the season's first race.

I signed on as crew in Juneau for the five-day Admiralty Island Sailboat Race. The skipper refused a tow to the starting line (because his engine was leaking coolant), so we missed the gun by two hours. It would cost us the race. By the time we finally shipped out, we were becalmed up against a buoy as the rest of the fleet disappeared around Retreat Point.

For the next four days, I learned how to work the foredeck. I swallowed nine waves during a midnight sail change, ripped a spinnaker during a jibe, and parboiled myself in a hot spring on Baranoff Island during the mandatory day's layover.

I learned how to read changing winds on the water, how to ease off the main sheet to reduce heeling, how to tighten the backstay, how to make cassette-tape telltales along the mainsail leech to read the wind in the sail, how to properly trim a sail, how to change a spinnaker, and how to steal another boat's wind.

By the time we raced and beat another boat down the final channel back into Juneau, we were in second place physically. But the layover and the handicapping rules for a thirty-seven-foot boat (the other boats were smaller, so we had to forfeit time) effectively put us in next to last place. The race left me tight with the sound of humming rigging, that "sweet" spot on the rudder where a boat *nestles* into the wind, and the uninterrupted roundness of my pate—indicative of not banging my head on a transom for weeks.

The duke's 1900 trip to the North Pole did not touch his success on St. Elias. He and Cagni (without De Filippi) split the narrative in the two-volume *Polar Star* about their expedition. The clarity of the duke's thinking, his understatement, his ability to grasp (and present) a myriad of logistics, and a refreshingly uncluttered prose made me wish that he had authored all of his expedition books. In the introduction, he summarized why his expeditions were successful: "I had comrades with me, rather than subordinates." Dogsledding was not yet an accepted mode of polar travel, so the duke concluded, "They have this advantage, too, that unlike horses and reindeer, they readily eat their fellows."

While wintering over for an early spring start to the Pole, the duke had a sledding accident in subzero temperatures. He wrote:

> The pain in my fingers grew worse, and gave me no rest by day or by night. Inflammation had set in at the junction of the living and the dead flesh. My fingers were of a dark colour; the skin rose from the part which had been frozen, and formed blisters full of serous matter.

A month later, he had the doctor amputate portions of two frostbitten fingers, and the duke reluctantly stayed behind to heal as Captain Cagni led the three sledding teams north. They fell short of the Pole, were forced to eat their dogs (one of Cagni's entries read, "We give the dogs what remains of the last victim's bones which have been already well scraped for our own meal"), and three men disappeared, which deeply fazed the duke, even though he was not present.

"Dr. Nansen's Feat Eclipsed" the headlines proclaimed. This time the duke returned home truly famous; the race to reach the Pole had long garnered worldwide headlines (unlike alpinism). His ardent nationalism even compelled him to lie in the book's narrative that he had been born in Turin, Italy, rather than Madrid, Spain. The duke sent a letter to the new king from Norway: "The steadfast courage and determination . . . acquired fresh glory for our country, by making its flag wave at the highest latitude which has hitherto been reached."

While he was gone, King Umberto (who underwrote the 922,000-lire North Pole expedition—three times the cost of climbing St. Elias) had been assassinated by an anarchist. The duke's cousin Vittorio Emanuele III inherited the throne.

The duke was apolitical, but when the satirical *Il Pasquino* magazine reported him as "the most handsome and popular Savoia," King Vittorio began to feel the same sort of envy he had felt years earlier as a pale and seasick landlubber accompanying his tanned and athletic cousin out to sea. Nonetheless, the young king bestowed the appropriate honors upon the duke, who had fired the imaginations of Italians, and elevated the status of the royal House of Savoy.

He spent the next few years as a seafaring diplomat, serving the whims of his insecure king. He raced cars (once being thrown out of his Fiat and wrecking it against a bridge piling; in Washington, D.C., he was pulled over by a policeman for speeding—diplomatic immunity got him off the hook). And he continued climbing in the Alps.

In 1906, he could not help but respond to the explorer Henry Stanley and his appeal about Africa to the Geographical Society: "that some person, some lover of the Alps, would devote himself to the Ruwenzori . . . exploring it from the highest to lowest points."

With the same attention to detail that marked his earlier expeditions, the duke—with De Filippi, Cagni, Petigax, and Sella—took Africa by storm. They mapped, surveyed, photographed, and climbed sixteen virgin (albeit casual) peaks while thoroughly exploring the region and finishing the work that Burton and Stanley had initiated. Another lavishly illustrated volume would be published (and translated into several languages).

It was a tour de force that won the duke more accolades than the St. Elias climb, but their lavishly outfitted African safari bore none of the uncertainty or back-breaking labor of his 1897 trip. Nonetheless, he grew cocky.

While elephant hunting with the duke on the way home, Sella wrote about his disappointment in his companions' lack of emotions, moral quality, and esthetic appreciation. He then shot an extraordinary photograph of his lifelong friend, sitting up in a chair while another subject sprawled on bare ground. The duke—prematurely balding with his forehead as wrinkled as a vulture—was lighting a cigarette and looking into the camera lens with princely contempt. Although never published, coming from Sella's keen eye, the photograph was a deliberate exposé.

Edward Whymper (world-renowned for his disaster on the Matterhorn) concluded in his booklet, *A Right Royal Mountaineer* about the duke: "To some perhaps, the narratives of his remarkable journeys would yield more attractive reading if their pages were occupied by relations of accidents and horrors. The absence of them, and the successes which have been attained, are evidence that unlimited time and trouble were spent in advance, in preparation."

I searched for Walter Harper's grave site, discouraged by the flowers and the more celebrated upkeep of the grave of the town founder, Joe Juneau. After several hours, I found it— half obscured by ground creepers. Harper and his bride had drowned, along with three hundred and forty-one others, when their ferryboat sank seventy-seven years ago. He was Athapaskan, and in 1913, he first stepped atop of Denali. Native Americans (like Mike Harry and Peter the Josher) lived with earth under their fingernails, close to some truth that I sought. I was perplexed by it, I wanted closure, some final message to take home.

I had come not because of any morbid fascination with graveyards (I generally avoid them), but because of the people who broke trail for me and provided inspiration. Life is nothing if not inevitable, and we all travel the same parabolas, doomed to repeat the follies and reexperience the successes of these doppelgängers from a distant and forgotten past.

By determining the course of Harper (and the duke), I wanted to set my own bearings. Modern climbers—clad in lightweight petroleum derivatives, equipped with unbreakable technology, supported by aircraft, and insured by cellular phones—call their new routes "innovations" and decry the pioneers of years past as "snow plodders." Regardless of the destination, regardless of how thick the hyperbole that the modern adventurer lays on his sponsors about "untrammeled" objectives, the fact remains that no matter how high or deep you get into trouble, it has already been stepped in before by some pioneer braver and more farsighted—usually dead by now too. You can go in winter, alone, by rowboat, au naturel, or on roller skates; you can walk backward, climb blindfolded, or even barefoot, but you're not likely to be the first. The movement in climbing today is to applaud one's futuristic vision, when most of the great problems were foreseen and overcome under greater hardship and risk— by Harper, the duke, or any number of nameless and forgotten climbers.

I n the spring of 1907, the duke was thirty-three and ready to get married. During one of his diplomatic sorties to the United States, he sent a letter to Sella, containing a postcard photograph of a brunette diva baring her breasts. On the back, he let down his guard, and wrote: "Here we are in the country of beautiful girls—like this one that I am sending to you—they make my head spin." He was referring to Katherine Elkins.

The previous fall, at Lake Como in Italy, he met Katherine, the twenty-one-year-old daughter of a wealthy American senator. The *New York Times* referred to her as "a princess . . . on West Virginian soil," who lived in a town named after her family. She indulged herself in tennis and horseback riding, and seldom spent a day apart from her mother. She grew up in one of the two thousand-acre houses "on the hill," as the lower and less affluent citizens of Elkins called it. The relationship between her and the duke would smolder for the rest of their lives, commanding front-page headlines on newspapers around the world for three years.

Now journalists trailed the duke everywhere, and given his experience with incourteous Americans and erroneous newspaper reportage ten years earlier, he sometimes traveled incognito, under his nom de plume, Luigi Sarto. When they mobbed him, he refused to grant interviews. One of only a few stories approximating a "scoop" appeared in the March 28, 1908, *New York Times:*

> "When will you return to America?" [the reporter] asked.
> "I can't tell," [the duke] answered.
> "Do you intend to return?"
> "I don't look like a disappointed man, do I?"
> The significance of this statement seems to bear out the general belief that the Duke has not met with a rebuff in love, as suggested by some American dispatches, but is simply going to Rome to get the King's permission to marry Miss Elkins.

Another story from the same week ran on the front page. The reporter tried to set up an interview; the duke replied that he had no story, but the reporter should come at 8 A.M. the next morning. "But, your Highness, the ship sails at that hour," said the reporter.

"Yes," chuckled the duke. "I know that."

The duke couldn't duck them all, however, and if they did not ask questions about Kathy, he sometimes held forth. In 1908, he told a reporter from the *New York World:*

> My life of adventurous exploration is nearly finished. I am now too old to make new polar expeditions, or to climb unexplored summits. The uproar that surrounds me seems strange and places too much emphasis on my deeds. I occupy the sixth or ninth place in the line of succession to the throne of Italy, and therefore it is improbable that I would ascend to the throne. . . . If the Americans would consider me an ordinary citizen I would be a lot happier.

Sella wrote to the duke (who characteristically had not told his friends about Kathy):

> The news is confirmed by the best [Italian magazine]. . . . Your Highness will make his own choice and also for an act, that in my opinion, shows stupendous logic for its common sense and physiologic reasons. You have decided to marry a young American girl of very rare qualities. To these, my sincere impressions, allow me to add the most cordial greetings of my wife with the very vivid desire that HRH can obtain real and desired happiness.

The *New York Times* carried the story of Napoleon Bonaparte's brother Jerome, who married a wealthy American woman in 1803, only to have Napoleon annul the marriage shortly afterward. Alongside the story was a satirical cartoon with a likeness of Katherine Elkins, feeding coins to a flock of foreign, crowned geese. Her brother, Richard, told reporters in Seattle that the duke "is better than the average of the titled foreigners they send over here for American wives."

Her father, Senator Stephen Elkins (former secretary of war and confidant of several presidents), had written a cryptic letter to his attorney just after the two lovers had met:

> I am willing to help about getting the leper [the duke was missing fingertips] out of this country and would be willing to make a small contribution to this end if you think necessary while he is in the Country. I have told our friends here that they should not let him want for anything. They say he does not need money but friendly treatment.

Trying to squelch the press, on November 16, the senator made an official statement that his daughter and the duke were not engaged to be married, and that he wished that the "constant publication of rumors . . . will now cease." The next day, the Elkins postmaster seized an undeclared package addressed to Katherine, from the duke, containing a five-thousand-dollar, six-karat ruby, clasped by an eighth-inch gold ring band.

Newspapers confirmed then denied the pending marriage for months, but eventually, a new theory was put forth that the queen dowager, Margherita, would only allow the marriage morganatically. If Katherine and Luigi bore children, they would have no claim to the throne or its riches (the duke and his two brothers were worth $30 million). Not only was Katherine a Protestant (Jewish according to some accounts), but to the oldest monarchy in Europe, she was considered "a commoner." The Elkins family was in an uproar because Senator Elkins, a self-made man—who told his family, "We are equal to this applesauce!"—had climbed from mediocrity to affluence and did not like being snubbed by the Italians.

There was little question that Luigi and "Kathy" were in love. They went touring in automobiles and horseback riding and were seen at various functions with her mother chaperoning. Kathy allegedly told reporters that the duke was the most charming man she had ever met and if he were an American she would marry him. The duke made numerous excursions to America, but felt pulled in two by his devotion to Italy (and the counsel of king and queen) and his pending rear admiral promotion, versus his need for a family without royal political chicanery.

"Abruzzi-Elkins" headlines faded from the American newspapers when the duke left for India in March 1909. Contrary to what he had told the *New York World,* he was not "too old." In the timeless fashion of memory-deficient alpinists, he had simply forgotten the suffering of previous expeditions and put together another climb to the penultimate mountain, K2. The team spent a month trekking in. They attempted several routes, but avalanches and steep climbing forced the duke to give up (K2 was not climbed for another forty-five years, via the "Abruzzi Ridge").

In early July, he began attempting the 25,110-foot Bride Peak (Chogolisa). On his second attempt, after climbing all day with Petigax and two other guides, he reached 24,600 feet in a blinding fog, amid monstrous cornices. They waited three hours in the cold, hoping the fog would lift. At 3:30 P.M., in his calm voice, he turned to Petigax and said, "Let us descend."

At base camp Sella anxiously asked, "Well, your Highness?"

"Barometer 308," he replied, which meant that he had climbed seven hundred feet higher than anyone else in the world (a record, albeit arbitrary, that would not be broken for thirteen years).

McClure's Magazine wrote of his return to Marseilles in September:

> The hair at his temples, beneath his yachting cap, had begun to turn gray. Of medium height, nervous and muscular, with an energetic head, and a smooth, deeply tanned face to which two very clear gray eyes imparted fire, he suggested, as he stood there enveloped in a huge, dark-colored ulster, the classical type of the Anglo-Saxon.
>
> Silent and courteous, he confined himself to shaking the hands that were offered, while his traveling companion endeavored to push aside indiscreet reporters. As soon as he reached the shore, he walked through the wind and rain straight to an automobile which was waiting near at hand, seated himself in the chauffeur's place, grasped the steering-wheel, and sped away.

He was promoted to rear admiral. Like many a weary and lonely expedition climber, the duke was now determined to marry Kathy and have a family. She traveled with her mother to France and checked into various hotels under the name "Ellis" in order to avoid the reporters. The duke dined with them as they shopped for Kathy's trousseau—then Senator Elkins arrived. Negotiations stalled.

McClure's quoted a Parisian actor, who observed the duke at an Italian resort:

> "We saw him arrive one day . . . a few weeks after his return from the Himalayas. He was alone. No one was expect-

ing him. He installed himself in a modest room on the second floor and went down to the table d'hôte, where he took his meals with the rest of us. . . .

"Naturally, he became the target for all the pretty eyes in the place, the object of all the coquetries. And I must admit that he was not insensible to these glances. He is a flirt—a taciturn flirt. One would never have imagined that the ardent and gallant man who was to be seen every evening flitting like a butterfly among the rocking-chairs could possibly be the bold explorer who had just broken the record for altitude, for his modesty was such that he never spoke of his exploits, unless in discreet allusions, when he referred to some piquant anecdote of his travels. His simplicity, which constituted his charm, was especially displayed in his attitude toward the lowly. . . ."

After that, one can understand the popularity that he enjoys in Italy.

It was rumored that the senator would not accept a morganatic marriage. He left Paris after an awkward meeting with the duke, while Kathy and her mother stayed, awaiting the final judgment of King Vittorio (ever jealous of his cousin). Royalty looks after its own, and considering that the duke was the sibling of an arranged marriage, it would have broken the House of Savoy's strict traditions to allow a prince to marry a non-European commoner. According to the duke's biographer, Speroni, the king could not condone the marriage under any form because Senator Elkins's background as a "swindler" and "speculator" (amending legislation and using his influence to award pork barrel contracts to his various business holdings) would taint the House of Savoy.

Short of renouncing Italy, the duke was powerless. A week later, the agency representing the king printed a release denying "rumors of a wedding of His Royal Highness the Duke of Abruzzi." Kathy's mother collapsed. Four months later Senator Elkins died of a heart attack. The duke vowed that if he couldn't have Katherine he would remain forever unmarried.

The mountain was pushing back against me like the Japanese Current as I tried to make southern headway. I tried to put Yasetaca out of conscious thought, but still its white tail fluke waved, beckoned, and called out to me in the horizons that are our dreamscapes. It became a wordless song playing in my head.

Justin Smith, a talented musician who answered my crew ad in Juneau, filled the lulls with his guitar playing as we hunted for wind. Sailing was not unlike playing music, and if Justin had been just a good mechanic or a sailor, I might not have learned to appreciate my boat. The *Heaven Sent* became an instrument rather than a machine. In light winds, Justin showed me how to sail wing and wing, holding the genoa sail out with a boathook-cum-spinnaker pole to starboard and spreading the mainsail to port as if the *Heaven Sent* were a butterfly emerging from its larval state.

Justin Smith.

We scrubbed the algae from the fenders. We scoured the gray-ness out of the teak railing with abrasive powder, then oiled it until the grains showed. By the time we had finished salving the hull with color brightener—buffing it topaz—the *Heaven Sent* rode like clear sky skimming the water.

Justin and I said our good-byes. The prospect of single-handing *Heaven Sent* the last six hundred miles from Prince Rupert to Seat-tle gave me the same tingly, lower-intestinal prompting that I had felt at the base of the mountain.

After Bride Peak and K2, the duke was finished with alpinism. As sabers were rattled at the outset of the Turkish-Italian War in 1911, the duke fired Italy's first shots against the Turkish aggressors. He wrote a news dispatch on September 29:

> I have arrived off Preveza [Greece] this morning and established a blockade. At 3 o'clock the officers in command of the flotillas signaled that two Turkish torpedo boats had left Preveza in succession. One flotilla gave chase to the first, which tried to escape to the north, and after a brief exchange of shots the Turkish boat made for the shore where she stranded after catching fire and remained *hors de combat*. The second Turkish torpedo boat, which was pursued by two destroyers, returned at once to Preveza without sustaining any damage.

Austria vetoed further military actions proposed by the duke (a bombardment of Preveza). Back in Italy, however, he was carried shoulder high by his countrymen as the band played the royal march.

Rumors flew about the king, so jealous of his debonair cousin that he posted him to the rear in order not to let him take any more com-mand or credit than necessary. Peace was drawn up in November

1912, although much of Europe was perched on edge, inevitably aimed toward World War I.

Back in the United States, in 1913, during a dinner party at the Elkinses, Kathy spontaneously announced her marriage to the tycoon Billy Hitt, son of a congressman, who had courted her for years.

The duke was shattered.

While he cruised the battleworn ports of Libya and Albania, World War I began. He was promoted to commander in chief of the Italian navy, commanding several vice admirals, including his *compagni,* Umberto Cagni.

The Italian books about the duke (and Italy) in action during World War I are singularly praiseful, but through the lens of history, the duke's greatest achievement was coordinating the French, British, and Italian ships to rescue more than 150,000 Serbian army refugees from sniping Albanians and advancing Austrians (a quarter of a million fleeing refugees had already been killed).

The English admiral Thursby, who was otherwise unimpressed by the Italian navy, wrote a private letter about the operation: "I do not think that with the scratch pack we have had to deal with, ships & material being supplied by 3 different nations, anyone but the Duke could have done it. In addition to being able and energetic, his position enables him to do more than any ordinary Admiral could do."

Another English officer, Herbert Richmond, also empathized in his diary with the duke, "the best man in his way that I have come across. He has listened and tried to do things, has adopted suggestions where he could; but has been blocked by the stupid staff at Rome in all important matters."

Two battleships were sabotaged or destroyed by mines while anchored in Italian ports—accounting for the deaths of over eight hundred men, mishaps eventually blamed upon the duke. Italy's navy was foundering, and eventually, the duke was forced to resign. Both the king and the duke of Aosta (who said, "My brother still believes he can make war as in the time of Garibaldi") wanted to can their cousin/brother, and did not try to fight the "scurrilous charges" about his womanizing, the frequent changes of chiefs of staff, and his supposed deaf ear to expert advice.

The day he left his ship in Taranto, there was, according to Paul Halpern's scholarly *Naval War in the Mediterranean,* a "large and spontaneous demonstration in which virtually every officer turned out to see him off." A British officer, Mark Kerr, said that if the duke had been fired in any time but war, all of the Italian officers would have quit. He added that the Rome bureaucrats had "shelved" Italy's best (the duke and Cagni) "in a hole & corner way."

There were rumors of his ill health, but as was his custom, the duke said nothing, leaving only a terse message:

> Officers and men: Today I leave as Commander-in-Chief of the Navy. For your work nobly given I thank you. [As] I depart from you I recall the past experiences together, and deeply and certainly I hope for the future, knowing well your good qualities that make me proud to have been the Commander of the Navy, they are the sacred heritage of the Navy of Italy. Take with you my wishes of gratitude and affection.

Now that the king had stripped the duke from three decades of navy service, he lived at the vacant residence of the duke of Aosta, who fought at the front. When Luigi asked if he could sign on under his brother's army command and fight, he was refused—again by the king.

He kept in close touch with his climbing friends. Sella sent him a card. The duke responded (with the traditional salutation):

> My very gentle Sella,
>
> I thank you for your good wishes for my birthday. Months go by, years go by, but Europe remains the same.
>
> Affectionately, Luigi d'Savoia

He lived alone, unable to serve the country for which he had disavowed love, lost his fingers, and climbed high peaks. By the age of forty-seven, he had become embittered and angry, and he left to begin an agricultural community in Somalia, turning his back on Italy and the Fascists (Sella's agricultural successes in Sardinia inspired the duke). His alpinism became a thing of the past.

Mountain expeditions used to seem like powerful metaphors. They are replete with challenge, strained communication, dead ends, uncertainty, leadership stalemates, and the overwhelming belittlement you always feel beneath the big mountain itself. If you could pull through this gauntlet, my theory was that you would have the tools to cope with the rest of life. But in practice, my life in the "real world" had none of the same grandeur. Expeditions no longer seemed my invaluable metaphor because the rest of my life had become a slow grinding series of routines, where I attended the cinema for vicarious excitement, and spent most of my time recounting the last great adventure and scheming for the next. I was going south alone in order to find the closure I was so desperately missing from the climb.

After abandoning the yuppie white pubs along the Prince Rupert waterfront, I trudged through the rain to the town center and spent my last evening in a Native American saloon called the Moby Dick. The band scratched out Eagles tunes and simulated smoke with a huge block of dried ice beneath a fan. On my way in, I got shoved to the floor and avoided having my liver carved out by offering to buy my adversary a drink. So we drank to one another's health while spoiling our own, and listened to one another. Pete was openly angry. His story was not unfamiliar to me, and because he spent a lot of time hunting in the wilderness, he understood what I was after as a "fucked-up mountain climber." Because I had nothing to lose, I told him that my climb had made me feel a failure.

"You'll figure it out, man," was all he said.

I asked him how and he replied that we always did things for a reason, and eventually it would come to me.

"What do you think my reasons are?"

"My grandpop always had sayings about these things," he replied.

"Like what?"

He looked temporarily befuddled, then said, "If I told you, then you wouldn't figure it out for yourself."

Single-handed sailing, twenty miles south of Prince Rupert, did not permit self-absorption. While sprinting from cockpit to foredeck I was determined to keep the motor off down the long and narrow Grenville Channel. The wind was blowing fifteen knots, but it was downwind sailing. Without a spinnaker I had to jibe every half mile to make progress. No less than a dozen boats, and several yachts with sails bagged, passed and blasted their air horns at me even though I (thought I) had the right of way.

While sailing south, I thought of how strong my legs felt while stomping in my crampons on brittle ice up to eleven thousand feet, how the final curve of ridge had beckoned me, and why we could have made it to the summit. My alpinism memory was failing me again.

My second night, moored at a wilderness hot springs, my palms were raw and oozing from sheeting in the genoa all day. I was wheezing with bronchitis and a lassitude brought on by two ineffective courses of antibiotics, so I soaked in the deserted hot pool until the heat and dizziness revitalized me. Stumbling back to the *Heaven Sent,* I found wintergreen leaves in the forest and filled my pockets in order to steep medicinal tea.

On impulse, I plucked a fiddlehead fern, with the idea of sending it to Jeff and inviting him back to Yasetaca—contrary to all my best intentions about quitting big mountains. That night I wrote the letter but in the end thought better of mailing it.

Five afternoons after leaving Prince Rupert, I nosed out into the big waters of Queen Charlotte Sound, a mere week north of Seattle. A broad-reaching wind swept over my right shoulder, the waves were splashing on deck, and for once, this supposed crux of the Inside Passage was not fogbound. My throat pounded with anticipation. I reefed the mainsail, hauled the genoa, and followed a course for the outside of Egg Island with the boat heeling like a banked race car as I clipped my chest harness into the high-side safety cable. Spray flew up over the boat's length. A week's worth of unwashed dishes clattered in the galley. Water gurgled disconcertingly in the bilge. I held the wheel with my feet, braced my arms back over the windward rail, and draped my hands into the cold Pacific.

After spending two hours correcting my steerage for a weathered helm, I shock-corded the wheel (there was too much sea for the doting autopilot), strode above decks, shook out the reefing, and fully extended the mainsheet. We heeled over a few more degrees and picked up another knot of boat speed. Now the mainsail balanced the big genoa. I yelled, *"Eeee-hahhhhhh!"* into the wind, steering around a big cedar deadhead, shutting off the marine radio, and wondering if I had been born a hundred years too late.

At 8 P.M., I doused the sails and motored into a twenty-yard-wide inlet leading to a sheltered cove. I threw out my rattling anchor, fed it 120 feet of line, and shut off the Perkins. A neighboring sailor invited me to tie our sterns together to minimize our drift.

Ev, a sixty-something Canadian, chucked me a Molson. He had run the Inside Passage a dozen times, so I pumped him for advice on dinghy dragging, how hard to reverse in order to set anchor, if his roller furling ever tangled, and all the questions left unanswered by my precious *Handbook*.

Once the beer was empty, I felt shot through with weariness. Sailing was so new and my learning curve was pitched so steep that I was exhausted every nightfall. The VHF reported an empty sailboat out at sea; I snapped the radio off. A warbler cried out plaintively as the bloodred sky clotted black and I fell asleep wondering why sad things always fascinated me.

Several days later, pulling anchor above Dent Rapids, Ev advised me that "a full-keeled sailboat could actually transit the rapids, provided you ride *with* the flood, hug the starboard shore, and keep Devils Hole to port. At the worst," Ev warned laconically, "you might spin round a couple of times in some of the smaller whirlpools."

"What about the *Sailing Directions* warning about 'dangerous eddies and overfalls' and 'waiting for slack tide'?" I asked.

"They wrote that book for weenies," Ev said. "Trust me. I've been through it at flood before."

"You going down?"

He nodded. "Yeah, I'll be right behind you."

Two hours later, as soon as I saw Devils Hole—wider than my boat's length and swirling ten feet deep—I wondered if Ev had sandbagged me. His Garden-30 was nowhere in sight. Normally the *Heaven Sent* pegged out at six knots, but as I plunged down the rapids the knot meter read "10" and the trees seemed to fly by like highway driving. Even a hundred yards to port, Devils Hole made me shiver involuntarily. I contemplated a quick parachute jump to shore, then saw that I would never make it—the smooth-watered tongue that I was riding V'ed out into a line of turbulent whirlpools and violent eddies. I aimed between two whirlpools. The boat swayed wildly—like Bogart's *African Queen* pitching through the waterfalls beneath the Nazi fort—until another whirlpool swirled out of nowhere, pitched the hull 40 degrees to port, and threw me down onto the lazaret with a percussion and cymbals accompaniment of pots and pans crashing in the galley as the boat spun 180 degrees to starboard and back toward the rocky shore. Without conscious thought I went with it and pulled the rudder around, then punched the Perkins up to full throttle to regain my way as the boat yawed wildly back and forth. I spun completely around in the whirlpool as cleanly as a rubber ducky above the bathtub drain, and just as I finished incanting Jeff's words from below the avalanche— "I'm dead meat"—the *Heaven Sent* pulled clear. I shook my head to clear the rain from my hair and straighten out the dizziness.

I aimed into a set of big eddies, contemplating how to break out of the rapids over into a mooring in Big Bay. I hit the *whoosh*ing and plunging eddies at ten knots: the bow fell as the stern shivered and shook. I accelerated as soon as the opposing wall of water shuddered against the keel, then punched out with a series of swift but balanced yaws. As I throttled it to hold against the dock current, no one offered to catch my lines, so after scraping a piling, I jumped out with the boat still under power, and promptly fell over backward on the greasy dock. It seemed unlikely that the gathering crowd was admiring my well-oiled teak, neatly tucked lines, or polished hull.

After eight years in Somalia, the Duke had built a thriving community of two thousand families with a mission, a mosque, a bazaar, medical facilities, and a school—seventy miles from Mogadishu. He had revamped the otherwise brutal sharecropper regime of the Italians. With his ear for language, he taught himself the three different Somalian dialects, because, he said, "If they comprehend you they can understand. If they understand you, they can be persuaded. Otherwise you will be a mistrusted stranger."

In 1921, in Paris, where she had waited for the king's marital pronouncement, Kathy was divorced from Hitt—whom she did not love and with whom she had no children. Increasingly concerned that the alcoholic Kathy needed help, the Elkins family convinced Billy Hitt to continue courting her. Two years later, they remarried in Washington. Their sprawling estate's front door was designed for the equestrian Kathy to enter *au cheval,* and foxes and parrots and numerous animals sat down with the guests for dinner. Few visitors missed the portrait of the duke hanging on the wall. Nor was it a secret that a locket of his hair hung around her neck.

The duke corresponded frequently with Kathy, who helped supplement the Italian sponsorship—24 million lire—for his sixty-thousand-acre agricultural project. He taught the Somalians how to fertilize, grow, harvest, then ship maize, sugarcane, and bananas from Abruzzi City to Mogadishu. Italian biographies promoted the duke as a visionary, diplomatically acting for the future of his country, but it was just as likely that the duke had been taken with the Africans since he had first visited Somalia.

His cousin, King Vittorio, had now hitched the House of Savoy's wagon to the Fascists under Benito Mussolini—good reason for the duke to avoid Italy. He lived with a young Somali woman, Faduma Au, in a two-story villa with a huge lawn. The duke had always believed in exercise, taking daily walks while wintering below the North Pole, or two-hour bike rides. But exercise would not alleviate his new and mysterious illness, so he traveled to spas and frequently consulted doctors. Newspapers reported him to be suffering from arterial sclerosis.

In 1926, after having been denied the only marriage he was interested in, he was required to pay Mussolini's Celibate Tax, imposed upon single men as incentive to increase the population. He traveled to Italy to attend the funerals of both Queen Margherita and Petigax. At his guide's funeral in Courmeyeur, he was characteristically terse: "I loved these men of the mountains, my guides." (Ollier, who accompanied the duke on other expeditions, also had a memorial plaque there.)

The duke was photographed consoling Petigax's widow, holding a cane, his fedora, and an envelope—with the largesse on which she could comfortably retire. He was gaunt, his thinning hair had gone white, and lines of anguish creased his forehead. He was fifty-three years old, but he looked seventy-five.

In 1928, he mounted an expedition to explore the headwaters of the Uebi Shebeli River that irrigated his fields. He had invited Sella to help make a motion-picture film about Somalia, but Sella turned it down. None of the duke's old cronies accompanied him.

In one hundred days, he covered 840 miles with a caravan of camels ridden by geologists, a linguist, and a surveyor. The expedition exacerbated his ill health; he was said to be suffering from undiagnosable African illnesses. He traveled to Italy and was diagnosed with diabetes. Pain debilitated him.

In the last two years of his life, after his brother and Cagni died, the duke lost his will to continue. Shortly thereafter, an Italian doctor diagnosed him with terminal prostate cancer, so he told his friends, "Don't ask for news of me anymore," and returned to his Somalian villa.

Near the end, high on sedatives, he cabled his brother a pre-arranged royal stoicism: "All's well." The pope sent a blessing, and then the sixty-year-old duke spent his last few hours in excruciating pain.

He departed at his favorite time, before the dawn, as was his custom in the Alps, on St. Elias, in the Ruwenzoris, on Bride Peak, and along the Uebi Shebeli. It was Saturday, March 18, 1933. Mussolini commanded the Italian press to suppress the news, so that mourning would not interrupt the visiting British prime minister MacDonald's "social program" on Monday in Italy.

On Sunday, thousands attended the funeral in Abruzzi City. As the governor of Somalia intoned the duke's name, the Somalians shouted, "Present," then began ripping out their hair in bereavement. Military planes bombed the mourners with flowers.

Mussolini's press release mentioned how the duke "went to die at the spot where he fought so gloriously [the duke had missed the brief shelling of Somalian ports thirty years earlier] . . . always directed toward the greatness and prestige of his country." Italian propaganda control also conveyed that the duke was only briefly visiting Somalia when he died.

In his simple granite-slabbed grave (he had demanded not to be interred in Italy), he was buried with a portrait of Kathy. His sole statement of public bitterness was etched onto his tombstone:

> *I would rather have Somalian women*
> *entwining their fantasies above my tomb*
> *than the hypocrisies of civilized men.*

The duke's simple grave in Somalia. He was buried with a portrait of his beloved Kathy. (Aldo Audisio photo)

Two years later, Mussolini invaded neighboring Ethiopia (formerly Abyssinia—where there had once been a movement to install the duke as king) and poison-gassed thousands of civilians.

Katherine Elkins continued to send money for road building and farm equipment. Three years after the duke was buried, at fifty years old, she drank herself to death.

More recently, the tombstone epitaph has mysteriously vanished.

While holding a point of sail along the shoreline, one minute after checking chart depths (showing twenty feet of water), I was thrown against the pilothouse door as the *Heaven Sent* ground onto a reef—it felt like driving a car over a boulder and ripping the oil pan out. I powered up the Perkins and put it in gear, and the hull shook off as the keel shuddered free. To make sure I wouldn't sink, I yanked open the bilge: no water. I double-checked the chart: no reef. Then I looked over the side: no visible damage. I decided to run for forty-mile-distant Vancouver.

All afternoon I rode a Canadian mistral down into the Strait of Georgia. I took an unoccupied Vancouver tideflat, drove the *Heaven Sent* alongside the pilings, and laced it tight with a system of equal-tensioned climbing ropes, crevasse pulleys, and molybdenum carabiners. Being a climber sometimes came in handy.

Eight hours later, the tide dropped enough for me to slop through the mud and inspect the keel: I had scraped off less bottom paint than Big Bay's docks had taken. For a total of twenty-two dollars at the local marina, I slopped a pint of gel coat on the keel and let it dry in the sun. While waiting for the tide to refloat us, I spent the afternoon scrubbing the hull, scraping off barnacles, and feeling the underside—as if this new knowledge of its shape, the grainy textured bottom paint, the curve of rudder, and its three-quarter-length, brick-hard keel (which bone-bruised my knuckles when I impulsively punched it) would impart some untold wisdom the next time I sailed.

My fingers were caked and tingling with creosote, blue paint, gel coat, powdered grime remover, the citrus smell of Goop hand cleaner, chemical burn (promoting a bad case of hangnail), and black mud (that would lodge in my fingernails for weeks). I had inadvertently gobbed tar on decks and mooring ropes. My back ached from yarding on the scrub brush. Yet it was the most satisfying workday I could remember.

On the chart, I drew a twenty-five-mile course for the Gulf Islands, then waited for flatter water—my two attempts to leave the protected harbor felt like riding a bronco and gave me vertigo. After a week's topsy-turvy ten-foot seas diminished, I could finally abandon the Granville Brewery.

I bounced out into the Strait of Georgia and hauled all of the sail I owned into a close-hauled southwestering breeze. Now that I understood the massive fin of lead below, I pulled apart the wind dodger, harnessed myself in, latched the portal shut to keep out errant waves, and ran into the wind. I leaned windward and hugged the transom, knowing that the *Heaven Sent* would not broach (so long as I didn't hit anything). The genoa hummed within a few feet of the sea. I unpocketed my grandfather's Hudson River pilot ring, slipped it on my wedding finger, and gave thanks to the hull carving water.

No sails furled the horizons. A riverine tide rippled south against my stern. Rafts of murrelets bobbed beneath the hull in perfect unison, like teams of synchronized swimmers, while the vast curve of land and sea continued scrolling alongside. All sense of time slipped away from me.

Eventually, I aimed my bow into American waters and watched Mount Baker appear off the bow, four months after leaving it. The mountain glowed vanilla bright in the late sun and I began visualizing Yasetaca with all the sudden, unwanted shock of an ice-cream headache.

Andy Kauffman—first to climb one of the highest mountains in the world, Hidden Peak in Pakistan—had written to me about his 1946 South Ridge climb "that St. Elias was the dream expedition of my life. I may dwell on Hidden Peak as long as I wish, but the fact is that our route on St. Elias was never-to-be-forgotten adventure and a real classic climb."

By the time I crossed the border, I was through debating about Yasetaca. I stuck the now brown, curled-cat-intestine fern into an envelope and unfolded the letter I had written to Jeff two and a half weeks ago:

> Enclosed more Alaskan fiddlehead fern for you, lest you forget the miracle roughage of the St. Elias range.
>
> Much to tell you about, re the boat and all, but mostly I am writing because my memory is poor and there is that one safe route and I think you and I could do it real quick as modern acclimated alpinists instead of Duke of Abruzzi wannabes. Winter would be best.
>
> Will you come?—JW
> In regularity We Trust.

That night I mailed it, figuring that Jeff would probably not reply, but it was a good start toward something inside me that needed a reckoning.

In a pub at Friday Harbor, I ordered a salad, then considered how the duke and I differed—while his climbing partners accompanied him on numerous expeditions, my own partners and I usually went our separate ways. This spoke in part to the growing narcissism of modern climbing. It was also true that the duke was a leader even without his royal status, while I was just as content to be alone. He was interested in mathematical tangibles and the highest things (St. Elias was thought to be the biggest mountain in North America, he wanted to set the high-altitude record, he clamored for the hand of a senator's daughter); I was interested in a mountain now unknown, my lungs didn't function well above twenty thousand feet, and my recent divorce left me feeling, as Voltaire wrote, that marriage is the only adventure open to the cowardly. Yet—in our familial isolation and interest in Yasetaca—the duke and I were not unrelated, so I had been composing a poem to describe what mountains meant to us. Suddenly, the waitress cleared her throat, the food sat in front of me, and she had probably been standing there for a long moment.

"You okay?" she asked.

I assured her everything was fine, thanked her, then spent the rest of the evening finishing the poem:

> *Taciturn half smile*
> *Lidded eyes*
> *Poker face*
> *cooling hurt amid*
> *glaciated mountains and oceanic infinitudes.*
>
> *Atop Mount St. Elias*
> *barely a man*
> *you descend to conquer a world too old for princes.*
> *Your Highness mother*
> > *sanctimonious*

leads you to the Rosaries
                and dies before you even know her.
       Your Highness father
            unattainable
            as K2 and the North Pole
            casts you to sea at six.
Your compagni
                revel at your
                shrewd mind
                dark wit,
        respecting your daring (royalty be damned),
                and vie to steal
       a vast weight your legacy to bear.

Your penultimate mountain,
    ocean gale,
    jungle disease,
    even your Great War
                are no respite.
                You rescue 150,000 Serbs.
                    Lose two fingers.
                    Irrigate barren Somalian minds.
                    Are denied Abyssinia's throne.
                    Skip middle age.
While your princess is not permitted.
Mrs. Katherine Hitt hung your portraits
                whispered "Luigi" in letters
                locketed your hair round her neck
                substituting your mountains, seas,
                and wars with murderous alcohol.
Your chest tremors
your gut metastasizes
                accompanying and defining your pain.
You bury your compagni
    one by one:

Cagni;
> *your brother;*
>> *At Petigax's grave*
> *you are 53 (looking 75)*
> *calming his widow*

Seven years from your own
>> *long-awaited,*
>> *merciful tomb,*
> *accompanied by Kathy's portrait*
> *epitaphed with rage.*

Your short full life
> *devoured you.*

High mountains and cold seas
> *exploit our sibling souls.*
> *While embracing primeval earth*
> *(your first expedition and my last)*
> *its terrible grandeur*
> *replenishes love denied.*

In a white dawn, I groped out of the harbor for my last of three weeks single-handing. An incoming ferry rudely cut me off, then blasted me with a deafening foghorn: I climbed atop the boom and squeezed my canned air bottle, and as the ferry pilot frowned down at me, I dropped my trousers and bent over into full-moon position. A deckhand and several passengers roared with laughter.

The Strait of Juan de Fuca was fogged in, but the waves were manageable, and a 157-degree course would allow me to ride the tide into Admiralty Inlet around noon. I sang aloud. I regularly plotted my chart position to avoid ramming any reefs or islands. And I kept the air horn in my pocket lest a freighter or another ferry loom out of the fog.

My present situation was remarkably similar to being up on the mountain. I realized that my greatest fear was not the sea so much as making the wrong decision by not listening to my instincts, then willfully crossing the strait (or an icefall) under dangerous conditions.

With the usual late, but seldom dumb, retrospection, I realized that I had feared myself. Not the mountain. I had been afraid of what I might do to myself on Yasetaca—not what the mountain would do to me. I had a glimmer of eternity beneath the South Face that had nothing to do with my arthritic knees, my fear of heights, or my own flesh and blood. I had learned that my dreams were indestructible when I had the courage to act on them. My dreams connected me to the stone-cold Yasetaca, to the Hollenbaughs, and to the long-dead duke.

I did not feel smug as my course came out true in Admiralty Inlet, under a following sea, a half mile shy of the Point Wilson foghorn. This would have been a good day for my former therapist to lie back on the hard lazaret and listen to my soliloquy from the helm:

I would never have a midlife crisis because I was lucky enough to have avoided the path that led to complete-life crisis. My "ruts" were simply falling back in with the status quo and being too eccentric to remain long down. Like all the other low points of my life, I reached up, chased ridgelines, and sought highness to get out.

Highness needs qualifying: I would not be accepting any invitations to Everest (I had already refused one, then been kicked off another when a lawyer thought I might write about his Sherpa servant) or any other commercialized expeditions. Climbing a new route on Yasetaca had reaffirmed my interest in eighteen thousand feet of untrodden quality and wilderness horizons, versus slogging with the crowds up Everest's (or some other name peak's) ofttrodden twenty-nine thousand feet of quantity.

What sustains me is in the dawn beside a hull spilling milky bright constellations into the dark sea. It is in the silent chaste hood of an avalanche seen from directly below its fall line. It is thousands of bird wings creating wind. And the inspiration of a man sixty-two years buried who turned his back on royal vestments for strenuous mountains. It is whales sharing our oxygen, sails giving shape to wind, porpoises playing eye tag, and a mountain that outlines desire.

More than anything—as the *Heaven Sent's* bow dipped disconcertingly, swung ninety degrees around in a tidal overflow and produced a similar adrenaline rush through my own inside passages—I found myself wishing that the trip would not end. I wanted to sail back north. I wanted to return to Yasetaca. My memory had once again failed me after only two months. All the longing to settle down and have children that I wrote about up on the mountain no longer compelled me. I swung the wheel against the tide rips to keep the bow pointing south.

My internal compass—for chasing the duke, learning how to sail, taking absurd risks, and incurring huge debts—was now oriented to the Yakutat Tlingits, Peter the Josher (the duke's porter) and Mike Harry (who rescued Jeff and me). An anthropologist cajoled Peter for the tribe's song about their mountain. Before he died he sang it aloud in his own tongue. It defines the duke's first climbing expedition, and my last, precisely:

> *Just as if you were the one*
> *That opened Yes,*
> *the world*
> *Yasetaca*
> *By It thus also you are to be happy*

SOURCES

Books

Amedeo of Savoy, Luigi (duke of Abruzzi). *On the Polar Star.* London: Hutchinson & Co., 1903.

Barzini, Lugi. *The Italians.* New York: Atheneum, 1977.

Basile, Cosimo. *Uebi-Scebeli nella spedizione di S.A.R. Luigi di Savoia; diario di tenda e cammino (2-ix-28–4-ii-29).* Bologna: L. Cappelli, 1935.

Bonacossa, Aldo. *Les Alpinistes Celebres.* "Les Duc Des Aruzzes 1873–1933," pp. 72–175.

Clark, Ronald. *The Splendid Hills* (Vittorio Sella biography). London: Phoenix House, 1948.

Cosimo, Basile. *Eubi-Scebeli nella spedizione di S.A.R. Luigi di Savoia.* Bologna: L. Cappelli, 1935.

Dainelli, Giotto. *Il duca degli Abruzzi; le imprese dell'ultimo grande esploratore italiano.* Turin: Unione tiporgrafico-editrice torinese, 1967.

De Filippi, Filippo. *The Ascent of Mount St. Elias.* Trans. Linda Villari. New York: Frederick A. Stokes Company, 1900.

———. *Karakorum and Western Himalaya.,* Westminster (England): Archibald Constable, 1912.

———. *Ruwenzori.* Westminster (England): Archibald Constable, 1908.

De Laguna, Frederica. *Under Mount St. Elias: The History and Culture of the Yakutat Tlingit* (3 volumes). Washington: Smithsonian Institution Press, 1972.

Fracchia, Umberto. *The Italian Navy in the European War.* Milan: Alfieri & Lacroix, 1918.

Halpern, Paul. *The Naval War in the Mediterranean, 1914–1918.* Annapolis: Naval Institute Press, 1987.

Heckstall-Smith, B. *The Britannia and Her Contemporaries*. London: Methuen, 1929.

Hutton, Edward. *Italy and the Italians*. London: W. Blackwood and sons, 1902.

Marder, A. J. *Portrait of an Admiral*. London: Jonathan Cape, 1952.

Marine Ministry. *The Italian Navy in the World War 1915–1918: Facts and Figures*. Rome: Provveditorato general dello stato, 1927.

Michieli, Adriano Augusto. *Luigi Amedeo Giuseppi Maria Ferdinando Francesco di Savoia duca degli, 1873–1933*. Milan: Fratelli Treves Editori, 1937.

Mummery, A. F. *My Climbs in the Alps and Caucasus*. London: Basil, Blackwell, Oxford, 1936.

Seton-Karr, H. W. *Shores and Alps of Alaska*. London: Sampson, Low, Marston, Searle & Aivington, 1887.

Speroni, Gigi. *Il Duca Degli Abruzzi*. Milan: Rusconi, 1991.

Stuck, Hudson. *A Winter Circuit*. New York: Scribner's, 1920.

Whymper, Edward. *A Right Royal Mountaineer*. London: Clowes & Sons, 1909.

Magazines and Journals

Dainelli, Giotto. "The Geographical Work of the H.R.H. the Late Duke of the Abruzzi." *The Geographical Journal* 82 (July 1933), pp. 1–15.

Ingraham, E. S. "The Ascent of Mount St. Elias." *The Mountaineer* 17 (December 15, 1924).

Ladd, William S. (Duke of the Abruzzi Obituary) *The American Alpine Journal*, (1933) pp. 113–116.

Lara, René and Franz Reichel. "The Adventures of a Modern Prince." *McClure's Magazine*, April 1910, pp. 589–604.

Russell, Israel C. "An Expedition to Mount St. Elias, Alaska. *The National Geographic Magazine* 3 (May 1891).

———. "Second Expedition to Mount St. Elias." Thirteenth Annual Report of the U.S. Geographical Survey for 1891–92. Washington, 1894.

Schwatka, Frederick. "Wonderland." *Alpine Journal* 12, 1891.

Thorton, C. W. "The Ascent of Mount St. Elias." *Overland Monthly* 31 (April 1898), pp. 291–300.

Diaries, Correspondence, and Personal Communication

Amedeo of Savoy, Luigi (duke of Abruzzi). Various letters to Vittorio Sella, 1897–1930. Fondazione Sella, Biella, Italy.

Andrews, C. L. Diary from the 1897 Mount St. Elias Expedition. University of Alaska, Fairbanks.

Elkins, Senator Stephen. *The Elkins Letters*. The Booth Library, Davis and Elkins College, Elkins, West Virginia.

Kelly, Katherine Elkins. Conversations with the author. 1995.

Putnam, Bill. Conversations with the author. 1995.

Richmond, Sir Herbert. Operations in the Adriatic (diary kept on board). National Maritime Museum, London.

Sella, Lodovico. Conversations and correspondence with the author. 1996–1997.

Sella, Vittorio. Correspondence to his wife, Linda, and to the Duke of the Abruzzi, 1897–1930; diary from the 1897 St. Elias expedition. Fondazione Sella, Biella, Italy.

Shandrick, Michael. Conversations and correspondence with the author. 1995–1997.

Other Sources

A multitude of stories and interviews about St. Elias and the duke's courtship of Katherine Elkins provided additional information. They include:

Alaska Daily Empire, 1933.
Appalachia, 1897–1933.
Colliers Outdoor America, 1910.
New York Journal, 1897–1910.
New York World, 1897–1910.
Philadelphia Enquirer, 1897.
San Francisco Examiner, 1897.
Tacoma Ledger, 1897.
The American Alpine Journal, 1933–1995.
The Alpine Journal, 1880–1950.
The Courier Record, 1897.
The Daily Evening Telegraph (Philadelphia), 1897.
The Herald (Boston), 1897–1899.
The New York Times, 1891–1995.
The San Francisco Call, 1897.
Scientific American, 1897.
The Seattle Post-Intelligencer, 1897.
The Seattle Daily Times, 1897.
The Times (London), 1897–1933.
Victoria Daily Colonist, 1897.
Yachting World (London), 1897–1898.

INDEX